The Politics of Deregulation

MARTHA DERTHICK and PAUL J. QUIRK

The Politics
of Deregulation

THE BROOKINGS INSTITUTION
Washington, D.C.

Library of Congress Cataloging in Publication data:

Derthick, Martha.
The politics of deregulation.

Includes bibliographical references and index.
1. Industry and state—United States.
I. Quirk, Paul J., 1949–   . II. Brookings Institution.   III. Title.
HD3616.U47D45   1985   338.973   85-16602
ISBN 0-8157-1818-7
ISBN 0-8157-1817-9 (pbk.)

2 3 4 5 6 7 8 9

THE BROOKINGS INSTITUTION is an independent organization devoted to nonpartisan research, education, and publication in economics, government, foreign policy, and the social sciences generally. Its principal purposes are to aid in the development of sound public policies and to promote public understanding of issues of national importance.

The Institution was founded on December 8, 1927, to merge the activities of the Institute for Government Research, founded in 1916, the Institute of Economics, founded in 1922, and the Robert Brookings Graduate School of Economics and Government, founded in 1924.

The Board of Trustees is responsible for the general administration of the Institution, while the immediate direction of the policies, program, and staff is vested in the President, assisted by an advisory committee of the officers and staff. The by-laws of the Institution state: "It is the function of the Trustees to make possible the conduct of scientific research, and publication, under the most favorable conditions, and to safeguard the independence of the research staff in the pursuit of their studies and in the publication of the results of such studies. It is not a part of their function to determine, control, or influence the conduct of particular investigations or the conclusions reached."

The President bears final responsibility for the decision to publish a manuscript as a Brookings book. In reaching his judgment on the competence, accuracy, and objectivity of each study, the President is advised by the director of the appropriate research program and weighs the views of a panel of expert outside readers who report to him in confidence on the quality of the work. Publication of a work signifies that it is deemed a competent treatment worthy of public consideration but does not imply endorsement of conclusions or recommendations.

The Institution maintains its position of neutrality on issues of public policy in order to safeguard the intellectual freedom of the staff. Hence interpretations or conclusions in Brookings publications should be understood to be solely those of the authors and should not be attributed to the Institution, to its trustees, officers, or other staff members, or to the organizations that support its research.

Foreword

ANALYSTS of American politics have generally been much impressed by the power of narrow interests. In particular, they have argued that, when engaging in economic regulation, government is prey to capture by the regulated industries. Therefore, when economists began arguing in the late 1960s and early 1970s that the economy would be more efficient if government substantially withdrew from the regulation of prices and entry in potentially competitive industries, few political observers expected this advice to be heeded. It seemed likely that the regulated industries, in concert with their unions, would easily thwart major reforms designed to deprive them of government protection against competition. It also seemed likely that their efforts would be reinforced by the regulatory agencies, seeking to perpetuate their missions.

Major acts of deregulation nonetheless occurred in a wide range of industries, and in this book Martha Derthick and Paul J. Quirk seek to explain why. They concentrate on the airline, telecommunications, and trucking industries because these are the most puzzling cases politically. In the airline industry, policy change was carried to the surprising length of abolishing the Civil Aeronautics Board and ending all regulation of domestic rates and routes. Though deregulation was less extreme in telecommunications and trucking, it was arguably even more puzzling because of the daunting nature of the opposition. The American Telephone and Telegraph Company and the trucking industry in combination with the Teamsters Union constituted industrial power as formidably organized as any in the American polity.

For all three cases, the authors examine why the regulatory agencies and Congress came to support reform, and why industry and union interests were largely ineffective in opposition. They conclude that policy change was achieved through the politics of ideas—specifically, the fusion of expert analysis with public opinion—and suggest that the political victory of a diffuse interest over particularistic interests, though due in part to special features of the cases, was not an aberration. Rather, it shows that the U.S. political system has a greater capacity for transcending narrow interests than has generally been acknowledged.

Most of the work for the book was done while the authors were on the resident staff at the Brookings Institution, Derthick as a senior fellow and director of the Governmental Studies program and Quirk as a research associate in Governmental Studies. Derthick currently is Julia Allen Cooper Professor of Government and Foreign Affairs at the University of Virginia, and Quirk is assistant professor of political science at the University of Pennsylvania.

Brookings received financial support for the project from the Esther A. and Joseph Klingenstein Fund and an anonymous donor. Derthick had the additional assistance in 1981–82 of fellowships from the John Simon Guggenheim Memorial Foundation and the Center for Advanced Study in the Behavioral Sciences, and in 1983–85 of an appointment in the Center for Advanced Studies of the University of Virginia. Support for the fellowship at the Center for Advanced Study in the Behavioral Sciences in turn came from the National Institute of Mental Health and the Exxon Educational Foundation. A grant from the Gerald R. Ford Foundation made possible research in the Ford Library in Ann Arbor.

For help with source material, the authors are grateful to Stephen M. Aug, James W. Callison, Richard M. Neustadt, Roy Pulsifer, William K. Ris, Jr., Stanton P. Sender, staff members of the Ford Library, and several officers of American Telephone and Telegraph, MCI, the American Trucking Association, and the Air Transport Association. Bradley G. Behrman provided research assistance at the inception of the project and made available material he had gathered on the Civil Aeronautics Board. Anton Naess, a graduate student at Ohio State University, helped assemble data for chapter 6. James E. McKee and John A. Clark, interns at Brookings, provided assistance with footnotes.

Gary C. Jacobson, R. Shep Melnick, Roger G. Noll, Paul E. Peterson, Roy Pulsifer, William K. Ris, Jr., Randall Strahan, and an anonymous critic read the entire manuscript and inspired numerous improvements, for which the authors thank them. The persistence, wide-ranging knowledge and contrasting disciplinary perspective of Noll were particularly valuable. R. Kent Weaver, Lawrence Baum, and William Gormley offered helpful comments on selected chapters.

At Brookings, Diane Hodges provided administrative support, ably sustaining the project even after the authors ceased to be in residence. Nancy Davidson edited the manuscript. Pamela D. Harris, Julie Bailes Legg, Robert L. Londis, Joan P. Milan, and Radmila Nikolič did the typing. Diana Regenthal prepared the index.

The views expressed here are the authors' alone and should not be ascribed to the persons or organizations whose assistance is acknowledged or to the trustees, officers, or staff members of the Brookings Institution. Taking joint responsibility for the contents, the authors wish to emphasize that their work has been thoroughly collaborative and, they believe, better on that account.

BRUCE K. MACLAURY
President

July 1985
Washington, D.C.

Contents

Tables

The Politics of Deregulation

CHAPTER ONE

Three Cases of Deregulation

COMMERCIAL air travelers, shippers of trucking freight, and subscribers to telephone service—which is to say virtually every business and adult individual in the country—can hardly have failed to notice major changes in the past several years in the services and facilities available to them and the pricing and promotional practices of the sellers.

Whereas a few years ago intercity airline routes were served by one, two, or three carriers, all charging the same fare, today both the number of carriers and their prices are highly unpredictable. Such competitive practices as restricted discounts, promotional fares, reduced off-peak fares, and premium services are commonplace.[1]

Much the same thing has happened in the trucking industry. A corporate traffic manager described negotiating for trucking service in the fall of 1981 as being "like walking into a candy store." About 90 percent of shipping rates are negotiated by individual shippers and carriers, with prices and services tailored to the shippers' needs. Big shippers, of course, are in the strongest bargaining position. Smaller shippers have found that they often need to consolidate shipments to take advantage of the new opportunity to bargain.[2]

---

1. For a summary and analysis of the changes, see David R. Graham and Daniel P. Kaplan, *Competition and the Airlines: An Evaluation of Deregulation,* Staff Report, Civil Aeronautics Board, Office of Economic Analysis, December 1982.

2. "Trucking: The Bitter with the Sweet," *Nation's Business,* October 1981, pp. 49–54; "Shippers Are in the Driver's Seat," *Business Week,* October 18, 1982, pp. 182–86; Interstate Commerce Commission, Office of Policy Analysis, "The Effect of Regulatory Reform on the Trucking Industry: Structure, Conduct and Performance," Preliminary Report, June 1981, pp. 81–82; and "Deregulating America," *Business Week,* November 28, 1983, pp. 80–96. Evidence on trucking rate levels and structures under deregulation is synthesized in Denis A. Breen, "Regulatory Reform and the Trucking Industry: An Evaluation of the Motor Carrier Act of 1980," submitted to the Motor Carrier Ratemaking Study Commission, March 1982, pp. 24–27.

Telephone users have found that they can shop for bargains in long distance service. Whereas American Telephone and Telegraph (AT&T) and the affiliates and "independents" that were tied to its network once were the only offerers of long distance service, competitors—of which MCI Telecommunications is the largest—offer service at rates substantially below AT&T's.[3]

Telephone users have also experienced changes in the choices of telephone instruments and other types of equipment, such as recording devices, switchboards, and machines with data storage and data processing capacity. Telephone answering equipment, once a costly luxury confined to businesses, has become an accessory affordable by many homeowners. Telephone instruments, once available only from telephone companies, now can be bought in drug, discount, and department stores in an array of shapes and styles ranging from severely functional to wildly frivolous. Users who want to attach other kinds of terminal equipment offered by manufacturers other than AT&T now can do so without fear that AT&T will punish them by withdrawing services as it once would have done. Increasingly, AT&T itself, through a subsidiary, is offering a variety of terminal equipment, including some with data processing capacities.[4]

These changes have occurred because government laws and regulations, which formerly discouraged competition, now encourage it—and consumers are not the only parties who are feeling the effects. Company managements are under pressure from new entrants. Low-cost airlines that are either new or have recently expanded into interstate markets, such as People Express, Southwest Airlines, Midway Airlines, Muse Air, and New York Air, were growing rapidly as of late 1983 and threatening the markets of bigger, older carriers such as United, Delta, Eastern, and

---

3. There are numerous journalistic accounts of the development of AT&T's long distance competitors. Among others, see N. R. Kleinfield, "The Monopoly's Challengers," *New York Times*, May 21, 1979; Jeffrey A. Tannenbaum, "Business, Consumers Step Up Use of Phone Service from Bell Rivals," *Wall Street Journal*, July 9, 1980; Bernard Wysocki, Jr., "Battling Big AT&T, Little MCI Keeps on Landing Sharp Blows," *Wall Street Journal*, September 28, 1981; Jody Long, "A New Breed of Phone Firm Starts to Grow," *Wall Street Journal*, April 29, 1982; and Virginia Inman, "MCI Races the Clock, Bets Billions of Dollars in Phone Competition," *Wall Street Journal*, June 14, 1983.

4. On the growth and composition of the terminal equipment or "interconnect" industry, see Federal Communications Commission, "Report by the Federal Communications Commission on Domestic Telecommunications Policies," September 27, 1976, Attachment B, "An Overview of the Domestic Telecommunications Industry and the Commission's Policies Concerning Terminal Equipment and Private Line Services," pp. 39-69.

Trans World Airlines.[5] In trucking, more than 27,000 carriers were licensed to operate at the end of 1983, compared with 16,600 in 1977. Carriers have broader operating authority, with many fewer restrictions as to territory, routes, and commodities, than they formerly had; as of May 31, 1984, more than 2,100 had been granted general, nationwide authority.[6] The value of operating rights, which once commanded high prices, has fallen precipitously. As of 1983, well over 200 companies were selling cut-rate long distance telephone service in competition with AT&T, most of them small resellers of its discounted bulk services. Firms that manufacture equipment to be connected with the telephone network—office switchboards for business use (PBXs), remote computer terminals, facsimile machines, answering devices, and dictation equipment—also number well into the hundreds. The $3 billion-a-year market for PBXs is so hotly competitive, according to the *Wall Street Journal,* that "manufacturers underbid their own distributors and think nothing of spreading rumors about the competition."[7]

The new competition has adversely affected the wages and working conditions of employees of the previously protected firms. Nonunion firms and nonunion subsidiaries of established firms have been proliferating in the transportation industries, exerting pressure on the unionized firms, whose contracts have saddled them with high wages and restrictive work rules. Between 1980 and 1984 locals of the Air Line Pilots Association accepted wage deferrals or freezes more than forty times. In 1982 the Teamsters Union agreed to a thirty-seven-month contract that raised total compensation only half as fast as inflation, and many Teamsters locals have accepted wage cuts of 10 to 15 percent at small trucking companies. The Communications Workers of America (CWA), once a militant bargainer against AT&T, was planning as of 1984 to spend several million dollars in an advertising campaign to help the company

5. William M. Carley, "Some Major Airlines Are Being Threatened by Low-Cost Carriers," *Wall Street Journal,* October 12, 1983. For a systematic analysis, see Graham and Kaplan, *Competition and the Airlines,* chap. 4.

6. "Industry Trends and Statistics," *Commercial Carrier Journal* (July 1984), p. 82; and interview, William Southard, director, Office of Transportation Analysis, ICC, October 24, 1984.

7. Richard E. Wiley, "The End of Monopoly: Regulatory Change and the Promotion of Competition," in Harry M. Shooshan III, ed., *Disconnecting Bell: The Impact of the AT&T Divestiture* (Pergamon Press, 1984), p. 37; Andrew Pollack, "The Man Who Beat AT&T," *New York Times,* July 14, 1982; and Peggy Berkowitz, "Rivalry Is Fierce in Growing Market for Telephone Switching Systems," *Wall Street Journal,* February 10, 1984.

sell its long distance service. In three years, CWA representation in the telecommunications industry dropped by 23,000 to around 524,000. Thousands of jobs of CWA members were redefined to require less skill and pay.[8]

Many of these changes were hoped for by the sponsors of deregulation, and none would have caused surprise. However, there have also been highly unpredictable changes in the fortunes of individual firms and classes of firms. The critics of airline deregulation predicted that big firms would swallow smaller ones, and not even the proponents anticipated that just the reverse would actually occur. The trunk airlines' share of domestic traffic has fallen, while that of carriers formerly called "local," such as Piedmont, Frontier, and Southern, has risen.[9] United Airlines, which argued for deregulation, has not conspicuously benefited from it, whereas Allegheny Airlines, whose president strongly opposed deregulation for fear of predation from bigger firms, has emerged as a big winner under the name of USAir.[10] In the trucking industry, the number of big carriers—those with operating revenues of over $5 million a year—has remained fairly stable under deregulation at around 1,000. By contrast, the number of carriers with revenues between $1 million and $5 million a year dropped by almost 50 percent between 1977 and 1983, from 3,100 to 1,600, while very small carriers, with revenues of under $1 million a year, have roughly doubled, from 12,400 to 24,400. This growth in the number of small carriers is presumably the result both of new entries into the industry and the fall in revenues of firms that formerly were larger.[11] In the telecommunications industry, there have been profound changes in the structure of AT&T, which has formed a separate subsidiary to manufacture and sell terminal equipment and to engage in unregulated competition with other suppliers. It has also divested its local operating companies in order to settle an antitrust action brought by the Justice Department with evidence derived from the record of the company's reaction to early reforms aimed at promoting competition.

8. "Airline Wages Are Set for a Long Slide," *Business Week*, April 9, 1984, pp. 127–28; "Deregulating America," p. 81; and "The Communications Workers Are Selling AT&T's Line," *Business Week*, August 13, 1984, p. 61.

9. Graham and Kaplan, *Competition and the Airlines*, pp. 31–36, 53.

10. On USAir's success, see Grant F. Winthrop, " 'Agony Airlines' Becomes a High Flyer," *Fortune*, June 30, 1980, pp. 104–08; and Charles W. Stevens, "US Air, Shaking Its 'Agony Air' Past, Profits from Routes Others Avoid," *Wall Street Journal*, February 28, 1984.

11. "Industry Trends and Statistics," p. 82.

The effects of changes in government regulatory policy are also evident in the government agencies that once did the regulating. The Civil Aeronautics Board (CAB) ceased to exist at the end of 1984.[12] Employment at the Interstate Commerce Commission (ICC) fell from 2,000 in 1976 to 1,300 in 1983. The Common Carrier Bureau of the Federal Communications Commission (FCC) has not been shrinking, but definitions of tasks and assignments of personnel have been more fluid than usual.

Finally, and of greatest importance in the eyes of the sponsors of procompetitive reform, the economy has been made more efficient. In the airline industry, planes are carrying fewer empty seats and the most efficient carriers are also the fastest growing. Fewer trucks are traveling empty on return trips. In both the airline and trucking industries rates are lower on average than they would have been without deregulation and are more nearly based on actual costs of service. In telecommunications prices have been reduced for certain services, prices and costs are better aligned, and more important, equipment and services have proliferated as technological advance abetted by competition has transformed the industry.[13]

The History of Change

Most of the changes in government policy that produced all this turbulence occurred between 1975 and 1980. By approving sizable discount fares, lowering barriers to entry, and proposing, except for minimal tests of fitness, to eliminate such barriers altogether in a case instituted in the spring of 1978, the Civil Aeronautics Board began to transform a protectionist regulatory regime into one that encouraged competition. Congress then proceeded in the Airline Deregulation Act of 1978 to confirm what the board had done and to lay the basis for much more.[14] Once the law was passed, the CAB proceeded to interpret it in a procompetitive way, so

12. "CAB Sheds Workers as It Prepares to Fly Slowly into Sunset," *Wall Street Journal*, November 11, 1980; and Ann Cooper, "The CAB Is Shutting Down, But Will It Set an Example for Other Agencies?" *National Journal*, vol. 16 (September 29, 1984), pp. 1820–23.

13. For a journalistic appraisal, see "Deregulating America." Official analyses for the airline and trucking industries are cited in notes 1 and 2 above. For an early effort at an official analysis of the rapidly changing telecommunications industry, see 61 FCC 2d 766–904 (1976).

14. 92 Stat. 1705. The actions of the CAB are chronicled in CAB, Bureau of Domestic Aviation, "Bibliography of Important Civil Aeronautics Board Regulatory Actions, 1975–1979," December 1979.

that after the spring of 1980 carriers deemed fit were essentially free to enter the industry at will and to determine what routes they would serve and what fares they would charge. Formerly, they had been required to obtain route certificates from the CAB by proving that the "public convenience and necessity" would be served, and the CAB had imposed a rigid fare structure that prevented price competition.

With a slight lag, roughly parallel changes occurred in trucking regulation in a roughly parallel way. The ICC enlarged the zones exempt from regulation that surround terminals and commercial areas in 1976, made it easier for applicants to enter the trucking business in 1978, and began many other similar proceedings in 1978 and 1979. The commission was well on its way to reform when Congress instructed it to slow down and let the legislature decide.[15] What the legislature decided, in the Motor Carrier Act of 1980, was to allow procompetitive deregulation to proceed.[16] The changes in law did not go nearly as far as the Airline Deregulation Act or as far as procompetitive reformers would have liked. The ICC remained intact, with a good deal of discretion. But it then used that discretion as broadly as possible to advance reform in what remained of 1980, and, after drawing back under a new chairman in the spring of 1981, resumed the advance a few months later. As a result, the trucking industry, like the airline industry, was changed for years to come. Whatever may happen in the future, the reforms effected in the late 1970s and early 1980s have been profound and far-reaching. Entrants into the industry must no longer prove to the ICC, as they once had to, that existing service is inadequate and that their proposed offering will respond to a public need and not harm existing carriers. The statutory presumption is in favor of the ICC's granting the application. Competitive pricing by individual firms is freely permitted, and collective rate setting, under antitrust immunity, is restricted almost to the point of abolition.

The chronology and pattern of regulatory reform in the common carrier portion of the telecommunications industry were different from those in transportation. On one hand, procompetitive reform began sooner. The landmark decision of the Federal Communications Commission that paved the way for competition in the provision of terminal equipment occurred in 1968. This was the *Carterfone* decision, in which the FCC

---

15. The ICC's actions are conveniently summarized in ICC, Office of Policy Analysis, "The Effect of Regulatory Reform on the Trucking Industry."

16. 94 Stat. 793.

prohibited AT&T from barring attachments that did not harm the telephone system.[17] Introduction of competition in long distance telephone service is usually traced to an FCC decision in 1969 that authorized MCI to offer private line services between St. Louis and Chicago and to a successor decision in 1971 that affirmed a policy of permitting new entry into the field of specialized long distance services.[18] But whereas for the airline and trucking industries Congress quickly followed the procompetitive initiatives of regulatory agencies with reform legislation, it has been unable as yet, despite a prolonged effort and general commitment to the goal of increased competition, to reach agreement on legislation that would define the terms of that competition in the telecommunications industry.

While Congress deliberated in the late 1970s and early 1980s, the FCC continued to pursue policies that encouraged competition, and it also began to retreat from traditional public utility regulation, which had involved, in principle at least, close supervision of both entry and rates. Until the late 1970s the FCC's policies had increasingly encouraged entry at the expense of the AT&T monopoly, but they had not, strictly speaking, been deregulatory. Rather than purport to forgo its traditional supervisory functions, the FCC continued to set standards for entry and mounted a much-increased effort to review the setting of AT&T's rates. But with the *Second Computer Inquiry* (Computer II) decision in the spring of 1980, the FCC clearly joined the general drive for deregulation.[19] Forced by the technological convergence of communications and data processing to define what it would regulate, the FCC responded in a remarkably self-denying way, entailing a substantial retreat from regulatory territory that it had been occupying for years. It decided to confine its regulation of service offerings to "basic services"—that is, the capacity for the transmission of information, of which long distance voice telephone service is the most familiar example. It stopped regulating "enhanced services," which use computer technology to store or restructure information. It withdrew regulation from all kinds of terminal equipment, from the basic telephone to far "smarter" and more complex alternatives. And, though it made no formal decision to do so, the commission more or less gave up any serious attempt at closely supervising AT&T's rates and

17. 13 FCC 2d 420–41 (1968).
18. 18 FCC 2d 953–1010 (1969); and 29 FCC 2d 870–983 (1971).
19. 77 FCC 2d 384–522 (1980).

cost accounting. Its decisions in the Computer II case were upheld by the Circuit Court of Appeals of the District of Columbia and, in the absence of congressional action superseding them, stood as government policy.[20]

Thus on close inspection the chronology of FCC action is more congruent with that of the CAB and ICC than it first appears to be. While the FCC, at least in the common carrier field (broadcasting is quite another matter), began procompetitive action sooner than they did, its commitment to procompetitive deregulation essentially coincided with theirs or lagged a bit behind it.

These numerous acts of the regulatory commissions and Congress substantially reversed regulatory policies that the federal government had been pursuing for decades. Federal regulation of interstate radio and wire communication was instituted by the Mann-Elkins Act in 1910 (and was under the jurisdiction of the ICC until the FCC was created by the Communications Act of 1934); that of the trucking industry began with the Motor Carrier Act of 1935; and that of the airline industry with the Civil Aeronautics Act of 1938.

The Critique of Regulation

These regulatory regimes had been rationalized largely as a way of guaranteeing service to the public by industries having the character of public utilities and as a means of protecting the public from monopoly pricing practices, including the destructive competition that was said to lead to the creation of monopolies. However, the agencies had instead— or as well—sheltered the regulated industries from competition and fostered very costly inefficiencies. Long a target of experts in administrative law, public administration, and political science, who found much fault with their structure and procedures, the commissions in the 1960s had become a target also of economists, who attacked their purposes by undertaking to show that the social costs of regulation far outweighed the benefits.

No one seems to have anticipated that these criticisms of regulatory policy would actually result in substantial reform. The fight for deregula-

20. *Computer and Communications Industry Association* v. *FCC,* 693 F. 2d 198–220 (D.C. Cir. 1982), *cert. denied,* 103 S. Ct. 2d 109 (1982). For a succinct history of the FCC's actions, see Wiley, "The End of Monopoly," pp. 23–46.

tion of transportation "has been the story of a few brave but lonely economists stubbornly attacking the American economy's largest legal cartel," one of the lonely economists told a conference of his colleagues in 1974.[21] (Loneliness is eased by going to gatherings of like-minded persons.) Another economist told the same conference that no regulatory agency was about to reduce its own powers. Such persons would have been incredulous had they been told that within a short time the regulatory commissions would begin taking steps toward reform that would culminate quite promptly in new laws promoting competition.[22] As economists were developing the case that regulatory agencies disserved the public interest, they were also producing their own version of a political theory explaining why this was so, which held that a pro-industry bias was deeply embedded in the functions of the agencies and in American political institutions and processes. A highly influential article by George Stigler presented without qualification the thesis that "regulation is acquired by the industry and is designed and operated primarily for its benefit." Stigler concluded that it was as appropriate to denounce the ICC for its pro-industry policies as it was to criticize the Great Atlantic and Pacific Tea Company for selling groceries or to criticize a politician for currying popular support.[23] The predominant view of both economists and political scientists was that regulation presented a case in which the benefits of government policy were concentrated in a few well-organized interests—the firms and unions that were protected from competition—whereas the costs were widely dispersed among consumers whose incentives to organize to protect their interests were insufficient to induce po-

21. Gary L. Seevers, "Prospects for Regulatory Reform," in James C. Miller III, ed., *Perspectives on Federal Transportation Policy* (American Enterprise Institute for Public Policy Research, 1975), p. 201.

22. But see the qualified analysis by Roger G. Noll, Merton J. Peck, and John J. McGowan in *Economic Aspects of Television Regulation* (Brookings, 1973), pp. 120–28, in which they append to an explanation of regulatory agencies' common resistance to change a list of forces for change, including an "entrepreneurial spirit" that causes some commissioners and staff members to want to be known by the reforms they institute. They conclude nonetheless that "in general, inertia appears to prevail enough of the time to inhibit both technological and institutional change" and that "those changes that occur reflect mostly the emergence of a new special interest."

23. George Stigler, "The Theory of Economic Regulation," *Bell Journal of Economics and Management Service,* vol. 2 (Spring 1971), pp. 3–21. For a more qualified but nonetheless compelling statement, see George W. Hilton, "The Basic Behavior of Regulatory Commissions," *American Economic Review,* vol. 62 (May 1972, *Papers and Proceedings, 1971*), pp. 47–54.

litical action. And the received wisdom of political science was that in clashes between a diffuse public interest and a tangible, well-organized interest, the former could be expected to finish a poor second.[24]

To be sure, scholars were beginning to revise this wisdom in response to events. Between 1967 and 1973 more than two dozen new laws for consumer protection, environmental protection, occupational health and safety, and other forms of social regulation were enacted, typically conferring benefits on the ill-organized general public at the expense of a well-organized few. James Q. Wilson has ascribed this unexpected development to the rise of "entrepreneurial politics," in which the entrepreneur "serves as the vicarious representative of groups not directly part of the legislative process." This entrepreneur is someone "who can mobilize latent public sentiment (by revealing a scandal or capitalizing on a crisis), put the opponents of the plan publicly on the defensive (by accusing them of deforming babies or killing motorists), and associate the legislation with widely shared values (clean air, pure water, health, and safety)."[25] Elaborating on Wilson's analysis, a leading practitioner of entrepreneurial politics, Michael Pertschuk, has suggested that this surprising wave of legislation was produced by a five-part coalition consisting of consumer advocates in Congress, a new strain of entrepreneurial congressional staff

24. The following succinct analysis by James Q. Wilson applies precisely to our cases: "When a program supplies particular benefits to an existing or newly-created interest, public or private, it creates a set of political relationships that make exceptionally difficult further alteration of that program by coalitions of the majority. What was created in the name of the common good is sustained in the name of the particular interest. Bureaucratic clientelism becomes self-perpetuating, in the absence of some crisis or scandal, because a single interest group to which the program matters greatly is highly motivated and well-situated to ward off the criticisms of other groups that have a broad but weak interest in the policy. . . . [A] major change is, in effect, new legislation that must overcome the same hurdles as the original law but this time with one of the hurdles—the wishes of the agency and its clients—raised much higher." "The Rise of the Bureaucratic State," in Nathan Glazer and Irving Kristol, eds., The American Commonwealth, 1976 (Basic Books, 1976), pp. 93–94. See also Wilson, Political Organizations (Basic Books, 1973), chap. 16. More generally, for major statements asserting the power of particularistic, well-organized interests at the expense of broad, diffuse interests, see Grant McConnell, Private Power and American Democracy (Alfred A. Knopf, 1966), especially chap. 10; Robert A. Dahl and Charles E. Lindblom, Politics, Economics and Welfare (Harper and Row, 1953), especially chap. 12; and David B. Truman, The Governmental Process (Alfred A. Knopf, 1951).

25. James Q. Wilson, The Politics of Regulation (Basic Books, 1980), p. 370. For a somewhat later statement by an economist, see Roger Noll, "The Political Foundations of Regulatory Policy," Journal of Institutional and Theoretical Economics, vol. 139 (October 1983), pp. 377–404.

members, advocacy journalists, organized labor, and private not-for-profit issue entrepreneurs, of whom the most prominent was Ralph Nader.[26]

If our cases were simply one more example of this political phenomenon, we would have been much less intrigued by them—but clearly they are not. Though some of the elements of the entrepreneurial politics of 1967–73 are importantly present and will constitute one theme of our analysis, there are also important differences from the pattern described by Wilson and Pertschuk. There was at most mild scandal in these cases, and no crisis of the sort that could stir the latent sentiments of a mass public. The public liked its telephone service and its airlines and evidently did not care that the trucking industry was heavily regulated by the government.[27] Ralph Nader and his associates had some part to play on behalf of consumers in these reforms, as we will explain in chapter 2, but Nader did not pursue procompetitive deregulation with anything like the sustained personal intensity that he brought to passing fresh consumer protection laws. More significant, though, than the mass public's indifference or Nader's low priority was the outright opposition of organized labor to the deregulatory reforms we describe. Employees in the transportation and communications industries were among the principal beneficiaries of anticompetitive regulation, and their unions came to its defense. In contrast, Pertschuk's account of consumer politics gives great credit to labor, calling it "a traditional political resource that dwarfed the efforts of all other consumer advocates combined."[28]

Finally, the intensity of industry opposition distinguishes our cases from most of the wave of new regulatory laws analyzed by Wilson and

26. Michael Pertschuk, *Revolt against Regulation: The Rise and Pause of the Consumer Movement* (University of California Press, 1982), pp. 5–45.

27. Louis Harris and Associates, "Public Attitudes toward Competition in the Telecommunications Industry," Study No. 782254, prepared for AT&T, July 1979; James W. Callison, "Deregulation—An Airlines' Perspective," unpublished speech, November 9, 1979; and private polls done for the American Trucking Association and cited in transcript, ATA executive committee meeting, February 14, 1979, and in ATA press release, April 29, 1980. In both of the ATA polls, only 3 percent of the respondents mentioned trucking when asked what industries should be deregulated. According to Callison, who was senior vice-president and general counsel of Delta Air Lines, various public opinion polls consistently showed that the airlines ranked very high among all industries in measures of consumer satisfaction and confidence.

28. Pertschuk, *Revolt against Regulation,* p. 29. A congressional staff source with considerable experience in consumer issues told us that the consumer movement seemed "almost as if it had been organized to help labor." Interview, Thomas M. Susman, July 14, 1980.

Pertschuk. With the conspicuous exception of automobile safety legislation, most of the new laws applied to industry generally, and they elicited a weak, diffuse, even defensive response. Pertschuk, who is presumably not disposed to understate the political power of business, recalls that "in the public political arena, business was quiescent—and defensive. Except for those industries that nestled comfortably in the protective shade of quota, tariff, or economic regulation, most American business, relatively undisturbed by Washington and flourishing, gave low priority to national political involvement."[29] What makes our cases profoundly different and of surpassing interest to a political analyst is that some of the most politically potent of American industries, in collaboration with organized labor, fought as hard as they could to protect their interests—and lost.

Political scientists would have been unlikely to foresee the defeat of the industries in these cases; and like the economists, they would also have been unlikely to foresee the willingness of regulatory agencies to engage in deregulation. Drawing on organization theory, they would most likely have predicted that any bureaucracy would seek to maintain and enhance itself; and, drawing on role theory, they would have observed that even if critics of agency missions were appointed to high positions in regulatory agencies, they would be forced to moderate their criticisms and adapt to organizational constraints.[30] The homiletic summation of the latter view—"where you stand depends on where you sit"—is renowned in Washington. Yet among the leading practitioners of entrepreneurial politics in these cases were regulatory commission chairmen who sponsored reversals in their agencies' roles.

Journalists too were skeptical of the prospects for reform, having received the views of the academic professions and reinforced them with a cynicism of their own about the relations among economic interests, government agencies, and congressional committees.[31] The general view was that a triumvirate (an "iron triangle") of regulators, regulated industries, and key members of Congress, influenced by campaign contributions

29. Pertschuk, *Revolt against Regulation,* p. 15.

30. Wilson, writing of bureaucratic inertia, observed that regulatory agencies would resist deregulation: "Any organization, and *a fortiori* any public organization, develops a genuine belief in the rightness of its mission that is expressed as a commitment to regulation as a process." "The Rise of the Bureaucratic State," p. 98.

31. For an extreme example, see Morton Mintz and Jerry S. Cohen, *America, Inc.: Who Owns and Operates the United States* (Dell, 1971), chap. 7.

from the regulated industries, constituted an insuperable barrier to any reform that was contrary to industry interests.

Why Did Deregulation Occur?

As political scientists, we shared some of the views that were confounded by events, and our purpose in this book is to solve the puzzle that the events present. Why did deregulation occur? How did a diffuse public interest, articulated by a "few lonely economists," get embodied in law, and why were the industry and union interests that had a stake in preserving regulation unable to protect themselves against change? Why did the regulatory commissions, which were expected to be one of the leading obstacles to procompetitive deregulation, instead take the initiative on behalf of it?

Our purpose is both practical and academic. Deregulation is of immediate practical interest as a successful reversal of well-established government policies. The steady and seemingly inexorable expansion of government activities has caused adversely affected interests, policy analysts, elected officeholders, and an increasingly disillusioned public to ask whether outmoded and excessively burdensome government policies can ever be revised. Proposed "sunset" laws signify the groping of public officials for a routinized means of review, as does the search for ways to make the budget more controllable. Most recent efforts at retrenchment have entailed relying on the budget process and trimming government programs by trimming expenditures.[32] These cases of deregulation therefore stand out as examples of the willingness of Congress to deliberately reexamine and fundamentally revise long-established government policies. More fundamentally, though, the recent history of deregulation raises the highly significant theoretical question of how particularistic, well-organized interests can successfully be subordinated to diffuse, far more encompassing, but ill-organized interests. We seek above all to specify the conditions and processes by which this occurred in a set of important cases.

---

32. For an account of retrenchment through the budget process, see John W. Ellwood, ed., *Reductions in U.S. Domestic Spending: How They Affect State and Local Governments* (Transaction Books, 1982).

Other Examples of Regulatory Reform

The three cases that we have picked to analyze in depth are not the only recent examples of regulatory reform. The Securities Acts Amendments of 1975, the Railroad Revitalization and Regulatory Reform Act of 1976, the Staggers Rail Act of 1980, and the Depository Institutions Deregulation and Monetary Control Act of 1980 included changes in federal regulation of the securities, railroad, and banking industries, all with the purpose of removing government restraints on competition.[33] We have chosen to concentrate heavily on the reform of airline, trucking, and telecommunications common carrier regulation because they are purer examples of the puzzles that intrigue us. They more clearly pitted particularistic interests against diffuse, widely encompassing interests, or they more clearly involved a retrenchment of government activity—deregulation, that is, as distinct from a mere procompetitive reordering and rationalization of regulatory techniques.[34]

For example, although the Securities Acts Amendments of 1975 withdrew official sanction from fixed commission rates on sales of securities, they also expanded the regulatory functions of the Securities and Exchange Commission in order to create a uniform national market system. While the abolition of fixed commission rates was opposed by most members of the New York Stock Exchange, it was very much favored by large institutional investors such as mutual funds. Indeed, the rapid growth of such investors and their increasing resort to regional stock exchanges, over-the-counter trading, and other evasions of the fixed commission rates of the New York Stock Exchange had introduced a considerable measure of competition into securities markets in the late 1960s and early 1970s. This made procompetitive policy change much more feasible po-

33. In addition, a thoroughly compromised deregulation of natural gas pricing was enacted in 1978 in the Natural Gas Policy Act. This much-contested case is so important to the politics of deregulation and had so qualified an outcome that we treat it independently in chap. 6 as part of an exploration of the limits of deregulation.

34. Arguably, deregulation in the transportation and telecommunications industries represented the substitution of antitrust policies for public utility regulation. So interpreted, it was a change in technique rather than retrenchment, yet for most industries most of the time, antitrust supervision is a less penetrating and pervasive form of intervention than public utility regulation, so that "retrenchment" remains a fair characterization. It may be questioned, however, whether it is a fair characterization of the government's relations with AT&T in the particular period we are describing. For AT&T in the late 1970s and early 1980s, reductions in regulation were closely correlated with and offset by profound government interventions through the medium of antitrust enforcement. See chap. 5.

litically than it otherwise would have been by making it a less than radical revision of the status quo and putting pressure on New York Stock Exchange members to accommodate to the new economic circumstances. Among those who split with the majority and favored an end to fixed commission rates was the largest brokerage house, Merrill Lynch, Pierce, Fenner and Smith, which accounted for about 10 percent of the total volume of the securities industry in the United States.[35]

Similarly, the rise of competition outside the established regulatory framework contributed to passage of a banking deregulation bill. Savers were withdrawing funds from commercial banks and thrift institutions, whose interest rates on deposits were limited by government regulation, in order to invest them in high-yield money market mutual funds, a new and unregulated form of financial institution that arose in the 1970s. This forced the banks and thrifts to accept changes in government policy that they would otherwise have thoroughly resisted. As its name suggests, the Depository Institutions Deregulation and Monetary Control Act of 1980 tightened some federal government controls and loosened others, with the net result that competition was encouraged nationwide, on a uniform basis throughout the affected industry. For example, the Federal Reserve Board secured the right to impose reserve requirements on all banks, not just those belonging to the Federal Reserve system; ceilings on interest payments on deposits in commercial banks and thrift institutions were removed; and certain provisions of state usury laws were preempted by the federal government.[36]

The Railroad Revitalization and Regulatory Reform Act of 1976, known as the 4-R Act, combined mild measures of deregulation that the railroad industry opposed with several billion dollars of fresh government benefits that the industry sought, and left much discretion with the ICC, which initially used it to perpetuate strict regulation of maximum prices. Only the threat of a veto by President Gerald R. Ford preserved even the limited amount of statutory reform that was achieved in 1976.[37]

35. Susan M. Phillips and J. Richard Zecher, *The SEC and the Public Interest* (MIT Press, 1981), chap. 4; and Andrew J. Glass, "Wall Street, Beleaguered and Divided, Tries to Shape Congressional Pressure for Reform," *National Journal,* vol. 5 (May 19, 1973), pp. 709–18.

36. A good summary of the law and its origins is contained in "The Depository Institutions Deregulation and Monetary Control Act of 1980," *Economic Perspectives,* vol. 4 (September–October 1980), pp. 3–23.

37. Gerald R. Ford, *A Time to Heal* (Harper and Row and Reader's Digest, 1979), p. 366.

The 4-R Act, which gave railroads much freedom to lower prices (as long as rates equaled or exceeded variable costs) but only limited freedom to raise them (given the ICC's decision to use its discretion over maximum prices in a restrictive way), had very little effect on the railroads' economic behavior but much on their political behavior. Their pricing practices did not change after passage of this act, but their perception of their interests did. By relieving regulatory restraints on minimum prices but not maximum ones and by curbing the functions of railroad rate bureaus, the act of 1976 undermined the railroads' interest in perpetuating regulation. They had lost its principal protective benefits and were left with only the restrictive burdens. In 1978, two years before the Staggers Rail Act passed, Conrail, the Chessie System, the Union Pacific, and the Southern Pacific formed a group known as Transportation by Rail for Agricultural and Industrial Needs (TRAIN) to support deregulation. After Southern Railway reached an accommodation with this group in the spring of 1979, only Burlington Northern among the major railroads continued to be opposed.[38] Thus the politics of the Staggers Rail Act in 1980 pitted the interests of the railroad industry, which had come to favor deregulation in the expectation of securing higher prices, against the interests of the shippers and users of rail freight, who feared higher prices.[39] It became possible to pass the Staggers Rail Act when these conflicting interests reached a compromise.

Three Hard and Clear Cases

By comparison with these others, our three cases are relatively clear and hard.[40] That is, the policy shift toward deregulation was unambigu-

38. David Bragdon, "Slow Train to Reform: The Politics of Railroad Regulation" (honors thesis, Harvard College, 1982).

39. "Bill Deregulating Railroads Approved," *Congressional Quarterly Almanac,* vol. 36 (1980), pp. 248–55.

40. A case that might be thought both "hard" and "clear" is that of cable television, which was substantially freed from anticompetitive regulation by the FCC in the period we are describing. Deregulation occurred despite strong opposition from the over-the-air broadcasting industry. Like AT&T and the trucker-Teamster combination, though for different reasons, the major television networks are thought to be very powerful in politics, and it would have been interesting to inquire why the government became willing to override their interests for the sake of improved competition. Nonetheless, we elected to omit cable television from our analysis. We did so partly for the sake of economy in exposition, but more fundamentally because federal regulation in this instance was much less well entrenched than in the other industries we concentrate on, with a more questionable statutory

ous, and at least at the outset the dominant industry interests were overwhelmingly opposed to this shift. Moreover, in two of the three cases the corporate and union opposition to reform was as formidable as any that American society has to offer. Measured by assets, AT&T is—or was at the time the crucial policy changes occurred—the biggest corporation in the country; and the Teamsters, who joined with the organized trucking industry in opposing deregulation, with 1.9 million members is the biggest union, although only a fraction of its members are truck drivers. AT&T, with its regional affiliates, and the nation's more than 16,000 regulated trucking firms, in conjunction with the Teamsters, had millions of dollars a year to spend on campaign contributions and mass advertising, and they had a virtually all-embracing network of contacts with members of Congress.

Airline deregulation alone might be thought not to be a hard case politically. The industry is not widely dispersed; corporate headquarters are located in a few major cities. Its unions are small. Furthermore, though industry opposition was intense through most of the debate, it all but collapsed before Congress completed action. (See chapter 5.) Nonetheless, the case remains politically hard and hence puzzling if only because reform occurred early, before the fashion and feasibility of deregulation had been demonstrated (it was mainly the airline case that had a demonstration effect), and because reform was carried to an extreme length. Here alone, Congress elected to abolish the traditional regulatory regime. The case appears hard, too, at least by comparison with air cargo deregulation, which passed immediately after being separated from airline passenger deregulation. In contrast with passenger deregulation, cargo deregulation was unqualifiedly endorsed by the CAB in 1976 and was never opposed by the so-called combination carriers—those like United, American, and TWA that carry cargo as well as passengers. Although their share of air freight in 1977 was more than 80 percent of total revenue ton-miles, this traffic accounted for less than 10 percent of their revenues. Continental, Delta, and Eastern found cargo so unprofitable that in the mid-1970s they ceased to carry it. And while the combination

---

foundation, and arguably, therefore, was relatively vulnerable to reform no matter what the traditional industry's power. Without specific authorization from Congress, the FCC undertook regulation of the cable industry in the late 1960s and equally at its own discretion began to abandon it less than a decade later. See Stanley M. Besen and Robert W. Crandall, "The Deregulation of Cable Television," *Law and Contemporary Problems*, vol. 44 (Winter 1981), pp. 77–124.

carriers were indifferent to cargo deregulation, the leading specialists in cargo favored it. Federal Express testified in favor of reform in 1976, and Flying Tiger did so in 1977. When Congress found that there was no opposition, it separated cargo deregulation from the more general deregulation bill and passed it in three weeks, whereas another year was required to complete action on the more contested general bill.[41]

Our goal is to learn whether and to what extent the success of deregulation has a common explanation in our cases. The causes of sociopolitical events generally are obscure, and individual causative factors are hard to isolate and weigh in relative importance; the reason for examining the three cases together is to make it more feasible, through comparison, to perform this analytic task. If a generally applicable explanation is attainable, it will be far more compelling and significant than an analysis confined to any one case.

However, we face the difficulty that the telecommunications case is unlike the other two in important respects. Given the fundamentally competitive structure of the airline and trucking industries, government regulation had only to fall away for the policymakers' underlying goal of enhanced competition to be realized. Reform was uncomplicated conceptually, and achievement of it was swift. The telecommunications case is quite another matter. Policy change has been far more prolonged, problematic, and inconclusive. Because of the size and monopoly position of AT&T, simply withdrawing regulatory restraints risked encouraging it to engage in predatory behavior. For roughly a decade beginning in the late 1960s, the FCC pursued procompetitive policy change without conceiving of it as deregulation; on the contrary, it thought of such reform as a strategy of regulation and a constraint on AT&T. But as the drive for deregulation gained momentum in Washington, it encompassed the FCC (chapter 3). Deregulation of telecommunications now joined greater competition as a goal of federal policymakers, with the result that the central issue became not how much competition to have—for everyone now professed to want the greatest possible amount—but what to do with or about AT&T. On what terms and with what corporate structure should it be allowed to engage in the new competition?

Because this momentous question has no parallel in our other two cases, we will pay relatively little attention to it. Our goal, more than

41. Lucile Sheppard Keyes, *Regulatory Reform in Air Cargo Transportation* (American Enterprise Institute for Public Policy Research, 1980); and Andrew S. Carron, *Transition to a Free Market: Deregulation of the Air Cargo Industry* (Brookings, 1981).

sufficiently ambitious, is to take the analysis far enough to explain the essentially deregulatory outcomes in all three cases, and we pursue only briefly (in chapter 5) the policymakers' subsequent attempt to reconcile the twin goals of deregulation and competition for telecommunications by defining new rules for the behavior and structure of AT&T.

Economic Theories of Deregulation

We would not have bothered to attempt this analysis were we persuaded that deregulation is explicable mainly by reference to economic events. One version of an economic theory of deregulation is that regulation crumbled because the original public interest rationale for it ceased to comport with economic reality—if indeed it ever did. Airline regulation was introduced to protect an infant industry, but the industry is now mature; trucking regulation was introduced to prevent predatory competition during a severe depression, but the economy has long since recovered; and telecommunications common carrier regulation was designed to restrain monopoly profits, but technological changes have undermined the natural monopoly of AT&T. Thus, changes were necessary in order to make policy serve the public interest under contemporary economic conditions.

Several things are wrong with this interpretation. First, by assuming that the economic rationales advanced in defense of regulation were the real reasons for the adoption of it, this explanation overlooks the political forces underlying regulation. Second, it overlooks the fact that economists' rationales, as well as economic realities, have been subject to change. As economists examined the operation of price and entry regulation in the 1960s and 1970s, the theoretical arguments for it began to seem less potent and persuasive than they had to an earlier generation of economists. A pervasive disillusionment set in. "The Supreme Power who conceived gravity, supply and demand, and the double helix must have been absorbed elsewhere when public utility regulation was invented," says a standard text on industrial organization published in 1970.[42] By then economic specialists in industrial organization had come to share a strong preference for relying on market forces except where cost structures indisputably led to the formation of monopolies. Finally, the interpretation overlooks the fact that original rationales and current realities

42. F. M. Scherer, *Industrial Market Structure and Economic Performance* (Rand McNally, 1970), p. 537.

quite commonly diverge without being subjected to intellectual scrutiny. It is precisely the policymakers' willingness to engage in scrutiny—and then to decide on change over the opposition of powerful vested interests—that constitutes the puzzle in this case, not the explanation.

A second version of an economic explanation of deregulation is that it occurred because under changed economic circumstances regulated industries or other comparably well organized and economically interested groups came to want it. Such an interpretation derives from the so-called economic theory of politics, which places nearly exclusive emphasis on the pursuit of self-interest as the motive of political action and defines narrowly and mostly in material terms the content of that interest. Elected officials, on this view, seek only reelection, while appointed ones seek only promotions or the maintenance or expansion of their agencies. Moreover, officials pursue these interests under conditions shaped almost exclusively by the relative success of contending interests in achieving organization and mobilization and thereby bringing tangible political resources to bear.[43]

An interpretation of this kind is hinted at, although not actually embraced, in essays on regulatory reform by Paul MacAvoy and George Eads, two economists who as government officials were deeply involved in the pursuit of deregulation in the 1970s. MacAvoy writes of the stress inflicted on economic regulation by inflation:

Since the mid-1960s, price and entry regulation has restricted profitability so widely that production growth has been slowed down in the energy and transportation industries. Rate increases have been less than cost increases, causing declines in capacity growth and production growth during the early 1970s. As a result most of the public-utility and common-carrier industries failed to extend service to new communities or customers at quality levels comparable to those in the 1950s and early 1960s.[44]

Eads argues that economic regulation failed to survive the 1970s because "it showed itself incapable of dealing with rapid structural change—change in the rate and direction of technological advance;

---

43. Among leading statements of the theory are: Anthony Downs, *An Economic Theory of Democracy* (Harper, 1957); Morris P. Fiorina, *Congress: Keystone of the Washington Establishment* (Yale University Press, 1977); and William Niskanen, *Bureaucracy and Representative Government* (Aldine-Atherton, 1971).

44. Paul W. MacAvoy, *The Regulated Industries and the Economy* (Norton, 1979), p. 105. See also Andrew S. Carron and Paul W. MacAvoy, *The Decline of Service in the Regulated Industries* (American Enterprise Institute for Public Policy Research, 1981).

change in individual factor prices, especially the prices of energy and
capital; change in the general price level; and change in the rate of growth
of the economy." Structural change, Eads argues, altered the issues that
regulatory agencies had to deal with and the frequency with which issues
had to be met, rearranged winners and losers within regulatory coalitions,
generated new potential entrants, and created customer dissatisfaction
with the services being received from regulated industries.[45]

Neither MacAvoy nor Eads is explicit about the political consequences
of these economic events, but one would predict a politics of deregulation
characterized by demands for deregulation from the regulated industries,
seeking to protect their profitability from the adverse effects of regulatory
lag in a time of inflation; new competitors demanding entry into regulated industries; dissatisfied customers of regulated industries; or possibly
the losers of whom Eads speaks, that is, the regulated interests newly
disadvantaged by structural rearrangements. This general approach to
explaining deregulation is unappealing and unpersuasive because there is
very little evidence that any of the parties putatively having an economic
stake in deregulation in fact asked for it or, at any rate, engaged in
enough political activity to have much effect on the outcome.

Most certainly, the regulated industries in our three cases did not ask
to be deregulated. The airlines all began by opposing deregulation, and
only United among the major carriers ever reversed itself, though most
others, as we have said, eventually ceased to be active in opposition. The
Teamsters Union and the thousands of regulated common carriers that
constituted the core of the regulated trucking industry never wished to be
deregulated and are no less firmly opposed now that deregulation has
actually occurred. The drastic drop in the value of operating rights speaks
for itself as an indicator of where the industry's interests lay. AT&T did
not wish to surrender its monopolies and be deregulated. Its executives
firmly believe today, as they believed ten years ago, that the regulated
monopolies of AT&T were in the public interest as well as AT&T's interest.[46] We will argue in chapter 5 that dominant industry interests in all of
our cases did retreat from their initial strong opposition to deregulation,
but that the cause of this retreat was reform initiated by government.

45. George C. Eads, "The Reform of Economic Regulation in Telecommunications and
Transportation," paper prepared for a conference on The Impact of Regulatory Reform in
Canada and the United States, May 20, 1982.

46. See Alvin von Auw, *Heritage and Destiny: Reflections on the Bell System in Transition* (Praeger, 1983), especially p. 88.

Without having encouraged policy change, these industries perforce accommodated to it. It would be a great mistake to interpret this accommodation as the cause of the change.

Because regulation restricted entry and because participation in the protected regime conveyed economic advantages, potential entrants were one likely source of support for deregulation. Some actual or potential competitors of the regulated industries did seek relaxation of regulatory restraints, but for the most part they were badly overmatched both economically and politically by the regulated industries and played only a peripheral role.

Airline deregulation received at least partial support from an assortment of commuter airlines, local service carriers, intrastate carriers in Texas and California, and charter operators. Indirectly, the charter companies may have had an impact. The application of one of them, World Airways, to the CAB in 1967 for authority to offer transcontinental service for $75 received a good deal of attention because the CAB delayed acting on the application and then declared it stale. The CAB's handling of the World application became one of the symbols that reformers invoked to demonstrate the perversity and ridiculousness of regulation. Similarly, action that the Department of Transportation took in 1974 to set minimum charter fares on overseas flights in order to give financial help to Pan American Airways elicited a sharp reaction from regulatory reform advocates newly active in the Senate Judiciary Committee, including brief hearings and a hard-hitting staff report that criticized the CAB as well as the Department of Transportation for putting a floor under charter rates. The CAB's restrictions on charters in the early 1970s also aroused the anger of Senator Howard W. Cannon, Democrat of Nevada, who was then chairman of the Aviation Subcommittee of the Senate Commerce Committee; Cannon was a partisan of the charters, though at the time no one took this to signify that he would be a partisan of deregulation.

Thus, by their mere existence and readiness to offer low-cost rival service to that of the regulated trunk carriers, which elicited a sharply anticompetitive response from government agencies, the charter airlines contributed something to the case for reform, but the contribution was indirect. Otherwise they were peripheral to the politics of deregulation. They were too few in number and too lacking in political resources to be important as direct advocates of policy change, and the same was true of the intrastate, local service, and commuter airlines. Having different priorities, the various classes of rival carriers did not combine to oppose regulation, and even if they had done so, they would not have had remotely the economic role or political visibility of the certificated airlines.

In the trucking industry, uncertificated owner-operators (independent truckers), private carriers (firms that hauled their own goods), and contract carriers (those that undertook to serve particular shippers exclusively) together hauled more freight than did the regulated common carriers as of the early 1970s, and their share was rising. Because the economy was becoming less dependent on the regulated common carriers, the risks of challenging them politically may have been declining too, though not necessarily in proportion. But the owner-operators, private carriers, and contract carriers were not in any other sense a significant force for change. Though politically active in the deliberations over trucking deregulation, they pursued narrow objectives designed to give them modest additional leeway without liberalizing competition more generally. Private carriers, for example, sought to increase their own operating flexibility, most importantly by reducing the constraints on services provided for compensation among subsidiaries of a common corporate parent. Owner-operators, who rarely had ICC certificates, asked for a liberal "back-haul" provision that would enable them to carry regulated freight when they returned from trips with unregulated shipments. Far from being responsible for congressional support of a broad deregulation program, these rival groups had only modest success even with the narrow liberalizing measures on which their efforts were concentrated.

Within the telecommunications industry, new rivals to AT&T became a very active and vocal political force, concerting action through Washington-based trade associations and using every possible avenue of influence over government policy with the ultimate aim, of course, of using the government to influence the behavior of AT&T. But the political activity of the new competitors followed from the FCC's grants of competitive rights rather than being the cause of them. The interconnect industry and the specialized common carriers such as MCI did not become a potent political force until FCC decisions and court rulings enabled them first to offer their products and services and then to prosper. As potential entrants, they had no independent political power in the 1960s other than that which they derived from their symbolism as incipient challengers of AT&T or from their own ingenuity and aggressiveness as manipulators of the regulatory process.[47] Once granted the right to compete, they grew rapidly, yet still were dwarfed by AT&T and its allies. At the time of AT&T's crucial legislative defeat in 1976–77 (see chapter 4), AT&T and its allies dominated interest group activity in telecommunications at least as thoroughly as did the regulated airline and trucking industries when they confronted the forces of reform. The main lobbying organization for competing common carriers, the Ad Hoc Committee for Competitive Telecommunications, was not formed until 1976. As products rather than proponents of procompetitive policies, AT&T's rivals cannot plausibly be given political credit, either, for bringing about the extensive deregulation that soon followed procompetitive change. Instead of deregulation, they wanted protection. Their overriding political objective, naturally enough, was to use government power to constrain AT&T, at least by regulating it and better yet by breaking it up.

What, then, of the consumers of the products and services of the regulated industries? As we have already said, there was no pervasive discontent or demand for change among the general public, nor even much awareness of the issues.[48] In particular, individual users of telephone service were an exceptionally satisfied group.[49] Business customers of all of

47. We allude in particular to MCI, whose exercise of the procompetitive rights granted by the FCC appears to have exceeded that which the FCC intended to grant. The FCC in its *Specialized Common Carrier* decision (1971) intended to restrict the new long distance offerings to private line service, but MCI proceeded to offer, with Execunet, what was in effect public service. When the FCC approved MCI's proposal of a "modular tariff," which embodied the prototype of Execunet, in 1975, it did not understand what it was approving. See Brian O'Reilly, "More Than Cheap Talk Propels MCI," *Fortune*, January 24, 1983, pp. 68–72. Later, when the FCC discovered the error and ordered a halt to Execunet service, MCI successfully appealed to the courts. See chap. 3.

48. A nationwide Harris poll done for AT&T in 1979 ("Public Attitudes toward Competition in the Telecommunications Industry") found that the public was evenly divided on airline deregulation, with 43 percent in favor and 43 percent opposed. This was eight months after Congress had passed the Airline Deregulation Act. In a similar survey in 1976, Harris had found that respondents favored airline regulation by 69 percent to 20 percent. In 1979, there was much more support for deregulation of industries generally than there had been three years earlier. For example, 52 percent of the respondents in 1979 favored regulation of the oil industry, but this was down from 73 percent in 1976. We infer from these data that public opinion was influenced by the advocates of reform and by government action rather than the other way around.

49. By 71 to 28 percent, respondents gave a positive rating to the quality of their telephone service; by 80 to 19 percent they judged the monthly rate for telephone service to be "reasonable" or "very reasonable;" by 64 to 36 percent, they had a high level of confidence in their telephone company; and 56 percent agreed with the statement that "as long as the present regulated telephone system works, it should be left as it is today." Ibid.

the regulated industries stood to gain from a reduction in costs through deregulation, and the business customers of AT&T did respond rapidly to rival offerings of terminal equipment and long distance service. Thus they gave economic impetus to the new competition, but until quite recently they were not politically active on its behalf. Businesses generally ignored airline deregulation, except for some that were located in small cities, where the airlines predicted particular harm.

Unlike consumers in the other two industries, shippers of trucking freight were sufficiently well organized, in the various business and trade associations and in a large functional organization, the National Industrial Traffic League, to make concerted action possible. They also stood to realize substantial savings from deregulation. However, with the exception of a few firms and associations they were so averse to uncertainty and fearful of having to compete with one another for shipping services that they hesitated to support deregulation or even opposed it. Insofar as business shippers cared about the reform issues at all, they tended to be concerned mainly with the impact of reform on their own industries or firms in comparison with competitors; from this standpoint, often as not, trucking deregulation was divisive or impossible to assess. Within the National Industrial Traffic League, an active minority pushed for strong support of trucking deregulation, but the majority did not agree, and throughout the debate the league's position on legislation was cautious and moderate.

In sum, even if procompetitive deregulation promised cost reductions and service improvements to users as a class, those were not objectives for which businesses, let alone the general public, mobilized. We detect little evidence that consumers of the products and services of the regulated industries, as a distinct economic interest, played more than a peripheral role.

This leads finally to the possible role of regulated interests that were newly disadvantaged by what Eads speaks of as structural rearrangements. As we have said, such rearrangements were at least an important precondition for and arguably a fundamental cause of procompetitive reforms of the securities and banking industries, in which new competitors challenged established interests before extensive change had occurred in government regulatory policies. As a result, the newly disadvantaged interests began to contemplate the possibility of changes in regulatory policies. Yet procompetitive deregulation was not the sort of response that new losers on the whole preferred. In the telecommunications industry particularly, AT&T staunchly denied that revolutionary technological changes called for a reversal of anticompetitive regulatory policy. Choosing to defend the status quo, this particular new "loser" argued that nothing in the new technology called into question the case for a single nationwide network of telecommunications services, centrally planned and managed and subject to government regulation.[50]

Technological and economic changes that alter the terms of competition within regulated industries occur all the time. Arguably, the pace of such change increased in the 1950s and 1960s. For a variety of reasons, the gap between costs and prices widened in certain markets—long distance telephone service and transcontinental air service, for example. Such gaps increased the likelihood that regulatory issues would receive political attention, for they constituted an incentive to new entrants and required regulatory bodies either to admit the new competition on controversial terms or, with equal or greater controversy, to suppress it. Either way, the irrationalities of regulation became more visible.[51] But even if they made general debate over regulatory policies more likely, such economic developments did not of themselves make it inevitable. Still less did they determine the particular outcomes of whatever debate arose. Destabilization of a protected industry by the rise of new rivals may lead to the elaboration of anticompetitive regulation. When the trucking industry arose as a competitor to the railroads earlier in the century, the government responded by extending regulation to trucking.

We infer that the success of procompetitive deregulation cannot be attributed to a change in the configuration of economic interests, nor can it be interpreted as the outcome of bargaining among interest groups. The most active and powerful organized interests were opposed to the policy change. In none of the cases did the regulated industries decide that regulation was no longer in their interests. In none was their defeat

---

50. "What has changed in the industry," AT&T argued to a federal judge in defending itself against a government antitrust suit, "is regulatory policy. The FCC has decided to permit new entry, notwithstanding the technology of the industry, in order to give telecommunications users alternative sources of supply." Defendants' First Statement of Contentions and Proof, *U.S.* v. *American Telephone and Telegraph,* 45 Civ. No. 74-1698 (D.D.C. 1979). On the extent to which the new telecommunications technologies caused the rise of competition, making it in some sense necessary or newly justifiable, see the excellent analysis in Gerald W. Brock, *The Telecommunications Industry: The Dynamics of Market Structure* (Harvard University Press, 1981).

51. We are indebted to Merton J. Peck for stressing this point to us.

brought about primarily by other well-organized groups that stood to gain by reform. Rejecting this interpretation of deregulation, we reject also the economic theory of politics from which it derives, offering not only a different account of these events but a different mode of interpretation. Although we make theoretical arguments, we will not offer a theory of politics comparable in structure and scope to the one we reject. In our view it is the implausible pretension of the economic theory of politics to extreme simplicity and yet general application that is its fundamental error.

The Case Studies and Analysis

The heart of the book is devoted to comparing our three cases and laying the basis for an analysis of those factors that led in common to reform. We begin in chapter 2 with an account of how deregulation, especially in its procompetitive form, developed into a powerful policy prescription. Chapters 3–5 seek to explain the most puzzling features of policy change that these three cases have crucially in common: the decision of the regulatory commissions to undertake deregulation; Congress's preference for diffuse interests as opposed to particularistic, well-organized ones; and the failure of interests as powerful as AT&T, the trucker-Teamster combination, and the (admittedly weaker) airlines to bring their political resources to bear more successfully.

Chapter 6, departing from the form of the rest, lays the basis for taking the analysis a step farther by describing bodies of government regulation that, though subject to sharp criticism by economic analysts, remained on the whole resistant to revision. Our purpose is to identify the limits of reform and thus to provide some basis for refining, in comparative fashion, the findings that emerge from our analysis of the three cases of successful policy change. Though we judge our cases to have been politically hard, others manifestly were harder still.

Making inferences from the commonalities among our cases and the contrasts with other cases, we attempt in chapter 7 to explain what it was that made momentous acts of procompetitive deregulation possible even when the political odds against them seemed impossibly high. We find the answers to lie partly in distinctive features of the cases, but partly as well in features of the U.S. political system that give it a greater capacity for

transcending particularistic interests than has generally been acknowledged.

Throughout this chapter we have treated regulatory reform or deregulation (for the time being using the terms more or less interchangeably) as
if it invariably had procompetitive goals. However, as the next chapter
will begin by explaining, this was not the case. Procompetitive deregulation was just one part of an effort by three successive presidents (Ford,
Carter, and Reagan) to broadly reduce unwanted government restraints
on private conduct—restraints that originate in law and then, typically,
are elaborated by administrative agencies. It was, however, much the
most successful part of this effort, and that is why we concentrate on it.
Though we are not especially interested in procompetitive policy change
per se, we are interested in the most important and intellectually puzzling
instances of deregulation, which happen to be procompetitive in nature.
By analyzing them in depth and other, less successful, cases more briefly,
we hope to comprehend the politics of deregulation generally and to learn
from it as much as we can about how policy is made and even, in rare
instances, reversed by the government of the United States.

CHAPTER TWO

The Reform Idea

" 'REGULATORY REFORM' is a cliché whose time has come," congressional Democrats acknowledged in 1975 in a response to reform initiatives of Republican President Gerald R. Ford.[1] "I grant you . . . that the notion of deregulation is the new religion in this town," the chairman of the Federal Communications Commission conceded in 1979 to a senator who was criticizing him for not deregulating fast enough.[2] From the recommendation of a few lonely economists writing in the early 1960s, deregulation had developed in roughly a dozen years into the prevailing policy fashion: much of Washington was doing it or professing to do it.

Our purpose in this chapter is to illuminate that evolution. But not to everyone, nor in all cases, did "regulatory reform" mean "deregulation," and it will be useful, as a prelude to our discussion specifically of deregulation, to say something of the vaguer, more inclusive term.

Presidents, Economists, and Regulatory Reform

Successive presidents beginning with Ford have made regulatory reform a leading part of their domestic agendas, conceiving of it broadly as a response to the excesses of government or at least of bureaucracy, often overlooking the fact that all regulation originates with laws that Congress has passed. "Rules and regulations churned out by federal agencies were

1. To be fair, the complete sentence was much qualified: "We note, however, that while 'regulatory reform' is a cliché whose time has come, one person's regulatory reform is another's environmental, consumer rip-off, unconscionable cancer risk, or return to the robber baronies of yesteryear." "Congressional Democratic Policy Statement on Regulatory Reform," June 25, 1975, in Box 26, Paul C. Leach papers, Gerald R. Ford Library.

2. *Amendments to the Communications Act of 1934,* Hearings before the Subcommittee on Communications of the Senate Committee on Commerce, Science, and Transportation, 96 Cong. 1 sess. (Government Printing Office, 1979), pt. 3, p. 2071.

having a damaging effect on almost every aspect of American life," Ford wrote in his memoirs. "Red tape surrounded and almost smothered us; we as a nation were about to suffocate."[3] With less hyperbole, Jimmy Carter wrote in his memoirs of the "problem of the federal bureaucracy— its complexity, its remoteness when people needed help, its intrusiveness when they wanted to be left alone, and its excessive regulation of the major industries to the detriment of consumers."[4] Carter's successor, Ronald Reagan, had been campaigning for years against big government and bureaucratic excess and entered office pledged to strong, swift action against "overregulation."

In criticizing regulatory excess all of these presidents no doubt were guided very much by political instinct—that is, by their sense of what was on the minds of the public—but in deciding what to do about it they were heavily influenced by the advice of economists on their immediate staffs. Long the locus of institutionalized concern about the efficiency of the federal government's own operations, the Executive Office of the President had also become the center of governmental concern about the efficiency of the economy as a whole, for which the president increasingly bore responsibility in his role as the economy's manager. Much as officials of the Office of Management and Budget (OMB) historically had advised the president on how to achieve efficiency in federal spending, members of the Council of Economic Advisers (CEA) now counseled him on how to reduce inflation, relieve the economy of unnecessary costs, and promote economic growth. And because many economists had become convinced that government regulations were contributing importantly to inflation, imposing unjustifiable costs, and retarding growth, they had advice to offer on how regulation should be reformed. Above all, they advised giving themselves a bigger role, and all three presidents issued executive orders to that end.

Presidents Ford, Carter, and Reagan prescribed rule-making procedures for line agencies (the independent commissions were excepted) that successively gave greater weight to economic analysis both by imposing requirements directly on the agencies and by lodging responsibility for central review in interagency committees or the OMB. Ford required the

3. *A Time to Heal* (Harper and Row and Reader's Digest, 1979), p. 271. Ford elaborated his point as follows: "Rules and regulations . . . were costing taxpayers an estimated $62.9 billion per year, . . . were increasing the cost of doing business . . . and thus contributing to inflation, . . . were perpetuating huge bureaucracies . . . stifling American productivity, promoting inefficiency, eliminating competition, and even invading personal privacy."

4. *Keeping Faith: Memoirs of a President* (Bantam Books, 1982), p. 69.

preparation of inflation impact statements (later called economic impact) to accompany major legislative proposals and rules proposed by the executive branch. "Impact" was to be judged by the costs to consumers, businesses, markets, or governments; the productivity of wage earners, businesses, or governments; effects on competition; and effects on supplies of important products or services. The OMB was designated to develop criteria and procedures for the preparation of these statements, but delegated its responsibility for regulations to the Council on Wage and Price Stability (COWPS), an agency created in 1974 to assist in controlling inflation.[5] In 1975 Congress gave COWPS authority to intervene in rule-making proceedings in order to present its views on inflationary impact.

Carter required agencies to apply formal economic analysis to all regulations whose effects on the economy amounted to $100 million or more or would cause major increases in costs or prices, and he created a unit in his Executive Office called the Regulatory Analysis Review Group (RARG), which was supposed to pick out important regulations for independent review, a step beyond what Ford had required.[6] RARG was in form an interagency group, but it was chaired by the chairman of the CEA; it was headed in fact by that member of the CEA who specialized in microeconomics (William Nordhaus and then George C. Eads); and it drew its professional staff from the CEA and COWPS.

Reagan in turn replaced the Carter executive order with one that sought to impose a strict cost-benefit test and gave the OMB broad powers of intervention and review.[7] The OMB was made subject to the direction of a Presidential Task Force on Regulatory Relief, composed of cabinet members and chaired by Vice-President George Bush. By its

5. Executive Order 11821, November 27, 1974, and Executive Order 11949, December 31, 1976.

6. Executive Order 12044, March 23, 1978. See also Timothy B. Clark, "It's Still No Bureaucratic Revolution, but Regulatory Reform Has a Foothold," *National Journal,* vol. 11 (September 29, 1979), pp. 1596–1601; "How RARG Has Regulated the Regulators," *National Journal,* vol. 11 (October 13, 1979), pp. 1700–02; and Lawrence J. White, *Reforming Regulation: Processes and Problems* (Prentice-Hall, 1981), chap. 2.

7. Executive Order 12291, February 17, 1981. For an official statement of the rationale for review, see *Economic Report of the President, January 1982,* chap. 6. For an evaluation of the various presidential review techniques under Ford, Carter, and Reagan, see W. Kip Viscusi, "Presidential Oversight: Controlling the Regulators," *Journal of Policy Analysis and Management,* vol. 3 (Winter 1983), pp. 157–73; and, for an extended account of the experience under Reagan, George C. Eads and Michael Fix, *Relief or Reform? Reagan's Regulatory Dilemma* (Urban Institute, 1984), pp. 57–65, 112–17. Whether the president has a constitutional right to review regulations gave rise to much debate and some litigation.

name (emphasizing "relief") and stature, this organization signified the Reagan administration's intense commitment to reducing the regulatory burden. Reagan halted new regulations for sixty days, largely to permit review of what had been proposed by the Carter administration as it left office, and he named Murray L. Weidenbaum, a prominent advocate of regulatory reform and the source of an oft-repeated estimate that regulatory costs amounted to $100 billion a year, as the chairman of his Council of Economic Advisers.[8] During the postelection transition, Weidenbaum had headed Reagan's advisory task force on government regulation.

In addition to these purely executive actions, both Carter and Reagan endorsed omnibus regulatory reform bills that would have incorporated in law analytic procedures such as they had prescribed in executive orders. Sharing the president's interest in regulatory reform, Congress in 1979–82 gave extensive consideration to bills framed as amendments to the Administrative Procedure Act of 1946, but was unable to pass one. Although the leading congressional critics of executive rule making wished to include provisions for a legislative veto of regulations and for broadening the authority of the courts to invalidate regulations, no president was willing to go that far in ceding supervision of executive agencies to rival branches. Nor did Congress find it easy to settle differences among contending interests—business on one side and labor, environmentalists, and the consumer movement on the other—over the precise provisions for economic analysis, for the latter groups saw in cost-benefit techniques a threat to the "new" or "social" regulation that they had won in the 1960s and 1970s.[9] This was regulation addressed largely to protect-

8. For the estimates, see *The Costs of Government Regulation of Business,* prepared for the Subcommittee on Economic Growth and Stabilization of the Joint Economic Committee, 95 Cong. 2 sess. (GPO, 1978); and Murray L. Weidenbaum, *Government-Mandated Price Increases* (American Enterprise Institute for Public Policy Research, 1975).

9. *Government Regulation: Proposals for Procedural Reform* (American Enterprise Institute for Public Policy Research, 1979); *Major Regulatory Initiatives during 1980: The Agencies, the Courts, the Congress* (American Enterprise Institute for Public Policy Research, 1981); Timothy B. Clark, "Regulatory 'Reform' May Lose to Regulatory 'Revolution' Advocates," *National Journal,* vol. 12 (June 14, 1980), pp. 969–73; Timothy B. Clark, "Regulating the Regulators," *National Journal,* vol. 12 (October 11, 1980), p. 1709; Alan Murray, "Regulatory Reform Measure Collapses at End of Session," *Congressional Quarterly Weekly Report,* vol. 38 (December 13, 1980), p. 3576; and Laura B. Weiss, "Administration Backs Regulatory Reform Bill," *Congressional Quarterly Weekly Report,* vol. 39 (April 11, 1981), pp. 627–28. For a critical appraisal of the application of cost-benefit analysis to regulations, see Marguerite Connerton and Mark MacCarthy, *Cost-Benefit Analysis and Regulation: Expressway to Reform or Blind Alley?* (Washington, D.C.: National Policy Exchange, 1982).

ing the health and safety of workers and consumers and rationalized on the ground that it was necessary to take account of the external effects of productive activity, such as the costs of pollution to the general public or the costs to children and families of flammable clothing or dangerous toys.

All three presidents saw regulatory excess as a problem, espoused regulatory reform (implying corrections of excess) as a general goal, and embraced economic analysis in rule making as a specific response, but there were important differences among them in the scope and degree of change they sought. The Republican presidents, Reagan especially, differed from the Democrat Carter in wanting to extend reduction to the new regimes—those with jurisdiction over health, safety, and environmental protection. Reagan, taking office after major statutory revisions of the "old" regimes of price, entry, and exit regulation had occurred—and after a campaign in which he had courted the trucking industry with hints that he would go slow on trucking deregulation—positively emphasized reform of the new regimes without, however, repudiating a commitment to deregulation in general.[10]

The difference between Carter and Reagan is dramatized by differences in appointments. Whereas a number of Carter's appointments to the independent regulatory commissions were intended to advance deregulation, for the newer agencies he chose persons identified with the consumer or labor movements whose idea of reform was to solidify and perfect the triumphs only recently embodied in such statutes as the Clean Air Act of 1970. Reagan, by contrast, named an Interstate Commerce Commission chairman who did not believe in deregulation and appointed to the newer agencies persons who had been their adversaries and critics. When he spoke of the need for reducing regulation in campaign appearances, he was fond of citing the more egregious actions of the Occupational Health and Safety Administration (OSHA).[11] Though Carter took

10. Reagan's positions on regulatory reform are anticipated and explained, in flattering terms, in James C. Miller III and Jeffrey A. Eisenach, "Regulatory Reform under Ronald Reagan," in Wayne Valis, ed., *The Future under President Reagan* (Arlington House, 1981), pp. 89–100.

11. On Reagan's appointments, see Timothy B. Clark, "OMB to Keep Its Regulatory Powers in Reserve in Case Agencies Lag," *National Journal,* vol. 13 (March 14, 1981), pp. 424–29; and on his campaign rhetoric, Rowland Evans and Robert Novak, *The Reagan Revolution* (E. P. Dutton, 1981), p. 138. Reagan's appointment of Reese Taylor, a Nevada lawyer backed by the Teamsters Union, as chairman of the ICC seemed to indicate a retreat from the proreform positions of his predecessors in regard to surface transportation. How-

pride in reducing the number of OSHA regulations, his public statements often emphasized the need for preserving the newer regulation. Carter's advocacy of deregulation was confined to particular industries—banking, airlines, trucking, communications, and railways. Among these were three—airlines, trucking, and railways—that had also been singled out by his predecessor for corrective action. Of course, where the positions of rival party leaders converged the chances of deregulation were very much increased.

In this chapter we will inquire how regulatory reform attained so high a place on the government's agenda and show that it entailed a heavy and bipartisan emphasis on what is often loosely called economic regulation, and specifically on instances of such regulation that we will call anticompetitive. In practice this kind of reform consisted of removing restrictions on price, entry, and exit from industries that had earlier been subjected to them on the ground, typically, that competition would be an inadequate safeguard of the public's interest in being served at a reasonable price. In theory at least, such regulation had been applied to natural monopolies that were "affected with a public interest," and accordingly it was called "public utility" regulation. The most significant of the regulatory reforms that took place in the late 1970s and early 1980s represented a judgment that public utility regulation had often been wrongly applied and that reliance on competition should be restored. To us "deregulation" is the removal, to whatever degree, of the earlier restrictions, and advocates of procompetitive reform very often advocated removing them entirely, thus arguing for deregulation in its strictest, most literal sense.[12]

We will describe the accumulation of political forces in support of procompetitive deregulation, but rather than portray this as a process of coalition building—the joining of political actors with shared interests in

---

ever, Reagan's other appointees to the ICC supported procompetitive change, with the result that the commission fell prey to internal feuds. Taylor nonetheless joined his colleagues in several important votes that advanced trucking deregulation. He came to the conclusion that the ICC's remaining regulation of truck licensing and rates had become "a wasteful, inane, monumental paper-shuffling operation with no benefits to anyone." Christopher Conte, "ICC Nears Paralysis as Its Members Feud Bitterly about Deregulation," *Wall Street Journal,* July 18, 1984.

12. For a typology of regulations and reform responses to them, see Stephen Breyer, "Analyzing Regulatory Failure: Mismatches, Less Restrictive Alternatives, and Reform," *Harvard Law Review,* vol. 92 (January 1979), pp. 547–609; and the more extended analysis in Breyer, *Regulation and Its Reform* (Harvard University Press, 1982).

support of a common goal—we portray it primarily as the evolution of a
political or policy idea through three stages. In the first phase, economic
analysts advocated deregulation as a way of reducing the social costs that,
they argued, often unnecessarily resulted from public utility regulation. In
the second phase, two presidents of the United States—Ford and Carter—and a leading senator—Edward M. Kennedy—advocated it as a way
of responding to widely shared desires, sentiments, and values. For them
it became, with differing emphases, a highly visible way to combat inflation, control the rise in consumer prices, reduce big government and
bureaucracy, and restore free enterprise. Finally, deregulation—by this
time often vaguely defined and loosely applied—became a preferred style
of policy choice in the nation's capital, espoused more or less automatically, even unthinkingly, by a wide range of officeholders and their critics
and used by them as a guide to position taking.

Deregulation as Analytic Prescription

In the late 1950s and early 1960s, academic economists began to produce a body of literature highly critical of price, entry, and exit regulation. Now regarded as classics, some of these early studies were abstract
and largely theoretical,[13] whereas others addressed the performance of
particular regulated industries and regulatory agencies and concluded
with highly explicit policy recommendations. Thus the basic message of
one work was "simply, that the major reason the transportation industries
have not grown and prospered as much as most industries is that transportation has been overregulated." The authors argued for "a substantial
reduction in government regulation of transportation and heavy reliance
on the forces of market competition to insure services and rates in the
best interest of the public."[14] Similarly, another author was quite critical
of the Civil Aeronautics Board and concluded by asking how public policy could "move, without serious transitional difficulties, from the present
system to one of relatively free competition."[15]

13. Harvey Averch and Leland Johnson, "Behavior of the Firm under Regulatory Constraint," *American Economic Review,* vol. 52 (December 1962), pp. 1052–69.
14. John R. Meyer and others, *The Economics of Competition in the Transportation Industries* (Harvard University Press, 1959), pp. vi, 270.
15. Richard Caves, *Air Transport and Its Regulators* (Harvard University Press, 1962),
p. 447.

An outpouring of related work followed these early beginnings, with results that were remarkably consistent. "In an era when economists are often accused of being unable to agree on anything," the authors of a review of the economic literature on regulation wrote, "we find comfort in the virtually unanimous professional conclusion that price and entry regulation in several multifirm markets [they cited agriculture, transportation, and oil and natural gas production] is inefficient and ought to be eliminated."[16] Their review included a bibliography of 150 items.

We are convinced that except for the development of this academic critique of policy, the reforms we are trying to explain would never have occurred; yet for the reforms to become possible, the academic critique had to cease being merely academic and enter into the stream of policy discussion in official Washington. That this happened is largely accounted for by three circumstances. First, the critique was taken up by precisely those organizations—foundations and policy-oriented research institutions—that specialize in linking social science analysis to public policy formation. Second, economists entered public service in large enough numbers, and in offices sufficiently influential and strategically placed, to constitute an important force for advocacy within the government. And, finally, several elements of the executive branch were disposed to promote procompetitive policies.

Between 1967 and 1975 the Ford Foundation granted $1.8 million to the Brookings Institution, a Washington-based public policy research organization, for a program of studies in the regulation of economic activity, an effort that resulted directly or indirectly in twenty-two books and monographs, sixty-five journal articles, and thirty-eight doctoral dissertations.[17] The grantors had no specific reform goals in mind; they merely had a hunch that here was a promising subject. By attracting scholars to the study of economic regulation, putting them in touch with one another through conferences and workshops, giving them a highly visible publications outlet, and encouraging them to address public policy issues, this very large effort by the Ford Foundation in collaboration with Brookings increased the volume of scholarly publication on government regulation, increased its salience to policymaking, and helped to equip some of the younger authors with the credentials that would be needed

16. Paul L. Joskow and Roger G. Noll, "Regulation in Theory and Practice: An Overview," in Gary Fromm, ed., *Studies in Public Regulation* (MIT Press, 1981), p. 8.
17. From documents in the files of the Brookings Economic Studies program.

for high government service. As the Ford grants expired, Brookings' research on regulation diminished, but another Washington-based organization, the American Enterprise Institute for Public Policy Research, at about that time took up regulatory reform as a policy cause and began to promote it with numerous pamphlets and conference proceedings.

Many of the leading academic analysts of regulation, authors of influential books and articles, served in Washington in the late 1960s or early 1970s as members of the Council of Economic Advisers or its staff, in the Office of Management and Budget, the Justice Department, or the Department of Transportation, or with presidential task forces and study groups. Given the rising scholarly interest in procompetitive deregulation as a policy goal, the near-unanimous commitment of economists to it, and the growing participation of economists in policymaking, it was inevitable that some proponents of reform would enter public positions; on the government's side, the existence of several agencies with an interest in procompetitive reform meant that there was no shortage of congenial receiving places.

For the Council of Economic Advisers, a position favoring procompetitive deregulation followed from its professional composition; this was an organization of economists.[18] For the Antitrust Division of the Justice Department, a procompetitive position was inherent in its mission, though it was not until the late 1960s that the division began to conceive of regulatory reform within the government as a proper way of fulfilling that mission and thus began, for example, to participate in regulatory proceedings; historically, it had functioned by bringing suit against antitrust violators.[19] For the Department of Transportation, a procompetitive position was largely an accident of the timing of its formation. Created in the mid-1960s in part to reform and rationalize transportation policy, it decided to intervene in regulatory proceedings in order to promote procompetitive policies. However, there was enough ambivalence in this position—and enough internal division over it, given the pressures on

18. For example, see the *Economic Report of the President, January 1971*, pp. 122–30, for a powerful argument against transportation regulation; and the remarks of Gary L. Seevers on the CEA's role in James C. Miller III, ed., *Perspectives on Federal Transportation Policy* (American Enterprise Institute for Public Policy Research, 1975), pp. 201–04.

19. Suzanne Weaver, *Decision to Prosecute* (MIT Press, 1977), pp. 115–18, 130–31; Richard E. Cohen, "Antitrust Division Emerges as Major Regulatory Watchdog," *National Journal*, vol. 6 (June 15, 1974), pp. 875–86; and interviews with Lionel Kestenbaum, July 20, 1980; Donald F. Turner, July 11, 1980; and Donald I. Baker, June 19, 1980.

the department to take a protectionist stance toward the transportation industries—to cause the department often to be at odds with other deregulators in the government establishment.[20] The Federal Trade Commission—and, during its seven-year life (1974–81), the Council on Wage and Price Stability—were other, lesser elements in this official coalition at the upper reaches of the executive branch. Bases of advocacy for competition, these agencies were also important training ground for advocates. Some of the scholars who wrote influential critiques of regulatory policies served in these agencies before doing so.

As of about 1970–71, there were enough active advocates of regulatory reform inside the government to constitute a small, informal community, loosely bound by personal acquaintance and commitment to a shared policy goal. What had begun as a random critique of government policies from private sources, with publication outlets in obscure learned journals and the book lists of university presses, in a decade had evolved into a moderately concerted effort with a substantial official and quasi-official base, whose written products included a stream of position papers internal to the government. Thus procompetitive regulatory reform was well and widely articulated as a policy prescription; but it remained a solution in search of a widely perceived problem, and its advocates remained in need of high-level political leadership.

It was insufficient to argue, no matter how persuasively, on the basis of reasoning and evidence that anticompetitive regulation was inefficient. For reform to begin to succeed, the need for it had somehow to be dramatized. Events could serve this dramatic function, and in 1970 the bankruptcy of the Penn Central, the nation's biggest railroad, did so to some extent. The collapse of the Penn Central drove federal transportation officials to a greater activism and discredited the regulatory practices of the ICC, which was condemned for forcing the Penn Central and other railroads to continue unprofitable operations. After the Penn Central failure, Transportation Department officials went to work on draft legislation for deregulating surface transportation, but when the Transportation Regulatory Modernization Act of 1971 went to Congress, it went from the department without benefit of presidential sponsorship.[21] President Nixon, the advocates of reform surmised, had caved in to the Teamsters.

---

20. Ann F. Friedlaender, *The Dilemma of Freight Transport Regulation* (Brookings, 1969), p. viii; and interview, Stanton P. Sender, July 24, 1980.

21. Interviews, John W. Barnum, July 15, 1980; and James C. Miller III, July 23, 1980.

There may be truth in this (we do not know), but it is true as well that the Penn Central bankruptcy, distressing though it was to transportation officials, did not constitute the kind of national affliction that necessarily evoked a presidential response. President Nixon could give in to the Teamsters (if that is what he did) because he did not feel compelled to sponsor a legislative solution to the "railroad crisis." And if the nation was experiencing a "transportation crisis," it showed no sign of comprehending that fact or of expecting the president to do something about it.

Deregulation as Policy Choice and Political Symbol

The existence of expert advocates, strongly committed to procompetitive deregulation and armed with analysis so abundant and consistent, created some probability that sooner or later political figures would respond. Officeholders are perpetually in search of program material—positions to advocate on the problems of the day—with the result that advocates, as the offerers of positions, have a fair chance of making matches with politicians who will become advocates in turn. On the other hand, plenty of advocates compete for the politicians' attention, and the higher ranking, more visible, and more powerful the politician, the more intense the competition becomes. Success for the advocates depends to some extent on more or less calculable factors such as strategic position, access to officeholders, the advocates' own professional status and prestige, and the ability to marshal arguments in a convincing and arresting way, but fortune too usually plays an unpredictable part. Typically, events must occur or background conditions of popular mood or opinion must develop in such a way that the politician sees in the advocates' prescription a way of responding to a problem of particular immediacy or of addressing the rising concerns of the public.

It was the happy fate of the advocates of deregulation in 1974–75 to make the best matches with officeholders that anyone could have conceived of—first with the most publicized Democrat in the Senate, Edward M. Kennedy, and soon thereafter with the new Republican president, Gerald R. Ford, who succeeded the disgraced Richard M. Nixon in the late summer of 1974. Both men espoused procompetitive deregulation as a policy choice and by their own actions and advocacy turned it into a political symbol of moderate potency.

Kennedy and Consumerism

Kennedy became involved when one of the expert advocates of regulatory reform, Stephen G. Breyer, became special counsel to the Subcommittee on Administrative Practice and Procedure of the Judiciary Committee, which Kennedy chaired. A professor of administrative and antitrust law at Harvard, Breyer had worked in the Justice Department's Antitrust Division in the late 1960s at the time it was beginning to get involved in regulatory proceedings, and with the economist Paul Mac-Avoy he was coauthor of a book that argued for deregulation of natural gas.[22] Though not an economist himself, he was very much part of the academic community that had built the analytic case for reform, and his arrival on Capitol Hill substantially bolstered the forces of advocacy in Washington.

Upon joining the subcommittee staff in the spring of 1974, Breyer urged Kennedy to consider airline regulation as a subject of investigative hearings, with the expectation that this would set the theme—regulation versus competition—for a whole series of investigations. He wanted to begin with the airlines because he believed that the analytic case for reform had been especially well established for that industry. Kennedy showed routine interest rather than great enthusiasm for the subject; he was willing to let the staff see what they could make of it. At any rate, he preferred it to Breyer's alternative proposal, which was for hearings on procedural changes suggested by the Watergate scandal. (This was another string to Breyer's bow; besides being expert on regulation, he had been on the Watergate Special Prosecuting Force.)[23]

Breyer believed that Kennedy was attracted to hearings on regulation by the prospect of achieving a concrete, worthwhile end. Under Kennedy's leadership for several years, the subcommittee had become "the fire brigade for liberal causes," according to an earlier counsel. The Nader

22. Stephen G. Breyer and Paul W. MacAvoy, *Energy Regulation by the Federal Power Commission* (Brookings, 1974).

23. Our account of the origin of the hearings and the relation between Kennedy and Breyer is drawn almost wholly from "Senator Kennedy and the Civil Aeronautics Board," a case study prepared by Donald Simon for the John F. Kennedy School of Government and the Law School of Harvard University in 1977. (Hereafter "Kennedy and the CAB.") In addition to the author's narrative, it contains copious quotations from Breyer and reproductions of two crucial memoranda that he wrote to Kennedy in May and June 1974. We supplemented it with an interview on July 14, 1980, with Thomas M. Susman, who was chief counsel to Kennedy's subcommittee.

Congressional Study Project had characterized it as "racing feverishly from one conflagration to another, leaving the rebuilding and analysis of source and solutions to others."[24] Perhaps in reaction to this rather unflattering reputation, Kennedy was now willing to undertake an issue that Breyer told him, not altogether correctly, would be "nonglamorous."[25] But it is more likely that Kennedy was attracted to the subject because he saw in it a response to consumerism, the political movement that addressed the interests of the consumer against big business or, in the case of regulatory regimes, the combination of big business and big government. As possible themes of the hearings, Breyer had suggested "help the consumer," "free the captive agency," or "more competition," and his memoranda to Kennedy defined prices as the central issue. Kennedy's opening statement in the hearings did so too: "Regulators all too often encourage or approve unreasonably high prices, inadequate service, and anticompetitive behavior. The cost of this regulation is always passed on to the consumer. And that cost is astronomical." "The way to get the press's and the public's and the senator's attention," a staff aide later said, "was with the consumer stuff," not just high prices, but also lost luggage and the suffering of household pets shipped as freight.[26]

There is not room here, nor is it necessary for our purposes, to recount the development of the consumer movement, except insofar as it contributed to the creation of a perceived audience for procompetitive regulatory reform. In that respect its most important activity was neither explicit advocacy nor direct lobbying (although there was some of both, to be described later). Rather, its influence lay in disseminating a populist critique of government regulation to the press and the attentive public.

The themes that anticompetitive regulation had a probusiness bias and that regulatory agencies were at best incompetent and at worst "captured" and corrupt had been driven home quite widely by the mid-1970s, even if price and entry deregulation was not, strictly speaking, a mass

24. The Ralph Nader Congress Project, *The Judiciary Committees* (Grossman, 1975), p. 221.

25. The phrase is from a memo that Breyer wrote to Kennedy on May 20, 1974, outlining a choice between two different sets of hearings, one on the CAB ("a nonglamorous, detailed, intricate, 'good government' job") and another on procedural changes that should follow from Watergate ("important and topical . . . more likely to receive publicity"). "Kennedy and the CAB."

26. Ibid.; *Oversight of Civil Aeronautics Board Practices and Procedures,* Hearings before the Subcommittee on Administrative Practice and Procedure of the Senate Judiciary Committee, 94 Cong. 1 sess. (GPO, 1975), vol. 1, p. 1; and Susman interview.

issue. Anyone who had an informed opinion on the subject could hardly have failed to have that opinion. Academic analysis played a part in this. While economists purported to show, with ever-increasing analytic sophistication, that anticompetitive regulation was inefficient and therefore contrary to the public interest, the literature of political science and history provided an explanation of why this outcome had occurred. Overwhelmingly, it portrayed regulatory agencies as excessively subject to the interests of regulated industries, although the authors differed over whether government regulation had been inspired by business interests in the first place or only succumbed to them with time through a combination of internal decay and the default of public supervision.[27]

Having gained considerable currency in academic settings, the view that regulatory agencies served the interests of the regulated was greatly amplified in the late 1960s and early 1970s by Ralph Nader and the political movement that formed around his person, purporting to speak for consumers generally. Nader's Raiders, Ivy League graduate students who were eager to expose the wrongdoing of regulators, fanned out through government agencies and produced a series of books on the incompetence and probusiness bias they believed they found there. These books had surprisingly large sales, partly as a result of their use as college texts. Nader's Raiders took the critique of regulatory agencies out of learned journals and gave it a semipopularized, widely accessible form.[28]

But it was through the press, rather than through these books, that Nader and his associates had most of their influence on public opinion and on politicians' perceptions of what they ought to be saying and voting for. Nader was news. He was an unusual personality, conflict surrounded him, and, as one writer shrewdly observed, the press, though inhibited by professional norms from putting out its own populist critique of America, was quick to respond when others skillfully supplied one. Certain reporters at elite papers—Morton Mintz of the *Washington Post,* who wrote Naderesque tracts himself, and David Burnham of the

27. Gabriel Kolko, *The Triumph of Conservatism: A Reinterpretation of American History, 1900–1916* (Free Press, 1963); and Marver H. Bernstein, *Regulating Business by Independent Commission* (Princeton University Press, 1955).

28. For a good account of the activity of Nader's Raiders, see Jay Acton and Alan LeMond, *Ralph Nader: A Man and a Movement* (Warner Paperback Library, 1972), pp. 86–133. For a penetrating review of one of their publications, see James R. Nelson, "The Ralph Nader Group Report on the Interstate Commerce Commission," *Bell Journal of Economics and Management Science,* vol. 2 (Spring 1971), pp. 330–36. The subject of Nelson's essay, *The Interstate Commerce Omission,* by Robert Fellmeth (Grossman Publishers, 1970), was a leading example of the Raiders' research style.

New York Times, who won a number of journalistic prizes for exposing government agencies—did investigative reporting that independently reinforced the work of Nader and his followers, while a much larger part of the press depended on them as subjects and sources. Nader and his coworkers became a "public relations bureau for the new populism," and tried to "restructure the American public's image of who governs the nation's political economy."[29] With help from the press and academia, Nader apparently made a good deal of headway. Eventually the idea that government regulation served business interests penetrated mass attitudes. In 1977 a poll for *U.S. News & World Report* showed that 81 percent agreed and only 8 percent disagreed with the statement that "large companies have a major influence on the government agencies regulating them." In a Sentry poll the same year, 46 percent agreed and only 24 percent disagreed with the statement that "on the whole, government regulation has done more to help business than to protect the consumer."[30]

Kennedy's hearings on the CAB, held early in 1975 after a half year of preparation by Breyer and a very able staff, were an outstanding dramatic success.[31] They set forth anew the academic findings about the adverse effects of airline regulation, uncovered abundant evidence of the agency's anticompetitive policies, and combined the two in a setting that exposed the CAB's inability to answer its critics. One whole day of hearings was devoted, for example, to showing that intrastate fares in Texas and California, for flights not subject to CAB regulation, were less than fares for comparable interstate flights, which were subject to regulation. This difference, which academic literature had already called attention to, appeared to constitute one of the most vivid and compelling indictments of regulation, but the CAB and the regulated airlines denied that regulation was the cause of it, arguing instead that differences in weather conditions, traffic densities, and aircraft types were to blame. The subcommittee staff gathered evidence with which to confirm regulation as the leading cause.

---

29. Simon Lazarus, *The Genteel Populists* (Holt, Rinehart and Winston, 1974), pp. 77–81.

30. "Regulators and the Polls," *Regulation,* vol. 2 (November–December 1978), pp. 10–12, 54.

31. The hearings, *Oversight of Civil Aeronautics Board Practices and Procedures,* were published in three volumes, with five additional volumes of appendices. Breyer's account of them, with inferences and advice for his successors in reform, may be found in *Regulation and Its Reform,* chap. 16, and in Stephen G. Breyer and Leonard R. Stein, "Airline Deregulation: The Anatomy of Reform," in Robert W. Poole, Jr., ed., *Instead of Regulation: Alternatives to Federal Regulatory Agencies* (Lexington Books, 1982), pp. 1–41.

Another day of hearings exposed the existence of a route moratorium, an informal, hitherto-unacknowledged policy of the CAB to deny the granting of new routes. Another day, dealing with what Breyer liked to call "frozen dogs," was designed to publicize miscellaneous consumer complaints unrelated to fares, such as overbooking and abuse of pets shipped as cargo. This particular hearing publicized the damning fact, uncovered by staff investigators, that the CAB's Bureau of Enforcement spent only 3 percent of its time on such complaints, whereas it spent 60 percent of its time on supervision of charter airlines whose typical offense was to offer fares below CAB-approved rates.

The function of the hearings was to provide vivid, concrete confirmation of the academic and populist critiques of economic regulation in a form readily accessible to the national press—indeed, calculated to attract it. Breyer and his staff briefed the press even before the hearings began on what they were planning to achieve and then had daily briefings while the hearings were going on. The national press in general responded with full coverage and admiring comment for what they judged to be an exceptionally successful effort at congressional oversight. In particular, Breyer formed a close relation with David Burnham of the *Times*, who covered the hearings in great depth because, as he later told an interviewer, they were "really aimed at substance"—"solid stuff" as opposed to mere scandalmongering. The hearings did not in fact pay much attention to instances of individual misconduct. They concentrated more on the limited competence of the CAB as a whole and on its inability to defend convincingly the practice of price and entry regulation. Therein for Burnham lay the real scandal and the real value of the hearings.[32]

Nonetheless, there was a suggestion of scandal more conventionally defined. The director of the CAB's Bureau of Enforcement committed suicide two days before he was scheduled to testify, after having surmised from files in his office that the CAB had prematurely closed an investigation into illegal campaign contributions from the airlines during the Nixon administration. Robert D. Timm, who was CAB chairman at the time of the investigation, and Richard J. O'Melia, who had been director of the Bureau of Enforcement then but had become acting chairman following the departure of Timm, were both implicated. The subcommittee held an inconclusive day of hearings on this unanticipated set of events, during which Timm and O'Melia gave conflicting testimony, and then referred the matter to the Department of Justice. A staff source later

32. "Kennedy and the CAB."

said that this episode saved the hearings from being too dull and academic, heightened the interest of Senator Kennedy and the Ford administration, and kept the press coming.[33]

Ford and Inflation

Except for the need to combat inflation, President Ford might not have become an advocate of deregulation. When he took office in the summer of 1974, inflation was the leading domestic problem, and his administration began with a series of summit meetings of influential citizens to discuss remedies for it. Nearly all economists at these meetings agreed on one thing only—that government itself was contributing to inflation with a variety of anticompetitive restrictions on the operation of markets. Hendrik Houthakker, a former member of the CEA, prepared a long list of offending yet well-established government policies, so-called sacred cows, that were potential objects of reform, such as the monopoly of the U.S. Postal Service, minimum wage laws, and subsidies for ship construction and operation.[34]

Slaughtering sacred cows is hard political work, and no one in the Ford administration could quite figure out in the fall of 1974 what to do next. The administration's initial response was vague and vacuous compared with its later effort. In a major address to Congress on the economy, the president identified "restrictive practices" as one of several areas in which government should act in order to combat inflation. To counteract such practices, Ford called for stricter enforcement of antitrust laws, surveillance of the inflationary effects of government action by COWPS, the preparation of inflation impact statements to accompany executive regulations or proposals for legislation, and the creation by Congress of a national commission on regulatory reform to examine the independent regulatory agencies.[35]

33. Susman interview.
34. Daniel J. Balz, "Summit Inflation Meetings Highlight More Questions than Answers," *National Journal,* vol. 6 (October 5, 1974), pp. 1503–05.
35. "Address to a Joint Session of the Congress on the Economy," *Public Papers of the Presidents: Gerald R. Ford, 1974* (GPO, 1975), pp. 228–38; and interview, Stanley Morris, July 8, 1980. Although Congress did not create a commission, the Senate Committee on Governmental Affairs did initiate an inquiry of its own into the conduct of regulatory agencies pursuant to S. Res. 71 of the Ninety-Fourth Congress. In 1976–78 the committee produced six volumes and an appendix of case studies under the general title *Study on Federal Regulation,* in addition to hearings.

This was not a prescription for fast or effective action, and it may have been a blessing for the executive branch proponents of regulatory reform that Congress did not act on the president's recommendation for a commission. Had it done so, policy change would probably have been delayed rather than advanced. Instead, an administration task force—the Domestic Council Review Group on Regulatory Reform (DCRG)—emerged in the summer as an analyst and advocate, less prestigious and less publicized than a national commission would have been, but also more cohesive, committed, expeditious, and effective, even though lacking a formal charter. The group met once a week in the White House, bringing together reform proponents from the Department of Justice, Council of Economic Advisers, Office of Management and Budget, Domestic Council, and Council on Wage and Price Stability.[36] It operated with considerable élan; slaughtering sacred cows, besides being hard work, is fun. It is fun, too, to have the backing of the president, and the commitment of Ford's staff members intensified and their pride rose as they became convinced of his willingness to challenge powerful interests. There is, for example, an oft-repeated story of a meeting at which the trucking deregulation bill was being considered. Ford, puffing on his pipe, turned to Secretary of Transportation William Coleman and said, "I understand the Teamsters and truckers are pretty opposed to this, is that right, Bill?" And Coleman replied, "Yes, that's right, Mr. President." Whereupon the president said, "Well, if the Teamsters and truckers are against it, it must be a pretty good bill." This exchange took place not long after a stormy meeting between representatives of the administration and the Teamsters.[37]

By the spring of 1975, Ford was speaking of regulatory reform as if it were an end in itself, not just one element in an anti-inflation program,

36. In the spring of 1976, when the DCRG was trying to enlarge its efforts, membership was broadened with representatives from a number of line agencies, including the Departments of Transportation, Labor, Agriculture, and Health, Education, and Welfare, the Small Business Administration, and the Federal Energy Administration. The Ford administration left office before the effectiveness of the expanded group could be tested.

37. Interview, William T. Coleman, July 28, 1980. The same incident is reported in Paul H. Weaver, "Unlocking the Gilded Cage of Regulation," *Fortune* (February 1977), p. 182. Similarly, a career official in the OMB told us that "Political arguments didn't appeal to Ford at all. He was very solid. He was always procompetition." Morris interview. Some of our sources compared Ford favorably with Carter in this respect. Susman, for example, saw no important differences in policies on transportation deregulation between the Ford and Carter administrations, but observed that Carter "was playing a lot more political games with us than Ford ever did."

and he was rationalizing it on grounds that mixed popular culture, individual psychology, and economics: "Reduced competition hurts . . . the entire free enterprise system," he told an audience in New Hampshire. "Competition—I think it is good in politics, I think it is good in athletics, and I think competition is the key to productivity and innovation." Two weeks later, before the annual meeting of the U.S. Chamber of Commerce in Washington, he gave a major speech in which the need for regulatory reform was the dominant theme, and the rationale was enlarged to encompass the need to combat big government in general. "A government big enough to give us everything we want is a government big enough to take from us everything we have," he admonished, in an aphorism borrowed from his predecessor.[38]

Thus, whereas Senator Kennedy had hewed consistently to a proconsumer theme, Ford's criticisms of regulation were variously addressed to consumer interests, business interests, the traditional American attachment to free enterprise, and popular hostility to big government. Mass distrust of government was growing, and so was resentment of the costs of supporting it and bearing its intrusions on private activity. A policy stance that promised to reduce government activity therefore had some potential for mass appeal (and some potential utility for a president who would soon be asking the national electorate to return him to office). Ford found that his speeches attacking big government and promising regulatory reform elicited a warm response.

The backing of powerful political leaders transformed the prospects of regulatory reform. What had been a gleam in the collective eye of a committed few suddenly became a leading item on the domestic agenda of the government—rather to the bewilderment of the press, some of whom were puzzled by the motives of a president evidently willing to risk this challenge to vested interests. John Osborne, a veteran observer of presidents for the *New Republic,* suspected that Ford was either naive or duplicitous. "The doubt remaining with me," Osborne wrote in the fall of 1975, "is whether the President adequately comprehends the extent of the challenge that he is posing or pretending to pose to powerful interests, notably labor and corporate interests, and whether, if he does compre-

38. "Remarks at the White House Conference on Domestic and Economic Affairs in Concord, New Hampshire," *Public Papers of the Presidents: Gerald R. Ford, 1975,* bk. 1 (GPO, 1977), pp. 518–24; and "Remarks at the Annual Meeting of the Chamber of Commerce of the United States," ibid., pp. 598–604. In his memoirs Ford names regulatory reform as one of his top domestic priorities for 1975.

hend it, he really intends to sustain and press the challenge."[39] The more politically oriented members of the president's staff were not happy with the emphasis he chose to put on this issue, nor was his vice-president, Nelson A. Rockefeller.[40] Understandably, those most closely involved in the reform effort seem to have been a bit incredulous themselves, and they occasionally sought reaffirmations of the president's concern.

In particular, late in 1975 the leaders of the DCRG, Edward Schmults and Paul MacAvoy, asked for a meeting at which they could secure Ford's personal views and guidance. The transportation bills had been sent to Congress, and the group was wondering what to do next. They also wanted to talk about how to get support from consumer groups, which they said had been only "lukewarm," and the general community of business, which likewise had not been very helpful. By contrast, the unions and corporations in the regulated industries were beginning to mount well-financed campaigns against reform proposals. And, with the presidential election approaching—Ford's one and only campaign for the office—they no doubt wished an opportunity to detect whether his commitment might wane on that account. In the meeting, which took place early in February 1976, MacAvoy put the question of politics to the president quite bluntly: he asked whether the president viewed the issue of regulatory reform as helping or hurting his political prospects and volunteered that sooner or later it was going to be clear that attacks on special interests would be counterproductive. Ford's answer must have been reassuring. Vested interests are always well organized, he said, and it was necessary to develop an effective counterforce to deal with them.[41]

By the way he used his office on behalf of reform, Ford demonstrated strong convictions. He argued for deregulation in speeches. He named a presidential counsel to specialize in regulatory matters and encouraged the DCRG in planning reform. He held one meeting with a select group of congressional leaders and two meetings with members of regulatory agencies to argue for reform, an exceptional showing of presidential inter-

39. John Osborne, *White House Watch: The Ford Years* (New Republic Books, 1977), p. 193.

40. Morris interview; and A. James Reichley, *Conservatives in an Age of Change* (Brookings, 1981), p. 400. In an interview on March 14, 1983, however, Ford could recall no dissension within his administration.

41. Memoranda, Edward Schmults and Paul MacAvoy to president, December 24, 1975, and Schmults and MacAvoy to president, February 2, 1976, in Box 30, Schmults papers, Ford Library; and "Notes on Meeting with the President," February 4, 1976, in Box 27, Leach papers.

est. He took an interest in the content of reform bills, and personally heard contending arguments of the Department of Transportation and Department of Justice. He sponsored the bills that interagency planning produced. He used his veto or the threat of it to bargain with Congress for legislation. Under him, the loose, informal subcommunity of reformers inside the executive branch was converted into a more organized force, aided by White House leadership to settle internal differences, and inspired by the belief that a president was prepared to take political risks on behalf of their cause.[42]

Progress was uneven, and priorities were unclear. The Domestic Council Review Group's interest in reform covered a very wide range of activities. For some—railroads, natural gas, financial institutions, repeal of "fair trade" laws—legislation was already pending before Congress when the DCRG was formed. For others—the Davis-Bacon Act, ocean shipping, insurance, agricultural cooperatives, the Postal Service, the activities generally of the "dependent" (or line) agencies—the DCRG made forays into regulatory terrain but achieved no progress substantial enough to approach the submission of bills. The greatest concentration of effort was on airlines and trucking, for which the administration submitted reform bills in 1975, and cable television and the Robinson-Patman Act (enacted during the Depression as a price-stabilizing measure to protect small grocers against supermarket chains), for which it came very close to doing so.[43] These were subjects on which a good deal of preparatory work had

42. The Ford administration's actions on regulatory reform are thoroughly chronicled in Louis M. Kohlmeier, "Ford Initiates Reform Offensive," *National Journal*, vol. 7 (July 7, 1975), p. 1000; Richard E. Cohen, "Ford Building Framework for Attempt to Change Policy," *National Journal*, vol. 7 (July 26, 1975), pp. 1078-83; Richard E. Cohen, "Justice, DOT Dispute over Airline Mergers Goes to Ford," *National Journal*, vol. 7 (September 27, 1975), pp. 1362-64; and Louis M. Kohlmeier, " 'Big Government' a Campaign Issue," *National Journal*, vol. 7 (November 1, 1975), p. 1520. See also *The Challenge of Regulatory Reform, A Report to the President from the Domestic Council Review Group on Regulatory Reform* (GPO, 1977).

43. Failure to submit legislation to lift the FCC's restrictions on cable television, despite the fact that Ford had said publicly that it would be submitted, gave rise to speculation in the general and trade press that he had yielded to pressure from the broadcasting industry. At least in this case, the stories intimated, he was unwilling to challenge powerful interests. The television networks were indeed very much opposed to the deregulation of cable, and politically oriented White House staff members argued that the president ought not to enter into a fight with them in an election year. In addition, the case for making the fight was thoroughly undermined by two circumstances: sharp differences between the DCRG and the Office of Telecommunications Policy over what kind of bill to recommend even if the

been done even before the DCRG was formed and for which it was possible to use the expertise of line or presidential staff agencies to challenge independent regulatory commissions. (Thus the Department of Transportation worked on bills affecting the CAB and ICC, the Office of Telecommunications Policy in the Executive Office of the President worked on those affecting the FCC, and the Department of Justice worked on all bills for procompetitive deregulation, but particularly those affecting the Federal Trade Commission.) Because the DCRG had no staff capacity for the preparation of bills, it depended very heavily on task forces drawn from executive agencies.[44] This may have been one of the reasons why the Ford administration found that it was harder to make headway with regulatory reform in the line agencies than in the independent regulatory commissions. Departmental secretaries generally were inclined to resist reform of regimes over which they presided, whereas Ford's secretary of transportation, William T. Coleman, actively cooperated in the administration's effort to modify the regimes of the CAB and ICC.[45]

---

president were willing to recommend one; and progress toward cable deregulation that was being made in the FCC and the courts even without the president's getting involved. It is scarcely conceivable that under such circumstances any president would have chosen to get involved. Paul MacAvoy sought a way out by arguing that more research was necessary. Memo, Paul MacAvoy and Edward Schmults to president, December 18, 1975, and enclosures; draft memo, Jim Cannon to president, February 23, 1976; memo, Lynn May to Edward Schmults and others, March 17, 1976; memo, John Eger to president, "Cable Television Regulation," no date; memo, MacAvoy to May, March 25, 1976; and memo, MacAvoy to DCRG, April 2, 1976, all in Box 22, Leach papers; and memo, Jim Cannon to president, March 11, 1976, and memo, Lynn May to Jim Cannon, November 15, 1976, both in Box 7, James M. Cannon papers, Ford Library.

44. The task force on transportation regulatory reform, for example, contained six members from the Department of Transportation, four from the Department of Justice, one from COWPS, and four from the OMB.

45. Too, the differences in organizational structure and patterns of authority and accountability appear to have created a different psychology. The Ford administration's approach to the independent regulatory commissions—which were not quite "of" the administration because of their ambiguous constitutional status (see chap. 3)—was overtly admonitory. The approach to department secretaries, who by contrast were unambiguously of the administration, was more tentative and solicitous. For example, the DCRG showed considerable deference in approaching Secretary of Labor John T. Dunlop. Enclosure to memo, Lynn May to Rod Hills, August 13, 1975, in Box 32, Schmults papers. In the Carter administration, Secretary of Transportation Brock Adams had to be admonished by the president to cooperate even in the reform of the regulatory regimes of the CAB and ICC. Interview, Stuart Eizenstat, April 13, 1981. The Ford administration's differing experience with the independent commissions and the line agencies is described in "A Task Force Proposal for Improving Agency Regulations," discussion draft, March 4, 1976, enclosure to memo, Ed Schmults to Bill Seidman, March 11, 1976, in Box 29, Cannon papers.

The Gathering Momentum of Reform

As work progressed and reform gained momentum and adherents, the goals of reform advocates became more ambitious. Within Kennedy's subcommittee, Breyer had initially had in mind rather modest procedural revisions of airline regulatory statutes that would have involved the Department of Justice and Department of Transportation more formally in regulatory proceedings. The committee report went further, calling for legislation designed to limit the CAB's powers to control prices, restrict entry, and confer antitrust immunity. In the hearings, Ralph Nader argued for abolishing the CAB. "Throughout the land," he said, "people are repulsed by arrogant and unresponsive bureaucracies serving no useful public purpose, and they are looking to this Congress to get on with the national housecleaning job that is needed. Can you think of a better place to start than the Civil Aeronautics Board?"[46] More important and surprising, in the summer of 1975 a study done within the CAB staff called flatly for ending entry, exit, and price regulation within three to five years.[47] What once had seemed impossible or absurd, and then unlikely, was now beginning to seem within reach after all—and it was beginning to be spoken of as "deregulation" rather than the more vague and ambiguous "regulatory reform," which was initially the prevalent term.

Not that "deregulation" failed to cloak a good deal of ambiguity. So remarkable was the convergence of the Ford and Kennedy positions that it became easy to overlook the fact that the convergence was in fact quite specific and delimited. It was confined to procompetitive deregulation—the removal of restrictions on price and entry.[48] As a conservative, Ford sought to embrace deregulation much more broadly and to reduce government intervention in business conduct on a wide front, but the consumerist orientation of Kennedy meant that his advocacy was much more narrowly confined. This was true for liberal Democrats in Congress gen-

46. This was the language in Nader's prepared statement, submitted for inclusion in the record. What he actually said to the committee was more conventional, focusing, for example, on changing the language of the CAB's statutory mandate and improving the quality of its membership. *Oversight of Civil Aeronautics Board Practices and Procedures,* Hearings, vol. 2, pp. 1150–68.

47. *Regulatory Reform: Report of the C.A.B. Special Staff* (CAB, 1975). When the report appeared, James C. Miller of the CEA circulated it among two dozen Ford administration officials, noting in a covering memo that because the report went beyond what the administration had been contemplating, "we may wish to reconsider our basically conservative approach." Miller to Rod Hills and others, July 22, 1975, in Box 28, Schmults papers.

48. And further to those particular instances of restriction on price and entry that had the effect of raising consumer prices. See the discussion of natural gas pricing in chap. 6.

erally and for Jimmy Carter, the Democrats' presidential nominee in 1976. In a campaign appearance at a Public Citizens' Forum chaired by Ralph Nader, Carter categorized his own beliefs as those of "consumerism," embraced the view that the economic regulatory agencies created during the New Deal had been captured by regulated interests, and called for reducing anticompetitive regulation—but said he wanted to strengthen regulation for consumer and environmental protection.[49]

Within the sphere of their agreement—airline deregulation being the immediate, specific case—the actions of Kennedy's subcommittee and the administration importantly reinforced each other. Breyer drew likeminded members of the administration into collaboration with the subcommittee staff, and the hearings helped to precipitate the formulation of an administration position. When administration witnesses appeared on the first day of the hearings, they argued the need for regulatory reform legislation and promised to submit a bill in the near future. Except for the catalytic effect of the hearings, they might not have made such a commitment so soon; formation of the administration task force was still two or three months away. When the administration was slow to fulfill its promise of a bill, the senator prodded the president with a personal letter, saying that "the delay . . . suggests to some a lessening of the Administration's commitment to genuine reform, making it correspondingly more difficult for me to maintain the same momentum on the congressional front."[50] When Kennedy's subcommittee issued its report, the senator and the president exchanged mutually encouraging letters that were made public, and the administration and the senator's staff continued to collaborate. A genuine alliance formed across the division of governmental branches and political parties, so strong was the shared commitment to a policy goal.

On the other hand, the symbolic, evocative power of the term "deregulation" did not lose much from the fact that the Democratic and Republican leaders of the gathering drive were far from fully agreed on their goals. Ambiguity is a great advantage in political symbols, and here was one that in a single phrase could be made to serve in two quite different ways. It could be used to affirm the traditional values of competition, free enterprise, and limited government, which were still widely held among conservatives and were enjoying a modest rediscovery among liberals. In

49. *The Presidential Campaign 1976,* vol. 1, pt 1: *Jimmy Carter* (GPO, 1978), pp. 470–75.
50. June 26, 1975, in Box 32, Schmults papers.

a more polemical fashion, it expressed a deep cynicism about government institutions that was central to the ethos of consumerism, was fast spreading to the public at large, and was injecting a new ambivalence into the policy positions of liberals. The development of deregulation as a political symbol associated with powerful political figures was a necessary precondition to the next stage of its evolution, as a fashion in policy choice.

Deregulation as Policy Fashion

Within a very short time, deregulation was transformed from a lonely cause with poor political prospects into a buzzword and bandwagon. Once coined—it first appeared as an entry in the *New York Times* index in 1976—the term entered swiftly into common and often gratuitous usage in Washington. Thus, for example, an extensive and varied reform of federal banking laws, under consideration for many years and with only one title of six having much to do with deregulation, was in 1980 entitled the Depository Institutions Deregulation and Monetary Control Act— much as the Federal Aid Highway Act of 1956 authorized a "national system of interstate and defense highways." Just as everyone in 1956 was in favor of defense, everyone in 1980 was in favor of deregulation.

The making of fashions in policy choice is more than a little mysterious, as is the making of fashions generally, but much can be inferred from what we have already said. Here was an idea, encompassable in a single if slightly awkward phrase, that responded to widely shared values, moods, and beliefs. That it could mean very different things to different people was an asset, not a liability; it suggested something worthwhile to virtually everyone. It also had very powerful and highly placed sponsors, and it suffered little or no loss in that respect when Jimmy Carter defeated Gerald Ford in the presidential election of 1976.

Whereas deregulation was manifestly congenial to Ford, a conservative Republican who rejected the notion that presidents are to be judged by their success in expanding the reach of federal government activity, a Democrat might have been expected to drop the issue in favor of giving priority to new programs. Carter did not say much about deregulation in his campaign, yet he promptly took up the cause after entering office and in early March 1977 endorsed airline deregulation in a brief message to Congress, signifying his interest in swift action. In its procompetitive form, deregulation was thoroughly consistent with Carter's professed commitment to consumerism, and, thanks to the efforts of his predecessor, it was a ripe issue to which he conveniently fell heir. Beyond that, the opportunity for fresh assertions of government power had been sharply reduced from the previous decade by budget deficits, stagflation, public disillusionment with big government, and liberals' loss of nerve and self-confidence. Increasingly, the activism of presidents was being channeled into rationalizing government rather than expanding it; hence the abiding interest in some version of regulatory reform.[51]

In addition to having acquired very powerful political sponsors, deregulation—again, in its distinctively procompetitive form—continued to benefit from having a broad base of support in academic opinion and analysis. In one way or another, the intellectual premises of this policy prescription had been adopted to an exceptional degree by academics, especially in the elite universities. The economists who argued for such deregulation, though perhaps not a large number, could not truly be called lonely. Virtually the whole profession agreed with them, as they rightly were pleased to point out to congressional committees. "The nice thing about being a student of industrial organization and regulation," one professor told Kennedy's subcommittee as hearings began, "is that you can get along with your colleagues, because you never have to run the risk of being dead wrong [in] saying regulation has been foolish in a particular sector. I know of no major industrial scholarly work by an economist or political scientist or lawyer in the past 10 years that reaches the conclusion that a particular industry would operate less efficiently and less equitably [without] than with regulation."[52]

Not only were economists agreed among themselves to an exceptional degree, but the agreement ranged, again to an exceptional degree, across the social sciences. The work of political scientists and historians had entered into the critique of regulatory conduct, and all of this work had had a telling influence on law schools, which were important because the practice of regulation had been the province of lawyers. Future regulators were trained there, and until the late 1960s and early 1970s they were

---

51. For the general argument, see Lawrence D. Brown, *New Policies, New Politics: Government's Response to Government's Growth* (Brookings, 1983).

52. Roger G. Noll, in *Oversight of Civil Aeronautics Board Practices and Procedures*, Hearings, vol. 1, p. 76.

generally trained in administrative law courses whose subject matter was overwhelmingly procedural and technical. But as the social sciences began to take up the study of regulation, their intellectual products began to invade law school curricula and publications. Some of the pioneering and influential critiques of public utility regulation appeared in law journals, and some of the influential advocates of reform—Breyer is the leading example—were members of law school faculties. Thus people who take their cues from the luminaries of the academic world would have come to think of procompetitive deregulation as a desirable thing, as would those who take cues from holders of the highest offices. Inside Washington, very few people indeed are impervious to both of these sets of cue givers. The press is attentive to both, and everyone is attentive to the press.

Apart from the properties of the fashionable idea itself and the properties of its sponsors, the creation of this policy fashion is to be understood also by reference to the nature of the community in which it reigned. Washington as the governing city is highly susceptible to fashions because it *is* a community—a collectivity overwhelmingly preoccupied with a common interest, the activities of government and politics, and positively saturated with internal communication. As a community, it is also internally competitive, intensely present-oriented, and status-conscious, which is to say responsive to the cues of leaders. Officeholders, thousands who serve them, and hundreds more who write and talk about them compete for political and policy successes. In this general quest, ideas as policy prescriptions are propounded in bewildering variety, and some succeed in the sense that they cease to be merely ideas; they are so widely approved within the Washington community, so often propounded, and so readily seized upon, that by sheer incantation they come to define styles in policy choice.

Though it puts us a bit ahead of our story, it is important finally to note that the appeal of deregulation as a policy fashion was immeasurably increased when its potential for political success began to be demonstrated. Incantation alone is unlikely to establish a fashion; some payoff in action is required. When Alfred E. Kahn as chairman of the CAB achieved well-publicized successes in deregulating through administrative action and when Congress then endorsed what he had done and carried it farther, deregulation became more than the policy preference of all right-thinking people. It became a proven winner in the competitive struggle for policy and political achievements, and everyone in Washington who wished to leave his mark on history could see that this was so.[53]

Conclusion

"There is a saying," Merton J. Peck observed in a gathering of lawyers and economists who were discussing regulatory reform, "that economists make bullets that lawyers fire at one another." In the late 1950s, Peck, an economist, had done research on the regulation of transportation, "and at that time no lawyers were taking the bullets." Peck thought that "what really dictates their demands for information are matters outside the purview of economists and their profession. . . . Changes in economic knowledge are less important in precipitating regulatory reform than events outside of economics."[54]

Much of our analysis supports this view. Economists had begun making the bullets of procompetitive regulatory reform fifteen years before politicians found them to be usable in particular battles they wished to fight. Drawing on the developing academic critique of transportation regulation, the Kennedy administration had sent a procompetitive reform bill to Congress in 1962 but elicited no response. In neither house was the bill even reported to the floor.[55] What ultimately, in the mid-1970s, made the economists' arguments relevant to politics were events that no one could have foreseen: the development of severe inflation, the rise of consumerism, and a vague but widely diffused disaffection with a government that seemed to grow uncontrollably and irreversibly. Ironically, the economists' arguments became relevant then largely because the profession was so thoroughly at a loss to offer any better, more plausible cure for inflation, and not because anyone seriously thought that the inefficiencies created by public utility regulation were a significant cause of the inflationary spiral.

53. See the remarkable data in John W. Kingdon, *Agendas, Alternatives, and Public Policies* (Little, Brown, 1984), pp. 12–13, on the impetus imparted to deregulation more generally by the legislative success in airlines.

54. *Unsettled Questions on Regulatory Reform* (American Enterprise Institute for Public Policy Research, 1978), p. 13.

55. *Congressional Quarterly Almanac,* vol. 18 (1962), p. 591. Louis M. Kohlmeier, Jr., suggests that the bill foundered on the unwillingness of the railroad industry to give up antitrust immunity. *The Regulators* (Harper and Row, 1969), pp. 99–102.

Still, we believe that Peck's argument probably goes too far. When events occur that call for a political response—an urgent public problem such as severe inflation, or a tide of public opinion—officeholders tend to cast about quickly for suitable responses and to make a choice from the current stock of conventional wisdom. They look to the latest and best thinking because events occur too fast and ideas mature too slowly for responses to be devised anew for each pressing situation. To return to Peck's phrase, politicians tend to select their bullets from the supply that happens to be available at any given time, and these typically are the results of the intellectual efforts of immediately preceding years. By engaging in advocacy, the expert proponents of regulatory reform created some probability that politicians would eventually pay attention to what they were saying, either because the politicians were routinely looking for bullets and stumbled upon these—which were lying around in great profusion as the result of sustained and coherent advocacy—or because events caused them to go looking for bullets of a particular sort and these, fortuitously, were found to be suitable.

In short, the existing stock of ideas shapes the response of political leaders to events by defining the conceptual alternatives from among which they choose. And then, having been endowed with political sponsorship, ideas acquire added force. The formation of political power may be viewed primarily as coalition building, and we have portrayed here the coalescing of a formidable set of political actors in support of procompetitive regulatory reform: expert advocates in academic settings; several executive agencies of the government, especially the CEA and the Antitrust Division of the Justice Department; the president of the United States; and a leading member of the Senate, supported by a skillful subcommittee staff. But beyond that, we have been trying to argue here, and to lay the basis for arguing in later chapters, that the notion of deregulation itself, as prescription turned symbol turned fashion, had an influence on events that was to some degree independent of the resources deployed by particular advocates. It tended to subtly permeate the perceptions and beliefs of officeholders everywhere—in Congress, the courts, even the regulatory commissions themselves. It constituted a powerfully enticing cue to political entrepreneurs—officeholders and their staff associates— who were seeking ways to shape the course of public policy. And it imposed an exceptionally heavy burden of proof on political actors who might advocate new forms of anticompetitive regulation or actively oppose procompetitive reform, contrary to prevailing views.

CHAPTER THREE

Why the Regulators Chose to Deregulate

THE reformers who sought to end or reduce anticompetitive regulation expected regulatory agencies to resist this change, both to satisfy the "normal" need of organizations to maintain and enhance themselves and to serve the interests of the regulated industries whose "captives" they were presumed to be and which were in most cases resisting procompetitive deregulation.

For the commissions to undertake procompetitive deregulation did in fact require fundamental reorientation, especially for the Civil Aeronautics Board and Interstate Commerce Commission, both of which followed a highly protectionist course in the early 1970s. The protectionism of the CAB—which was denying new route awards, approving capacity-limitation agreements and a rigid fare structure, and curbing low-cost charter flights—was so extreme as to constitute a very important stimulus to reform. Nothing so enlivens reform as egregious examples of what is believed to need reforming. It is often said in Washington, not altogether facetiously, that the CAB chairman who should be credited with bringing about deregulation was neither John Robson (1975–76), who instituted competitive pricing practices, nor Alfred E. Kahn (1977–78), who moved to end controls over entry, but Robert D. Timm, who was responsible for the unprecedentedly protectionist policies of 1973–74. The *New York Times* reported in the spring of 1973 that airline executives considered Timm's appointment as CAB chairman one of the best things that had happened to their industry since the invention of the jet engine.[1] Timm's

---

An earlier version of this chapter appears in Roger G. Noll, ed., *Regulatory Policy and the Social Sciences* (University of California Press, 1985).

1. *New York Times,* April 8, 1973.

counterpart at the ICC—George Stafford, who was chairman from 1969 to 1977—told a congressional committee in the spring of 1975 that less regulation would cost consumers more in the long run, and the ICC's annual report for that year opened with a stiff and righteous statement that refused even to discuss regulatory reform.[2] In 1983 Gerald Ford recalled that when, as president, he had called a meeting of commission chairmen at the White House to exhort them to reform, the only one who acted uncooperative was the chairman of the ICC.[3]

The Federal Communications Commission is a more complicated case because, at least in a circumscribed way, it began admitting competition to AT&T in long distance communications and terminal equipment in the 1960s, several years before anything like a movement for procompetitive deregulation developed within the Washington community.[4] This early anomaly is to be explained, we believe, mainly by the search of the Common Carrier Bureau, a fledgling organization in the 1950s with a new

2. Linda E. Demkovich, "ICC Resists Ford Move to Cut Its Power over Rails," *National Journal*, vol. 7 (July 5, 1975), p. 996; and Interstate Commerce Commission, *Annual Report, 1975*, p. 1, which says: "The rhetoric that surrounded the continuing debate over the benefits and obligations of transportation regulation this year is not to be found in this report, nor should it be. This is a report of the manner in which the Interstate Commerce Commission carried out its responsibilities, with an analysis of the condition of the industries regulated. As such, it is hoped that the report illuminates the need for regulation."

3. Interview, March 14, 1983. Stafford's prepared statement for the White House meeting argued that free competition would depress rates and cause bankruptcy and instability among carriers, leading ultimately to higher prices, poor service, and the elimination of competition. "Statement of George M. Stafford, Chairman, On Behalf of The Interstate Commerce Commission, Issued at the President's Regulatory Summit Meeting, July 10, 1975," in Box 26, Paul C. Leach Papers, Gerald R. Ford Library. The Ford administration tried to replace Stafford as chairman but failed. In February 1976 the president nominated Warren Rudman of New Hampshire to a vacancy in the ICC and announced that upon confirmation he would be appointed chairman. However, after four months the Senate had failed to confirm the nomination and Rudman withdrew. He was later elected to the Senate. Memo, Douglas P. Bennett to the president, February 3, 1976, and "Statement of Warren B. Rudman," June 11, 1976, in Box 160, White House Central Files, Ford Library.

4. The procompetitive evolution of common carrier regulation is documented and analyzed, among other places, in *Agenda for Oversight: Domestic Common Carrier Regulation*, Subcommittee Print of the Subcommittee on Communications of the House Interstate and Foreign Commerce Committee, 94 Cong. 2 sess. (Government Printing Office, 1976); and Gerald W. Brock, *The Telecommunications Industry: The Dynamics of Market Structure* (Harvard University Press, 1981), chaps. 8, 9. This evolution might be traced as far back as the *Above 890* decision of the FCC in 1959, which authorized private long distance microwave systems. In retrospect, the decision in *Above 890* was very important, but in contrast with decisions of the late 1960s it appears not to have expressed a consciously procompetitive policy. "Briefing Paper on the Evolution of Common Carrier Regulation," presented by Walter R. Hinchman to the Subcommittee on Telecommunications, Consumer Protection, and Finance of the House Energy and Commerce Committee, May 20, 1981.

chief in 1964, for a more satisfying conception of self and purpose. (Industry-oriented bureaus—broadcasting and common carrier—were formed in 1952. The FCC had previously been organized along functional lines, with accounting, legal, and engineering divisions.) The Common Carrier Bureau was initially uncertain how to behave toward a giant monopolist whose service was generally applauded and whose service charges, thanks both to technological progress and to the rapid growth of its market, tended to fall even in the absence of regulatory pressure. However, the bureau began to be more aggressive and self-consciously independent of the regulated industry in the 1960s after being criticized in congressional hearings for being too lax with AT&T.[5] In response to issues raised by entrepreneurs with new technologies—and in response also, we believe, to the gigantism of AT&T, which belied any need for protection and instead fostered feelings of frustration and hostility among official regulators—it undertook as a conscious regulatory tactic to admit competition to AT&T within limited spheres. However, the procompetitive trend of Common Carrier Bureau action in this period, in contrast with later decisions, was not deregulatory. On the contrary, because AT&T was in a position to use predatory pricing against the new competitors, the FCC mounted an increased effort at supervising AT&T's rates. Not until 1979 or 1980 could the FCC be said to have undertaken to deregulate the common carrier industry. Thus, despite differences in the timing of their retreat from protectionism (and differences as well in the political explanations for that retreat), it is fair for our analysis of deregulation to discuss all three commissions together.

That the three commissions undertook to change policy themselves, and to change it in a deregulatory, self-denying way, is puzzling indeed, and the purpose of this chapter is to account for it. Besides being important and profoundly puzzling in themselves, the commissions' actions are worth analyzing because they had very important consequences for the subsequent politics of reform. They increased pressure on Congress to act, because Congress felt its prerogatives were being challenged, and specifically to act in a strongly procompetitive way, because it became very hard for Congress to endorse any less reform than the regulatory

5. Interview with Bernard Strassburg, former chief of the Common Carrier Bureau, October 4, 1979; and Strassburg, "Case Study: FCC's Specialized Common Carrier (SCC) Decision," in "Organization Analysis of the Regulatory Process: A Comparative Study of the Decision Making Process in the Federal Communications Commission and the Environmental Protection Agency," The Urban Institute, November 30, 1977, pp. III-30–31.

commissions themselves chose to undertake. The commissions' actions also compelled the protected industries to reexamine their opposition to reform by thoroughly destabilizing, and thus reducing the protectionist value of, the regimes in which they had a stake.

We attempt to show that an array of external forces together pushed the commissions in the direction of procompetitive deregulation, but because the chairmen were the focus of these external influences and the medium or agent of their conversion into commission action, our analysis will concentrate on them—their role, their powers, and the way in which they defined policy goals. Before beginning this analysis, however, it will be helpful to review the main properties of independent regulatory commissions and their historic place in the U.S. government.

Commissions as a Governmental Form

The commissions are multimember bodies whose distinctive property, according to one distinguished student of administrative law, has been that they embody an administrative, instead of judicial, method of enforcing regulatory statutes. Rather than rely on criminal prosecution or private action for damages in the courts, the legislatures of the United States (state legislatures as well as Congress) created an administrative form that would impose restraints on private conduct in advance of actual injury in those instances "where there would be no assurance that private action in the form of a damage suit would be taken at all or taken often enough to serve as an effective deterrent of a public evil."[6]

A central feature of the commission form and of the regulatory method that it was created to administer has been a broad and vague grant of statutory power. Congress laid down only the general outlines of a mandate or a standard of private conduct to be enforced and left the commissions to fill in the detailed requirements. The statutory standards were embodied in such phrases as "public interest, convenience and necessity" and "just and reasonable" rates, classifications, or practices. Thus, for example, a crucial provision of the Interstate Commerce Act dealing with trucking regulation provided that the ICC:

---

6. John Dickinson, "Commissions," in *Encyclopaedia of the Social Sciences* (Macmillan, 1931), vol. 4, pp. 36–40.

may from time to time establish such just and reasonable classifications of brokers or of groups of carriers included in the term "common carrier by motor vehicle", or "contract carrier by motor vehicle", as the special nature of the services performed by such carriers or brokers shall require; and such just and reasonable rules, regulations, and requirements . . . to be observed by the carriers or brokers so classified or grouped, as the Commission deems necessary or desirable in the public interest.[7]

The term "public interest" recurred in these statutes. This was in principle the touchstone of commission action; the theory on which it rested was that experts would regulate with that standard as a guide. Congress could have enacted detailed regulatory statutes, but preferred that experts with broad delegations of regulatory authority act on its behalf.

Just how to think of these agencies (whether as legislative, administrative or judicial, for they partook of all three), how to rationalize their anomalous place in the constitutional system, and how to order their relations with Congress, the president, and the courts, have troubled constitutional and administrative law for decades.[8] In the early part of this century it was argued that they violated the separation of powers prescribed by the Constitution and that Congress had made unconstitutional delegations of power to them, but the courts ruled in favor of their existence. The courts also ruled that the president could not remove members at his own discretion because of differences over policy. In a landmark case arising out of President Franklin D. Roosevelt's attempt to remove a member of the Federal Trade Commission, the Supreme Court said that the commission "must be free from executive control" and "free to exercise its judgment without the leave or hindrance of any other official or any department of the government."[9] In turn, precisely because of their immunity to executive supervision, the President's Committee on Administrative Management (the Brownlow committee) roundly condemned the commissions as a "headless 'fourth branch' of the Government, a haphazard deposit of irresponsible agencies and uncoordinated powers."[10]

Just as troubling as these constitutional and administrative questions have been the commissions' alleged failures in pursuit of the public inter-

---

7. *The Interstate Commerce Act, Together with Text of Supplementary Acts and Related Sections of Various Other Acts* (GPO, 1973), p. 144.

8. Robert E. Cushman, *The Independent Regulatory Commissions* (Oxford University Press, 1941), chap. 6.

9. *Humphrey's Executor* v. *United States,* 295 U.S. 602 (1934).

10. The President's Committee on Administrative Management, *Report of the Committee with Studies of Administrative Management in the Federal Government* (GPO, 1937), p. 40.

est. A wave of attack in the 1950s and 1960s addressed not their form, but the performance of their functions. That they served the regulated interests rather than the public became at this time a settled theme of academic comment, especially among political scientists.[11]

Thus when economists mounted a critique of their own in the 1960s and 1970s they were well within a long tradition of dissatisfaction, but their perspective was different and their critique was more fundamental. They began to ask, as perhaps only they among the academic disciplines credibly could, whether the regulatory function itself, as entrusted to the commissions, was correctly conceived. They began to argue that it was possible after all to rely more heavily on the market and, if necessary, the courts to protect against the public evils that regulation was designed to prevent. That the commissions' form and performance had been so much criticized for so many years increased the likelihood that the economists' challenge to their underlying function would succeed, but ironically the economists' challenge would not have been so successful had not the form itself been well suited to respond. For when the commissions decided to make sweeping procompetitive changes in policy—even, in some cases, virtually to cease exercising their functions—they could cite the broad powers with which they had been vested and the vagueness of a "public interest" standard.

Moreover, to the extent that the commissions did decide to moderate or cease anticompetitive regulation, the consequences for economic behavior could be counted on to develop promptly, for they did not depend on any elaborate process of implementation by the government. It was in the nature of procompetitive deregulation that once these new policies and rules were promulgated by regulatory agencies they were largely "enforced" by the private actions of firms in the newly competitive markets. Deregulation, after all, granted permission for at least some firms—the would-be price-cutters and entrants into hitherto restricted markets—to do what they wished to do, and it thereby forced others, the hitherto protected firms, to follow suit and compete whether they wanted to or not. That was the logic underlying deregulation. It meant that the compli-

11. For summaries of and excerpts from this literature, see Samuel Krislov and Lloyd D. Musolf, eds., *The Politics of Regulation: A Reader* (Houghton Mifflin, 1964); and Commission on Law and the Economy, American Bar Association, *Federal Regulation: Roads to Reform* (1979), chap. 2. Two leading examples are Bernard Schwartz, *The Professor and the Commissions* (Knopf, 1959); and Marver H. Bernstein, *Regulating Business by Independent Commission* (Princeton University Press, 1955).

ance of private actors was not generally problematic, and that the success of policy change did not depend on changing the attitudes or administrative behavior of far-flung field staffs (which in these cases did not even exist).

The Chairmen

One important legacy of the management experts' criticism of the commissions—their plea for more efficient internal operations and greater external accountability, such as was found in the Brownlow report—was strong chairmen who owed their offices to the president. Although the commissions were in form collegial, the chairman had in fact emerged as the chief executive and dominant figure.[12] The president had been given the power to name the chairmen, and the chairmen in turn had been given executive functions such as the appointment and supervision of personnel (typically with the appointments subject to commission approval); the distribution of business among personnel and among administrative units; and supervision of the use of funds. The CAB was so reformed in 1950 and the FCC in 1952, although it was not until 1969 that Congress acceded to a presidential request to similarly restructure the ICC.[13] Until then, executive power in the ICC was lodged in three division chairmen, commission members who attained their positions through seniority. The chairmanship rotated among the remaining members with the result that the overall chairman, rather than having exceptional power, had an exceptional lack of it. But once the anomalous case of the ICC was dealt with at the outset of the Nixon administration, all of the commission chairmen were in the position of chief executives, owing their appointments as such to *the* chief executive in the White House.

12. For detailed, inclusive evidence, see David M. Welborn, *Governance of Federal Regulatory Agencies* (University of Tennessee Press, 1977).

13. Reorganization Plan No. 13 of 1950, 64 Stat. 1266; 66 Stat. 712; and *Public Papers of the Presidents: Richard Nixon, 1969* (GPO, 1971), item 274, pp. 534–36. The formal grant of authority to the FCC chairman is relatively weak and moreover is hedged in by an administrative order of the commission dating from 1956 that, according to Welborn, grew out of the members' belief that chairmen had become overbearing (*Governance of Federal Regulatory Agencies,* p. 23). FCC chairmen have been only slightly hampered by these restrictions, however. The difference is minor between their dominance and that of other commission chairmen who are formally more powerful. See ibid., p. 133; and Donald A. Ritchie, *James M. Landis: Dean of the Regulators* (Harvard University Press, 1980), chap. 13.

As chief executives, the commission chairmen in general expected and were expected by others to conform to type: to be active, to have an "agenda" or "program," and to measure their success by the amount of the agenda they accomplished. And, as of 1975–76, it was very hard to conceive of any agenda that would not somehow respond to the gathering support for procompetitive deregulation—an effort at policy change that originated with experts in academic settings and eventually was embraced, as chapter 2 has shown, by several executive agencies of the government, especially the Council of Economic Advisers and the Antitrust Division of the Justice Department; by the president of the United States, after Gerald Ford's ascension in 1974; and by a leading member of the Senate, Edward M. Kennedy. Commission chairmen were uniformly influenced to accept procompetitive deregulation as a policy goal and in varying degrees to promote it no matter what their prior policy convictions, if any.

Nominally independent, the regulatory commissions are in truth derivative organizations, heavily dependent in various ways on the three major branches of government. The members and chairmen owe their appointments to the president, even if he cannot remove members at will. The commissions as a whole owe their existence to Congress, whose statutes govern them, and they need from it not just tangible support in the form of appropriations, but continuing approbation of what they do. Federal courts can overturn their decisions. When important elements of all three branches adopt a shared approach to regulatory policy, chairmen are likely to respond. To some extent, this is what happened with respect to procompetitive deregulation.

Despite their advocacy of procompetitive deregulation, Ford and Carter did not give explicit instructions on regulatory policy to their appointees, perhaps because their own positions weren't clearly enough defined or deeply enough held to make instructions possible, perhaps because they thought instructions inappropriate for appointees to "independent" agencies, or perhaps because they had enough confidence in their appointees to make instructions seem unnecessary. They signaled support for procompetitive deregulation mainly in two ways: by endorsing reform legislation and by appointing to the regulatory commissions several persons who were advocates of such reform or at least were expected to be open-minded about it. Even though the use of presidential appointments was insufficient in the short run to create procompetitive, deregulatory majorities in the commissions (and hence does not by itself account for

the policy changes we seek to explain), along with other presidential actions it constituted a cue to chairmen and members generally that these
presidents favored deregulation and thus might be expected to reward
with reappointment those who supported it. For procompetitive deregulation to occur within the commissions when it did, some members had to
switch policy positions—and presidential cue giving undoubtedly contributed to these switches.[14]

In Congress, it was leading subcommittee units—or, more precisely,
their chairmen—who became advocates of procompetitive deregulation.
Oversight hearings and committee reports were powerful weapons with
which to embarrass and ridicule the regulatory commissions for anticompetitive conduct. Senator Kennedy, as chairman of the Subcommittee on
Administrative Practice and Procedure of the Senate Judiciary Committee, applied these weapons to the CAB in 1974–75. Three years later, as
chairman of the Subcommittee on Antitrust and Monopoly, Kennedy
held hearings as well on trucking regulation, though these were less dramatic, less publicized, and less well staffed than the hearings on the CAB.
Kennedy's lack of jurisdiction over regulatory legislation may have
tended to limit the effect of his activities, but if so this limitation was
amply offset by his ability to attract the press and exert pressure on the
Senate subcommittees that did have jurisdiction. With Kennedy showing
so much interest in procompetitive regulatory reform, it became very hard
for Howard W. Cannon, who was chairman of the Subcommittee on
Aviation of the Senate Commerce Committee and after 1978 chairman of

14. John Robson, who instituted important procompetitive, deregulatory changes as
chairman of the CAB in 1975–76, told an interviewer that he never talked to anyone in the
Ford administration about his views on airline regulatory policy. "Now, I can't tell you that
somebody in the Ford administration didn't think that [deregulation] was what I *would* do,"
Robson said. "But they never talked to me about it." (Interview with Richard Smithey of the
Yale School of Organization and Management, July 24, 1981. All subsequent quotations
from Robson are from this interview, a condensed version of which appeared in *The Bureau-
crat*, vol. 11 [Summer 1982], pp. 32–38. Our interview with President Ford confirmed Robson's hunch that the president was confident that Robson's views on policy would conform
to his own.) Similarly, A. Daniel O'Neal, who instituted procompetitive deregulation while
chairman of the ICC in 1977–79, told us that he had talked to President Carter only once
before his appointment and that the president had asked him only one vague question about
deregulation. (Interview, December 10, 1979.) Before Alfred Kahn was appointed chairman
of the CAB he paid a visit to the White House during which Carter and his staff provided,
not instructions, but assurances of the depth of their own commitment to deregulation and
their desire that he accept the office. (Interview, Mary McInnis, White House domestic
policy staff, January 6, 1981.)

the full committee, to show none. Cannon too began holding hearings, though his were in the nature of legislative explorations rather than critical oversight of the commissions and began with an impartial tone.

In telecommunications affairs, in contrast with trucking and airline regulation, congressional interest in procompetitive deregulation originated within a subcommittee that did possess legislative jurisdiction—the Subcommittee on Communications of the House Interstate and Foreign Commerce Committee. This subcommittee was created as a distinct entity in 1975 (communications had previously been combined with energy in the subcommittee structure) and acquired its own staff, concurrent with the general development of subcommittee staffs in the House. With the blessing first of subcommittee chairman Torbert H. MacDonald, Democrat of Massachusetts, and then of his successor, Lionel Van Deerlin, Democrat of California, the staff plunged promptly into regulatory reform, then burgeoning as a field of political and policy action. It prepared hearings and issued a staff report that roundly attacked the FCC for anticompetitive restrictions on cable television, and held oversight hearings in 1975 on domestic common carrier regulation, which stressed the inability of the FCC to regulate effectively, followed the next year by hearings on competition in the telecommunications industry.

Among the federal courts, the Circuit Court of Appeals for the District of Columbia became the leading critic of anticompetitive regulation, and because this court was much the most important single reviewer of regulatory agency action (sometimes called the "supreme court" for regulation), its attitude was especially influential. To some extent this court as a whole, and clearly Judge J. Skelly Wright in particular, had come to credit and to expound the reigning academic and populist critique of the regulatory agencies. Thus, in *Moss* v. *CAB,* a case in 1970 that involved the board's procedures for determining air fares, Wright wrote that the essential question was "whether the regulatory agency is unduly oriented toward the interest of the industry it is designed to regulate, rather than the public interest it is designed to protect." In devastating language that came as a shock to the CAB, he concluded that it was.[15] Far from encouraging deregulation, this opinion led the CAB to make an elaborate effort at systematizing its rules for setting rates, but subsequently the court began to expound an explicitly procompetitive position. Thus, in *Continental Airlines* v. *CAB* in 1975, speaking through Judge Harold Leventhal,

15. 430 F.2d 891 (D.C. Cir. 1970).

it found that the Federal Aviation Act required the board to "foster competition as a means of enhancing the development and improvement of air transportation service on routes generating sufficient traffic to support competing carriers."[16] In *P.C. White Truck Line* v. *ICC* in 1977, the court in a *per curiam* opinion ruled that the ICC could not deny an application for operating rights solely on the ground that the applicant had failed to prove the inadequacy of existing service, but was required to weigh the possible benefit to the public from increased competition.[17]

But much the most significant action of this court for our purposes was its decision against the FCC in the Execunet case in 1977. In 1975 the FCC had found that the offering of Execunet, a long distance service of MCI, one of AT&T's new competitors, was unlawful because MCI had been authorized to offer only private line services, whereas Execunet was essentially a public telephone service, allowing a subscriber to call anywhere MCI had facilities. The Circuit Court found that the FCC had erred in rejecting MCI's Execunet tariff because it had failed to determine that the public interest would be served by creating an AT&T monopoly in public interstate long distance telephone service. In its closing sentences, the court said: "the Commission must be ever mindful that, just as it is not free to create competition for competition's sake [a reference to a landmark decision of the Supreme Court, *FCC* v. *RCA Communications,* in 1953] it is not free to propagate monopoly for monopoly's sake. The ultimate test of industry structure in the communications common carrier field must be the public interest, not the private financial interests of those who have until now enjoyed the fruits of *de facto* monopoly."[18]

The institutional influences that we have described thus far were mainly in the nature of sanctions—punishments inflicted or threatened for carrying out anticompetitive regulation—and while they might explain the moderating of anticompetitive positions, they do not suffice to explain why regulatory commission chairmen began promoting procompetitive deregulation. To understand that, it is necessary to understand that for the chairmen these external influences also created opportunities and promised rewards.

16. 519 F.2d 944 (D.C. Cir. 1975).

17. 551 F.2d 1326 (D.C. Cir. 1977).

18. *MCI Telecommunications Corp.* v. *F.C.C.,* 561 F.2d 365 (D.C. Cir. 1977). More generally on the aggressiveness of this particular court of appeals, see Daniel D. Polsby, "F.C.C. v. National Citizens Committee for Broadcasting and the Judicious Uses of Administrative Discretion," in Philip B. Kurland and Gerhard Casper, eds., *The Supreme Court Review, 1978* (University of Chicago Press, 1979), pp. 1–37.

Persons who wanted to achieve procompetitive deregulation of course detected an opportunity in the developments we have described and were therefore more attracted to office in the commissions at this time than they otherwise would have been. The best illustration is Alfred E. Kahn, a distinguished academician who had been serving as chairman of the New York Public Utilities Commission and who, even in 1977, very nearly preferred staying in New York to heading the CAB. But he found it hard to say no to a personal plea from President Carter and to resist service in the very place where legislative action seemed imminent.[19]

Less predictably, chairmen with no independent commitment to procompetitive deregulation also responded to the opportunity for action that the gathering momentum for reform created and proved quite willing to embrace the increasingly prevalent definition of what ought to be done—perhaps because they became persuaded that the prevailing view was correct on the merits, or perhaps because to be guided by prevalent views increased their chances both of achieving *something* and of being widely applauded for what it was they had achieved. The attitude of John Robson about service as CAB chairman illustrates this prototypical will of the chief executive to act:

The fact is I didn't have very many views on [airline regulatory policy]. I had talked to the Ford administration about some other posts in government. Then I said to myself, "You are in a time when government isn't going to have any money; no agency is going to have money. You aren't going to be able to do much from the standpoint of new domestic programs. . . . But you know you have the airline deregulation issue on the table because it has already surfaced." It was a topic I believed had gained some momentum and attracted some attention. The intellectual underpinnings were available. . . . Then Ted Kennedy had surfaced the issue in hearings he held late in 1974 and 1975 so that deregulation became politically more visible. It seemed to me that the CAB provided a unique opportunity to do something—to be at a place at a time when something was happening. It was clear there was going to be action on the CAB frontier. . . . In terms of personal reward you don't get a chance to change things significantly very often in your life.

Though action tends to bring its own rewards (in fun, excitement, and a sense of accomplishment), audience approval adds to the satisfaction, and the regulatory commissions as of 1975 had a growing audience. For some decades they had been one of the backwaters of American govern-

19. *Nominations—June-August,* Hearings before the Senate Committee on Commerce, Science, and Transportation, 95 Cong. 1 sess. (GPO, 1977), pp. 55–56; McInnis interview; and interview, Alfred E. Kahn, June 23, 1981.

ment, attended to mainly by client groups, the lawyers of the client groups, and a small number of professors of law and political science who were intermittently assigned by presidents or the Congress to study them, invariably with highly critical results. Except when scandals broke out, they received little or no attention from the national press, which for official Washington is an overwhelmingly important audience in its own right as well as the medium through which other audiences are reached. This changed when the movement for regulatory reform got under way with some seriousness. What the consumer movement, Senator Kennedy, and two presidents thought was important the press was inclined to cover, and, what's more, was helped to cover by passage of the Government in the Sunshine Act in 1976, which for the first time opened meetings of the regulatory commissions to the press. Regulatory commission chairmen became the subject of news. Partly this was because as leaders of reform they were causing action to occur, but it is equally the case that a heightened exposure to press coverage gave them additional incentives to act in pursuit of procompetitive deregulation, which the press uniformly approved of. Editorials throughout the country overwhelmingly supported it, and a few members of the Washington press corps followed the story closely and sympathetically.

Finally, among the external influences bearing on the chairman one must take account of other chairmen, at least after Kahn achieved his well-publicized successes in deregulation at the CAB. He became a model for other chairmen to emulate and the standard by which the press, congressmen, and other audiences judged their performance. Thus, for example, a fellow commission member intimated that the FCC under Charles Ferris was trying to "out-Kahn Alfred."[20] A story about the FCC in the *New York Times* that compared Ferris with Kahn elicited from a member of the Senate Commerce Committee the unflattering observation, to Ferris's face, that his performance did not merit the comparison.[21]

Largely in response to this varied combination of external influences, all chairmen of the ICC, CAB, and FCC in the late 1970s moved toward procompetitive deregulation no matter what their seeming preferences. Whether as a grudging necessity (presumably the case for chairmen who

20. "Remarks by Commissioner Joseph R. Fogarty before the New England Conference on Public Utilities Commissioners, Inc.," May 30, 1979, FCC files.

21. *Amendments to the Communications Act of 1934,* Hearings before the Subcommittee on Communications of the Senate Committee on Commerce, Science, and Transportation, 96 Cong. 1 sess. (GPO, 1979), pt. 3, pp. 2070–71, 2082–84.

began from a protectionist position) or as a prized opportunity (for those who entered office as ardent deregulators), all acted as the rising critique of regulation prescribed that they should.

In George Stafford's last years as chairman, the ICC backed away from its stiff, unyielding defense of regulation and began to acknowledge some need for reform. In 1975 alone the Department of Transportation counted three "favorable final decisions" by the ICC and six cases that showed "signs of movement." A White House staff memorandum in the fall of 1975 noted Stafford's flexibility on several issues and suggested that the ICC was changing its position on freedom of entry "primarily due to the pressure and publicity brought to bear by two GOP administrations."[22]

Stafford's successor at the ICC, A. Daniel O'Neal, had a record as an ICC member that showed him to be "consumer-oriented" and "interested in protecting the little guy" but uninterested in if not downright hostile to deregulation. He told the Senate Commerce Committee in 1973 that "vigorous enforcement of regulatory laws . . . probably is the best course to follow."[23] As late as 1975, he remarked to a conference sponsored by the American Enterprise Institute that "there is . . . something cavalier about the attitudes of those who appear willing for others to sustain serious losses so that we can test some economic theories."[24] To yet another conference, he remarked that although regulation didn't work well enough, "for what most citizens expect from transportation, it will work better than the marketplace."[25] Yet soon after his elevation to the chairmanship, he began arguing for easier entry into the trucking business and he instituted a wide array of procompetitive policy changes. Under O'Neal deregulation became the goal of the ICC.

Because Ford replaced Robert Timm as chairman of the CAB at the end of 1974, he did not have much chance to show what kind of chairman he would be in a changed environment, but there is persuasive evidence of

22. Memo, Peter McPherson to Douglas P. Bennett, September 18, 1975, in Box 160, White House Central Files, Ford Library.

23. Nominations—February–March 1973, Hearings before the Senate Committee on Commerce, 93 Cong. 1 sess. (GPO, 1973), p. 174. The characterizations of O'Neal's record at the ICC are his own, from our interview with him.

24. Regulatory Reform: Highlights of a Conference on Government Regulation (American Enterprise Institute for Public Policy Research, 1976), p. 35.

25. Transportation Policy Options: The Political Economy of Regulatory Reform (Public Interest Economics Foundation, n.d.), p. 150.

his adaptability. Early in 1975 the CAB began a self-study under prodding from the Office of Management and Budget, and Timm, despite his record as an arch-protectionist, all but urged that this study endorse deregulation:

This reappraisal committee . . . must go far beyond administrative or housekeeping concerns. . . . They should question the continuing viability of the Federal Aviation Act and specifically whether the mandate to "promote" an infant industry is necessary or advisable in the changed circumstances of the present day. . . . If deregulation by function (rates, routes, etc.) seems indicated, they should further examine how and in what time span the phasing out should occur. The group should examine the wisdom of regulation per se and should set standards and prerequisites for the imposition of regulatory controls.[26]

Timm's successor at the CAB, John Robson, entered office "objective and agnostic" but soon became a deregulator and in the spring of 1976 testified before the Senate Commerce Committee that "economic regulation should be redirected so domestic air transport is, in time, essentially governed by competitive market forces."[27]

Charles Ferris, a Carter appointee who presided over deregulation at the FCC, arrived in office as a self-professed generalist, or, alternatively, a specialist in figuring out how to make action in Washington occur. He had served for some years as a staff member to the Democratic majority in the Senate and, more briefly, to the Democratic Speaker of the House. Initially agnostic on the issues before the FCC, especially common carrier issues, he began before long to promise deregulation in both broadcasting and common carrier affairs.

Even Kahn, whose independent commitment to increased competition is beyond doubt, seems to have sensed the pressures of role and context that dictated immediate action when his academician's instinct was to pause for inquiry. He told an early audience that "very much like the Red Queen in *Through the Looking Glass,* I am in the interesting position of being responsible for executing the sentence first, with the verdict already in, and the trial postponed until some indefinite date in the future, when I may be able to return to more leisurely academic study. I regard it as my job to preside over an effort to restore this industry as much as proves

26. Memo, Robert Timm to Richard O'Melia, "Committee on Regulation," January 15, 1975, CAB files. O'Melia served as acting chairman before Robson took over.

27. *Regulatory Reform in Air Transportation,* Hearings before the Subcommittee on Aviation of the Senate Commerce Committee, 94 Cong. 2 sess. (GPO, 1976), p. 346.

feasible to the rule of competition, cautiously, thoughtfully, and sensitively, even though my own preference would have been to study it for several years first."[28] Initially committed to gradualism, he later favored "something as close to total deregulation as the law will permit, to be achieved as quickly as possible."[29] Kahn himself seems to have been unsure of the reasons for his initial restraint. At one point he wrote to a staff member: "I do not myself know to what extent I declare a commitment to gradualism insincerely, merely to reassure Congress and the industry that I am not a madman, and that I am solicitous of the financial fortunes of the industry, and anxious not to impair them. I am sure I do so also because I don't believe in *any* economic prediction with more than, say, 65% conviction. Undoubtedly an additional reason is my lack of opportunity to have absorbed the work of others who have studied this industry."[30] Much as the agnostics became believers, this believer became more deeply committed to acting on his beliefs. The experience of office tended to move all the chairmen toward more deregulation than they were initially committed to.

The one exception to this generalization was Darius Gaskins, an economist appointed by Carter in 1980 to head the ICC. Strongly committed to procompetitive deregulation, Gaskins was constrained by congressional sources. One such source was Senator Cannon, who admonished the ICC in a speech in October 1979 not to make major moves in trucking deregulation that could preempt congressional action. Another was the Senate Appropriations Committee, which more or less simultaneously instructed the ICC not to implement any policy changes while new legislation was pending.[31] Commission action under O'Neal had attained enough momentum to elicit this counteraction from Congress, which sought time to make the decisions about trucking deregulation itself. In a letter responding to Cannon's speech, O'Neal as chairman and Gaskins as his impending successor pledged to take no final action in

---

28. "Deregulation of Air Transportation, Getting from Here to There," speech presented by Alfred E. Kahn at Northwestern University, November 6, 1977.

29. Alfred E. Kahn, "Applications of Economics to an Imperfect World," paper prepared for the 1978 annual meeting of the American Economic Association.

30. Memo, Alfred E. Kahn to Roy Pulsifer, "Your Comments on My January 20 Talk to the Security Analysts," January 24, 1978, CAB files.

31. *Department of Transportation and Related Agencies Appropriation Bill, 1980*, S. Rept. 96-377, 96 Cong. 1 sess. (GPO, 1979), p. 50. The conference committee repeated this instruction. *Making Appropriations for the Department of Transportation and Related Agencies*, H. Rept. 96-610, 96 Cong. 1 sess. (GPO, 1979), p. 15.

major deregulatory proceedings before June 1, 1980, the date by which Cannon had promised to produce passage of a bill. Thus Gaskins was forced to defer to the legislature, yet he continued the ICC's independent pursuit of procompetitive deregulation with actions that he judged to be within the terms of his agreement with Cannon.

The Staffs

The commission chairmen were variously pushed or drawn toward procompetitive deregulation as a policy goal. But if external forces moved them in that direction, why did not internal forces hold them back? How were they able to overcome the opposition of their staffs to a fundamental revision of agency missions?

In none of the three cases was internal opposition insurmountable or even a serious obstacle. In all three, staffs eventually either acquiesced in procompetitive deregulation or became influential advocates of it. In attempting to explain why, we again approach the analysis from the perspective of the chairmen. We will argue that they found support for procompetitive deregulation from four classes of staff members: dissidents, newcomers, deferers, and converts. Before very long, these categories embraced virtually everyone who mattered.[32]

Dissidents

Within the regulatory commissions there were a few staff members who from personal experience or exposure to external criticism had come more or less to disbelieve in what they were doing even before reform-oriented chairmen arrived, and when the drive for reform developed under Ford, they were available to fulfill a variety of influential roles.

32. One group of officials that proved especially resistant to deregulation, both at the ICC and CAB, was administrative law judges. Historically, nearly all route cases in the CAB came before such judges, who presided over prolonged hearings and then produced elaborate decisions. Those hearings were the "epitome of administrative justice" under the old regime of public utility regulation, one source remarked to us. Deregulation threatened to destroy them, and with them the function of their presiding officers. The CAB's chief judge, Nahum Litt, opposed the procedural changes characteristic of deregulation with such bluntness and vehemence that reformers feared his language might be used against them in court. In memoranda, he charged, for example, that interested parties were being denied due process. Interview, Frederic D. Houghteling, July 14, 1982. The cooperation of administrative law judges was not, however, essential to achieving deregulation.

One case was that of Betty Jo Christian, who had for some years been a litigation attorney in the ICC general counsel's office and then chief of the litigation division, and who had become convinced during her years as a litigator of the need to reexamine policies and practices of the ICC that she found hard to defend in court because they violated reason and common sense.[33] After Ford appointed her to the commission in 1976 she proceeded to vote consistently for granting entry and liberalizing entry policies.

Another case was that of J. Michael Roach, a lawyer who held various staff positions in the CAB between 1967 and 1974 and who, he told us, came to a dissenting view on airline regulation through "one of those Paul-on-the-road-to-Damascus experiences." Late in 1969, he had been assigned to write the board's decision in a route case with no instructions whatever except the name of the winning airline. The "revelation" was "sitting down with a blank legal tablet" and realizing that it was up to him to contrive the board's reasons for the decision. And after he was done, the board did not change a word of what he had written.[34] It came to him as vivid proof of what many in the CAB knew or sensed: that the board's alleged rationales for route awards were not the real rationales, but artifices designed to give the gloss of legal reasoning to awards made privately by the board on other grounds. Not that there was anything corrupt about these other grounds, as staff members understood them. Roughly, the board acted in a commonsensical way to make sure that every carrier got a reasonable share of new route authority and that none was exposed to financial hazard.[35]

Not everyone was disillusioned by the need to rationalize these decisions in ways that would make them seem the work of experts and enable them to survive tests in court. Some very intelligent people found the exercise to be fun, "much in the way that doing crossword puzzles is fun."[36] But persons with a strong moral sense could be outraged or guilt-

33. Interview, Betty Jo Christian, February 12, 1980.
34. Interview, J. Michael Roach, November 26, 1980.
35. There is a remarkably candid acknowledgment of this approach in "Southern Tier Competitive Nonstop Investigation," Docket No. 18257, *Aviation Law Reports* (Commerce Clearing House, 1969), sec. 21,872.03, p. 14,776.
36. The source of this quotation, a career civil servant, asked to remain anonymous. Another interview source, a veteran career official, also spoke of the experience as a game: "The math was lovely. You could really get into it. . . . The numbers people produced this stuff in volume, and it was pretty on the page. God, we had a lot of fun with those numbers." Houghteling interview.

stricken, as was Roach. "I realized that I was spending my time constructing lies," he recalled. "It was an evil thing I was participating in." It was
not "the worst of evils—not like dropping napalm in Vietnam," but still
wrong. And it wasn't even very sensible or practical, Roach thought,
because in "passing out cookies," the board "often passed out the wrong
cookie." Carriers did not get the routes they "really" wanted or "ought"
to have. Roach left the CAB at the end of 1974 and for several months
worked on an airline deregulation bill as a staff member of the Council on
Wage and Price Stability, one of the agencies that was represented in the
Ford administration task force on regulatory reform. He left the government in the fall of 1975 but returned two years later to work as special
assistant to the new chairman of the CAB, Alfred Kahn.

Dissidents such as these, having become expert in regulation through
the practice of it, brought special skills and credibility to the reform
effort, but such persons were likely to leave the jobs that they no longer
fully believed in performing, and hence to cease being dissidents. In the
period we are analyzing, Christian was no longer on the staff of the ICC,
having been elevated to the commission, and Roach was no longer on the
staff of the CAB, although he was on the chairman's personal staff.

Nonetheless, dissidence had a significant influence in the CAB, at
least. For several years, staff members of the Bureau of Operating Rights
had been showing a disposition to doubt the board's anticompetitive policies. Some of this questioning may have arisen from personal experience,
such as Roach related to us, but another important source of it was the
bureau's assistant director, Roy Pulsifer, who was an avid reader of the
economics literature that criticized airline deregulation and who encouraged other staff members to study it too, challenging them to disbelieve in
what they were doing. If there was intellectual inquiry in this, there was
also a measure of iconoclasm. There was outrage and moralism in Pulsifer
too. He came to see first the protected industry and later the whole government establishment in Washington as parasitic and in a profound
sense corrupt. When we interviewed him in his office in the CAB in 1980,
he had become a radical libertarian, with a picture of the famous free-
market economist, Milton Friedman, displayed on his desk.

It may seem inexplicable that early in 1975, when the CAB undertook
a self-study, it turned to Roy Pulsifer to do the job. Pulsifer's attraction,
in addition to a dozen years of highly competent service at the CAB, was
of course that he would be credible because he was known to be critical.

Members of the OMB, in urging on Chairman Timm an appraisal of the CAB's functions, had also urged the use of an independent outside consultant in the belief that the CAB's staff could not be disinterested. The choice of Pulsifer was apparently designed to demonstrate that the OMB was wrong. Promised independence, Pulsifer formed a study group consisting of three CAB staff members and an independent economist, Lucile S. Keyes, who was one of the earliest critics of airline regulation and still a very active one. In July 1975 this group recommended flatly that federal law be amended to eliminate protective entry, exit, and price control in the domestic airline industry in three to five years.[37] Incredibly, the CAB's own inquiry had ended in a radical recommendation for deregulation, an event that impressed attentive congressmen and their staffs as well as the White House. If the CAB's own study concluded that regulation was harmful, surely the case for it must be very weak. Within the CAB, the report helped enable John Robson and a staff task force that he assembled to take a surprisingly strong stand in favor of deregulation.

Pulsifer's radical dissent and his opportunity to express it in an official document were unique. Outside of the CAB, dissenters did not become an important asset to reform-oriented chairmen. Ironically, not even Pulsifer was personally consulted or relied on. Robson, judging Pulsifer to be idiosyncratic and moreover not wishing to be upstaged by a staff member, refrained from embracing his report. Instead Robson created his own staff task force to study the need for changes, within which were several doubters whose doubts owed much to Pulsifer's personal influence. Under Kahn, Pulsifer felt ill-used by the newly arrived advocates of deregulation with whom the chairman staffed the top levels of the CAB and deprived of credit for a reform that he had advocated two or three years before, at some risk to his career, when the new arrivals were still in their university chairs, or wherever.

Newcomers

The earlier reforms that gave the chairmen a chief executive's administrative powers proved very important in securing staff support for procompetitive deregulation. In all the commissions the chairman could appoint personnel, reorganize administrative units, and reassign func-

37. *Regulatory Reform: Report of the C.A.B. Special Staff* (CAB, 1975).

tions, although in the ICC these powers were so recently established and had been so little used by their first holder, George Stafford, that both O'Neal and Gaskins faced a very different sort of challenge than did their counterparts at the CAB and FCC. As of 1977, the ICC chairman still had to secure his right to executive leadership, whereas at the CAB and to a lesser extent the FCC that right was taken for granted. It is not surprising, therefore, that at both the CAB and FCC the chairmen used new appointments and reorganizations as major techniques for securing staff support for their policy goals. At both places, but especially at the FCC, new appointees to the staff in turn became an important source of influence on the chairman, strongly urging deregulation on him and boldly inventing the means to achieve it rather than merely helping him to attain what he had independently defined.

Kahn at the CAB at first sought to work with the incumbent staff, but he soon grew frustrated. As his own goals became clearer with experience in airline regulation, it also became clear that incumbents at the top of the staff were not likely to help him attain those goals. They were inclined to emphasize what law and precedent said could not be done rather than look for enlarged definitions of what could be. With the aid of an intensely loyal managing director whom he had brought from New York, Kahn began to make changes, and after six months his own choices had been installed at the top of the organization.

The bureaus in charge of routes and rates were consolidated into a single Bureau of Pricing and Domestic Aviation with a director from outside the organization. A new Office of Economic Analysis was created. A new general counsel and a new personal assistant to Kahn were brought in. All were associated through professional training, personal experience, or academic publication with the rise of procompetitive deregulation. The new general counsel, Philip J. Bakes, Jr., had been assistant chief counsel to Kennedy's investigation of the CAB. The new special assistant to Kahn was J. Michael Roach, the former member of the routes staff who had the "Paul-on-the-road-to-Damascus" experience that revealed to him the evils of CAB route setting. The head of economic analysis was Darius Gaskins, an economist with strongly procompetitive views who would later be named chairman of the ICC by President Carter. The head of the new consolidated bureau (the consolidation was the price of his coming, after Kahn decided he *had* to have him) was Michael E. Levine, a law professor, with training also in economics, who had made his professional debut in 1965 with a seminal article in the *Yale*

Law Journal criticizing airline regulation.[38] They were all young and very bright; several were brash, especially Levine, who rode roughshod over the industry and staff alike; they were willing and eager to push the Federal Aviation Act to the outermost limits of permissible discretion; and they were equally willing and eager to take on any arguments in court over where those limits might lie.

Veteran careerists of high rank, genuinely respected by this group yet rejected, left the organization, were bypassed, or withdrew into passive dissent. Arthur Simms, who headed the rates bureau and had run the domestic passenger fare investigation, a massive and meticulous effort of the early 1970s to establish rules for rate setting, left when it became clear that there was simply no longer a tolerable place for him. Pulsifer stayed but grew hostile to the newcomers. Both felt, in Simms's words, that what the new arrivals were doing "was just goddamned illegal and wouldn't stick. I felt that they were twisting the statute beyond all legal recognition and the government ought not to do that."[39]

At the FCC, Ferris did not install prominent advocates of procompetitive deregulation as deliberately as did Kahn at the CAB, but what he did was tantamount to that. He enlarged the role of economists in policymaking by enlarging the functions of the FCC's Office of Plans and Policy and naming an economist to head it. Both this economist, Nina W. Cornell, and Ferris's general counsel, Robert R. Bruce, were strongly critical of traditional public utility regulation; as such, they exemplified the "latest and best thinking." Walter Hinchman, who was chief of the Common Carrier Bureau when Ferris took office and who favored procompetitive policy changes without a retreat from regulation, left in 1978 out of sheer fatigue. He was replaced briefly by an economist from within the FCC and then in 1979 by a lawyer, Philip L. Verveer, who had been lead counsel for the Department of Justice in the preparation of its antitrust suit against AT&T. When Cornell and Bruce, as generalists in favor of procompetitive deregulation, were joined by a Common Carrier Bureau chief who shared that objective, the way was prepared for the outcome of the Computer II inquiry in the spring of 1980. This outcome represented a sweeping retreat from traditional public utility regulation, with its focus on rate setting, and the embrace instead of a structural approach to pre-

38. "Is Regulation Necessary? California Air Transportation and National Regulatory Policy," *Yale Law Journal*, vol. 74 (July 1965), pp. 1416–47.

39. Interview, Arthur Simms, November 25, 1980.

venting predatory conduct that relied heavily on requiring AT&T to form a separate subsidiary and on authorizing resale of its services. This result incorporated the beliefs of leading staff members, which in the course of internal discussion became the beliefs of the chairman too.[40]

There were no veteran careerists left in the Common Carrier Bureau to pose an obstacle to the Computer II decision. Much of the career staff left in the late 1970s, often in order to avoid the effects of newly harsh conflict of interest laws that threatened to limit their employment opportunities upon departure from the civil service. So weakened was the bureau that the Senate Appropriations Committee in 1979 took note in a report of its "apparent disarray" and expressed disappointment with "the high turn-over of key personnel and the lack of progress in key areas."[41] Rather than being a bastion of veteran careerists, the bureau was badly in need of rebuilding, and it was rebuilt under Verveer with persons who had no experience of or commitment to traditional public utility regulation.

Even if veteran careerists had been present, they might have had a hard time mounting a strong defense of regulatory practices that were widely acknowledged to be hapless and ineffective. The FCC's regulation of common carrier affairs was uniquely vulnerable to criticism that was more pragmatic than principled. Whether or not critics thought regula-tion of AT&T ill conceived (and there was much more room for dispute on this point than in the airline and trucking industries, which had none of the characteristics of a natural monopoly), all agreed that the FCC had achieved very little control over AT&T's rate setting. This point was not merely conceded, but was given particularly convincing expression by various FCC commissioners, administrative law judges, and the chief of the Common Carrier Bureau for four years, Walter Hinchman. Hinch-man's public statements argued with equal vehemence both the necessity of regulating AT&T and the futility of doing so. This confession of help-

40. Interviews, Nina W. Cornell, April 24, 1981, and Charles D. Ferris, July 28, 1981. The regulatory philosophies of influential staff members are set forth in speeches: "Remarks by Robert R. Bruce before the Federal Communications Bar Association," June 21, 1979; "Remarks by Philip L. Verveer before the Federal Communications Bar Association," Janu-ary 25, 1980; and, most pointedly, "Telecommunications Regulation and Competition in a Post-Industrial Society," presented by Nina W. Cornell before the Armed Forces Commu-nications and Electronics Association, January 11, 1979.

41. *Departments of State, Justice, and Commerce, the Judiciary, and Related Agencies Appropriation Bill, 1980,* S. Rept. 96-251, 96 Cong. 1 sess. (GPO, 1979), pp. 65–66.

lessness made it easier for the committed deregulators of the Ferris administration to argue for their alternative structural approach.[42]

Deferers

By "deferers" we mean staff members who did the staff work in support of procompetitive deregulation because it was what incumbent authorities—the chairmen or commission majorities—instructed them to do. Some measure of deference is of course always to be found in hierarchical organizations; they can't function without it. And in this instance, the normal authority of officeholders was importantly reinforced by the authority of expert opinion and other sources of external criticism. Though commission staffs were not under the same compulsion as chairmen to define agendas for action, they were hardly more immune than the chairmen to the currents of critical opinion swirling around them. Intangible sanctions—embarrassment, ridicule, the opprobrium of informed opinion—were falling heavily on these agencies, which therefore were suffering a loss of pride and self-esteem. Beliefs in the correctness of their mission were undermined to some immeasurable extent, and the staffs were under much pressure to demonstrate that they were capable of renewal and improvement.

Deference to leadership was especially important in the ICC, whose staff historically had lacked a critical spirit. Whereas the CAB staff not infrequently talked back to the board, according to one consultant's study (the Barber report) it was unusual in the ICC for the commission and staff to talk to each other at all.[43] The ICC staff traditionally was preoccu-

42. For an analysis of the obstacles faced by the FCC, see Robert W. Crandall, "The Impossibility of Regulating Competition in Interstate Communications Markets," paper prepared for the 1979 Eastern Economic Association meeting. For Hinchman's views, see "The Future of AT&T: For Whom *Does* (the) Bell Toll??" remarks before the Communications Networks Town Meeting, Houston, January 13, 1981. He asserted that "the FCC has never been able to hold Bell accountable to the just, reasonable, and nondiscriminatory standards of the Communications Act"; that its effort to do so reached a high-water mark in 1970–78, with consequences for Bell's pricing behavior that were "virtually nil"; and that after 1978 the commission "retreated in disarray from this admittedly difficult task" and largely dismantled the few regulatory mechanisms that offered any hope of constraining Bell.

43. *The Interstate Commerce Commission: Application of Its Resources in a Changing Environment,* a report prepared for the chairman, Interstate Commerce Commission, by Richard J. Barber Associates, June 1977.

pied with—indeed overwhelmed by—the agency's routine tasks. (It processed over 5,000 pages of tariff filings per working day, and as of 1976 decided on 5,000 applications for operating rights annually.) Perhaps because its own routines were far less burdensome, the CAB staff appears to have had more time to think critically about them, and when it was invited to think critically, through creation of the special staff study, Pulsifer as chairman of the group did not hesitate to make a response so radical and heretical that board members, as John Robson later said, treated it "like a new father with a dirty diaper, sort of holding it out in front of them with two fingers." In the ICC, on the other hand, when O'Neal as chairman created a staff task force in 1977 and invited the members to think critically, they responded with moderate procompetitive proposals of the sort they supposed the commission wanted. In an interview, the head of the task force attributed its generally procompetitive tone more to the commission than the staff. "It was a reaction to changes that were in the wind," he told us. "There was probably a majority on the commission for reform by that time," though the task force "didn't realize how quickly things were changing on entry in the commission" or "it might have gone farther than it did." Nor did Darius Gaskins, O'Neal's successor, find the ICC staff in general to be resistant to the policy changes he sought.[44]

Staff deference was also relatively important to the ICC chairman because it was harder for him than for his CAB and FCC counterparts to bring newcomers to the staff. The chairman's authority was so much less well established at the ICC that he could not count on the commission to acquiesce in his choices of personnel. In comparison with Kahn at the CAB, O'Neal made relatively few staff changes at the ICC, though he too resorted to reorganization. Besides securing his own authority by abolishing the specialized, highly autonomous units characteristic of the old subdivided commission, he created an Office of Policy and Analysis, put an economist in charge, and began to draw on it for analytic advice on the progress of procompetitive reform. When Gaskins succeeded O'Neal, he made a few personnel changes, including the appointment of persons who had participated in deregulation at the CAB, but he continued to rely heavily on incumbent staff members and to find them in general respon-

44. Interviews, George Chandler, February 19, 1980; and Darius Gaskins, January 28, 1981.

sive. "We have been able to persuade the staff that we're moving in the right direction," he told us.

How much use a chairman could make of deference depended importantly on how far he wished to carry policy change. Up to a point, deference could be elicited even in the CAB, with its deeper tradition of staff independence. Their pride wounded by the Kennedy hearings and the faint scandal associated with the Timm chairmanship, veteran careerists at the CAB cooperated with Robson in the spring of 1976 in preparing the CAB's own procompetitive reform bill. However, this legislative proposal was far milder than Robson's oral presentation of it seemed to promise; even under him there was a visible gap between the goals the chairman was professing and what the highest-ranking, most prestigious members of the incumbent staff were willing to concur in. When Kahn after Robson persisted in pursuing radical goals—and through commission action rather than awaiting statutory changes—veteran careerists did not defer, but were replaced or pushed aside. That this sort of contretemps did not develop at the ICC is to be explained not just by the greater propensity of that staff to defer, but also by the fact that as administrative deregulation at the ICC became radical Congress intervened to stop it and to take legislative action instead.

Converts

Some incumbent careerists, without having been dissidents before the development of procompetitive reform, nonetheless became believers in it—"converts" who enthusiastically cooperated with the new leadership. They may have been convinced on the merits; they may have been acting opportunistically, to obtain higher ranks and salaries; or they may have been caught up in the excitement that typically accompanies significant policy change.

Converts appear to have been especially important at the CAB. "There were a lot of lawyers willing to do what we wanted—young ones receptive to opportunity," according to Elizabeth E. Bailey, an economist whom Carter appointed to the CAB and who was, if anything, a more zealous deregulator than Kahn. According to Bailey, the new unit heads whom Kahn found in turn "found people—sub-groups of young lawyers—there [at the CAB] between four and nine years, 15s but not 17s, 14s but not

18s, who became upwardly mobile."[45] The sense of excitement out of which converts could be made was especially keen at the CAB because of the wit, dynamism, and expertise of Kahn.

The bright, young, ambitious staff members who were potential converts may have been more numerous proportionately at the CAB than elsewhere because the CAB was an elite organization, with a staff generally believed to be of superior competence and élan. "The selectivity at the CAB was a notch above that at the ICC," according to an administrator who had held high-ranking positions in both. "We hired fewer lawyers, with the result that they tended to be more inquisitive, more receptive. . . . The whole ethos was different."[46] The CAB housed converts for some of the same reasons it housed dissidents. While the contrast with the FCC was less clear and direct than with the ICC, if only because the functions were much less similar, a civil servant in the CAB who had come from the FCC told us he had found the CAB a much better place to work. Particularly during the period of reform under Kahn, a time in which he had achieved rapid promotion, it had been "incredibly exciting, a wonderful challenge." He could not "conceive of a better time."[47]

Drawing on some combination of these four categories of supporting staff members, proreform chairmen could secure with reasonable promptness staff support for what they sought to do and congenial advice on what they ought to do. If there were staff members who did not cooperate, they could be bypassed. "The pricing group two years after deregulation still comes up to us with the same old boilerplate," Elizabeth Bailey remarked. "You tend to build around a group like that."[48] All of the proreform chairmen "built around" old groups by enhancing the size and functions of policy analysis units, staffed mainly with economists, though none could rely exclusively on generalist staff units.

45. Interview, Elizabeth E. Bailey, May 6, 1980.
46. Interview, Gary Edles, April 22, 1981.
47. Interview, Paul Gretsch, July 11, 1979.
48. Bailey interview. There was no cluster of dissidents in the rates staff comparable with that in the routes staff, perhaps because the rates staff had had a more satisfying relation with the board in its protectionist years. At least after the domestic passenger fare investigation of the early 1970s, which produced an elaborate, refined scheme for regulating rates, the board had deferred to the rates bureau. Rates had come to seem an arcane, technical subject on which it was necessary to solicit staff advice, in contrast with route awards, which were made by the board on commonsense or "political" grounds and left to the staff to justify.

In addition to the powers and authority of the chairman as chief executive, one other very important factor common to the commissions helps
to account for the surprising ease with which staff support was induced.
Not very much behavior needed to be changed. "It was all done by
twenty people," Michael Roach remarked of the CAB, probably without
much exaggeration. These were small agencies. The CAB had only 780
employees; the ICC, 2,200; the FCC, 2,100, of whom 240 were in the
Common Carrier Bureau. More to the point, the major operational sub-
units were not numerous. Regulation of transportation entailed controls
over entry ("routes" or "operating rights") and supervision of prices
("rates" or "fares"). In the CAB, a Bureau of Economics was in charge of
fares and a Bureau of Operating Rights was in charge of routes (before
Kahn consolidated them into a single bureau). In the ICC, the main
organizational unit was the Office of Proceedings, with sections for finance, operating rights, and rates. In the FCC, the crucial unit was the
Common Carrier Bureau. To achieve rule and policy changes, proreform
chairmen needed either to control these components or to circumvent
them with the aid of personal assistants and generalist staffs, such as
offices of policy analysis or general counsels. This was not a task of vast
scope.

Commission Members

Chairmen needed the support of other commission members as well as
staffs. Including the chairman, in 1975 the CAB had five members; the
ICC, eleven; and the FCC, seven. To achieve reform chairmen had to
command a majority of these votes. In none of the commissions did new
appointments under Ford and Carter occur to a sufficient extent, with
sufficient swiftness, or with a sufficient policy bias to provide such majorities by themselves. The CAB did not have a majority of Ford-Carter
appointees until September 1978, and the ICC did not have such a majority until April 1980. The critical burst of initiatives on behalf of procompetitive deregulation in both agencies occurred too soon to be accounted
for solely by these appointments, even if they all had been made primarily
for the purpose of securing deregulation, which was not the case. The
Ford administration came only gradually to the realization that it cared
enough about deregulation to scrutinize appointments with that particu-

lar end in view. Thus in the spring of 1975 it appointed to the ICC Robert J. Corber, member of a well-known Washington law firm and former chairman of the Republican party in Virginia, because he was well qualified by training and experience as well as by party service—and then administration officials were surprised to discover that Corber regarded deregulation as "a prescription for disaster."[49] The Carter administration, in making appointments to the FCC in the years crucial to deregulation, paid much attention to appointees' sex and ethnic identity as well as to their policy orientations.

Despite the failure of even Ford and Carter consistently to appoint commissioners who were above all reliably proreform, reformist chairmen were not seriously hampered by the opposition of fellow members. When the chairman and staff collaborated, commission members generally deferred. With some qualifications, this was the pattern in both the CAB and the FCC. Given the lack of a tradition of executive leadership, the ICC was again a rather different case.

Commission members tended in general to defer to the chairman. The formal executive powers that all of the chairmen possessed gave them a great advantage over commission members, who theoretically were confined to consideration of policy and who in practice found it difficult to participate effectively even in policy without having command of the staff. In truth, commission members had very little to do and few resources with which to do it. "I don't know why anyone would want to be a member of a multimember agency," Robson told an interviewer. "I think it would be devastatingly boring." Tenney Johnson, who was a member of the agency of which Robson was chairman, thoroughly agreed with this view. "You don't think you're doing anything," he said. "It's enervating to anyone with a mind. The chairman is the focal point, constantly embroiled, but as a member you have to play a lot of golf."[50] That members may have shared this low estimate of their jobs is suggested by

49. Corber, apparently feeling a need to explain himself to the man who appointed him, wrote a letter to the president in July 1975, setting forth his position on regulatory reform. Ford apparently either did not see this letter or remember it, because he was surprised later to read in a Grand Rapids, Michigan, newspaper the report of a speech by Corber that criticized deregulation. The president clipped the story and, in a note, asked of his staff: "Isn't this one of 'ours'?" Letter, Robert J. Corber to President Ford, July 7, 1975, in Box 30, Schmults papers; Memo, Jim Connor to Ed Schmults, with enclosure, April 17, 1976, and Memo, Schmults to Connor, April 27, 1976, in Box 39, Schmults papers; all in Ford Library.

50. Interview, R. Tenney Johnson, November 20, 1980.

high rates of turnover. The median length of commissioners' service has been less than their terms of appointment.[51]

Being the president's choice also helped the chairmen. (The CAB chairman was appointed by the president for a one-year term; the chairmen of the ICC and FCC serve at his pleasure, for unspecified terms.) This created some presumption that the chairman was pursuing policies that were also the president's policies and that he was therefore entitled to support from those commission members who were of the same political party as the president and the chairman. He was entitled, in short, to a working majority. To the extent that the White House shared this presumption, it was disposed to appoint commission members who were known to be acceptable to the chairman. To the extent that commission members of the dominant party shared this presumption, they would routinely vote with the chairman, both to give him his working majority and, for those interested in extended service, to enhance their own chances of reappointment.[52] Neither for the White House nor for commission members were these considerations always controlling, but enough appointments were designed to support the chairman and enough members were willing to support him to make the creation of majorities ordinarily manageable rather than problematic.

In the CAB and FCC, it was a rare chairman who could not achieve dominance—perhaps with the resentment of the members, but dominance nonetheless. A disgruntled member of the FCC, wishing to expose the dominance of Ferris in his first six months in office, calculated that in 502 votes from October 25, 1977, to May 31, 1978, there were splits on only 19 occasions. Otherwise, the commission unanimously supported the chairman. This was, however, no different from the pattern under Ferris's predecessor. "The chairman is dominant for reasons of law and proce-

51. Data are summarized in Barry M. Mitnick, *The Political Economy of Regulation: Creating, Designing, and Removing Regulatory Forms* (Columbia University Press, 1980), pp. 229–32.

52. By law a vacancy occurs each year in each agency, and the partisan advantage of the majority is restricted to a margin of one vote. Also, resignations are not uncommon. These facts in combination mean that a president can soon expect to secure a majority for his own party, and even to install a majority of his own appointees, depending, of course, on the size of the commission. (A president could more quickly place a majority of appointees on the five-member CAB than the eleven-member ICC.) For a discussion of the appointment power and other techniques of presidential influence over the commissions, see William E. Brigman, "The Executive Branch and the Independent Regulatory Agencies," *Presidential Studies Quarterly*, vol. 11 (Spring 1981), pp. 244–61.

dure," this member told a state broadcasters' association. "He selects the general counsel and other key staff. He and his personal staff meet regularly with bureau and office chiefs to plan and discuss upcoming agenda items. Some draft policy recommendations are submitted to him alone; while the staff is hard put to decline sharing them with commissioners on request, commissioners are not informed that they exist."[53] (When this member's term expired, Ferris let the White House know confidentially, via his administrative assistant, that he did not want her to be reappointed, and suggested someone to consider in her place. The president appointed the person whom Ferris suggested.)

John Robson secured the unanimous support of CAB members for the agency's presentation to Congress in the spring of 1976 and thereby assured its effect, despite the fact that none of the members had shown any interest in procompetitive deregulation. In fact, one of them, Lee R. West, had developed a very strong personal antipathy to Robson and resented his highly assertive style of leadership. Robson's explanation for this unanimity was that it "came from an amalgam of persuasion, loyalty, fear of political retribution, institutional pride, and tactic." It was not based on "true conviction."

Kahn as chairman had all the advantages normally attaching to his office, plus one fellow Carter appointee (Bailey) who was ideologically committed to procompetitive deregulation, plus quite exceptional personal powers of persuasion, expertise, and ability to exploit the opportunities for publicity freshly made available by the Sunshine Act and the press's interest in deregulation. Kahn made sessions of the CAB more than the public meetings that by law they now must be; he consciously made them public performances, a form of theater, at which the audience—the general press, the trade press, the industry, the CAB staff—watched him pursue with his pedagogue's passion for reasoned inquiry the questions of *why* airline regulation was as it was and *why* it could not be done differently. Within the board he needed only one more vote to add to his own and Bailey's, and he was able to get it from one or both of the other Democrats on the board, West or G. Joseph Minetti, even though his procompetitive goals far surpassed what they had previously endorsed under Robson, let alone what was presumably congenial to them.

53. "The FCC: An Inside View," delivered by Margita E. White before the Georgia Association of Broadcasters, February 1, 1979.

The ICC by contrast posed a challenge to its chairman because of its large size and its legacy of independent, decentralized functioning. Under Carter the ICC was allowed to shrink for the sake of making it more manageable. As members left they were not replaced, and because these departing persons had been protectionist, the commission grew more reformist by default. Thus it was at first the president's willful abstention from his appointment power, rather than a conscious exercise of it, that contributed to creating a procompetitive majority at the ICC. Later, in 1979, sympathetic members were added, and in the meantime one member had switched to the procompetitive side on questions of entry. Even so, Chairman Gaskins found that securing cooperation of the commission was more difficult than securing cooperation of the staff. This was in sharp contrast with the other commissions, where the chairman, with the acquiescence of the commission, secured control of the staff and then, with the support of the staff, pursued procompetitive, deregulatory goals that the members generally agreed to because they had little choice.

As was true in relations with the staffs, how much deference the chairman could expect to elicit from other commissioners—even in the FCC and CAB—depended very much on how far he wished to go. Both Ferris as chairman of the FCC and Verveer as Common Carrier Bureau chief had suggested publicly that, as a condition of allowing AT&T to compete in deregulated markets, it ought to be subjected to divestiture, and they apparently were prepared to claim that the FCC had the authority to impose divestiture.[54] But they drew back because divestiture was going too far—way too far for most FCC members, just as it was obviously way too far for most congressmen (though under threat of adverse judicial action, divestiture of local operating affiliates turned out not to be going too far for AT&T). Two members of the FCC dissented in the Computer II decision on the ground that the structural requirements imposed on AT&T were too drastic, although there was no disposition within the commission to resist the sweeping withdrawal from regulation embodied in the decision.

At the CAB, Kahn had a majority but not unanimity for his radical changes. Richard J. O'Melia, the Republican who had been appointed to the board in 1973 by Nixon after many years on the staff, persistently

---

54. *Telecommunications Reports*, vol. 45 (November 12, 1979), p. 5; *Amendments to the Communications Act of 1934*, Hearings, pt. 4, p. 3106; and *Second Computer Inquiry*, 77 FCC 2d 384 at 486 (1980).

dissented from Kahn's proposals in strong terms. Kahn's Republican predecessor, Robson, believed that O'Melia had supported him, despite being intellectually opposed to deregulation, out of political loyalty. "I think Dick had a very strong sense that when his people were in he had an obligation to follow the chairman's lead," Robson told an interviewer. But it was also the case that Robson's actions, mainly involving reductions in fares and liberalization of charter rules, were much easier to reconcile with the board's historic practices than was Kahn's pursuit of multiple permissive entry, which involved abandoning traditional tests of public convenience and necessity and the competitive award of routes. Veteran staff members readily concurred in what Robson did or proposed, and this in turn encouraged Democrats West and Minetti to go along with Robson. Under Kahn high-ranking veterans within the staff were estranged. In this situation, O'Melia, as both a staff veteran and a Republican, had no reason to do anything other than follow his own convictions.

In relations with members, as in relations with the staffs, the chairmen between 1975 and 1980 all benefited intangibly and immeasurably from the backing of prevailing opinion—particularly elite, expert opinion. The very fact that turnover rates among commission members were high suggests that these organizations had a limited capacity to socialize new members to the performance of agency functions, and, as a consequence, had some latent vulnerability to criticism. Moreover, to the extent that members did wish to retain their positions, they were quite vulnerable to pressure from the White House. Even in these years, the White House never made appointments to any of the regulatory commissions solely on substantive grounds, but because of the interest of Ford and Carter and their staffs in procompetitive deregulation, substance was playing a larger part than usual. On both the CAB and ICC, crucial votes for procompetitive deregulation were cast by at least one member who was nearing the end of his term and was believed to be disposed to cooperate at least partially on that account. In addition, the sanctions imposed by critics in Congress and the courts had an effect on commission members, even those veterans who did identify closely with their organizations. For CAB members as well as that agency's staff, the Kennedy hearings came as a particularly nasty blow to their pride. Joseph Minetti, who had been on the CAB since 1956, liked to call it the "Tiffany" of regulatory agencies; restoring the shine became important.

No member of any of these agencies became an outspoken and well-publicized defender of traditional regulation, if only because none had sufficient stature to command general attention.[55] With the exception of one member of the FCC whom a high-ranking staff source referred to caustically as the "member from AT&T," none seems to have been thought of by procompetitive activists as a consistent spokesman for, let alone a "captive" of, the regulated firms. By the end of the 1970s, capture was nowhere in sight.

Conclusion

Broadly speaking, the commissions behaved in 1975–80 much as the original theory of them stipulated that they would. Possessed of vague, encompassing delegations of power that gave them broad discretion to act, they served as vehicles for converting the disinterested views of experts into public policy, even if the expert views had originated largely as criticisms of their own conduct and had come to prevail inside the commissions because, rather than being "independent," they were highly vulnerable to the appointive, oversight, and review powers of presidents, congressional critics, and judges.

It was the convergence of external influences on the commissions—the simultaneous tendency of the president, congressional critics, courts, and elite opinion in general to push them in the direction of procompetitive deregulation—that largely accounts for the commissions' choosing that course of action. Ideas advanced by economic analysts and then disseminated by Washington-based advocates of procompetitive reform were the underlying source of the convergence. They were a coordinating force in a governmental universe that is normally chaotic. It is impossible to tell to what extent the commissions were influenced by the ideas themselves or by the sanctions and rewards disposed of by influential institutions: the president's power to make appointments to the commissions; the capacity of the Congress to call them to account and embarrass them in public; and the right of the courts to reverse their decisions and chastise them. Together the two types of forces were powerful enough to cause all the commissions largely to abandon anticompetitive behavior.

Prevailing theories of "capture," which purported to explain the pro-industry bias of regulatory agencies, could not account for, let alone pre-

---

55. It is worth noting that President Ford learned of Robert Corber's dissent by reading the *Grand Rapids Press,* which covered a speech that Corber gave locally. He could not have learned of it in the *Washington Post,* the *New York Times,* or the *Wall Street Journal,* which would not have judged the speeches of ICC members to be newsworthy.

dict, this development. The most common of these explanations stressed the regulated industries' monopoly of information needed by the regulators; the atrophy of support and scrutiny over time from political actors purporting to serve a general interest, especially the president and broad political movements; the use of appointments to regulatory agencies to gain political favor with affected industries, or at least to avoid giving offense; the development of economic incentives, particularly the prospect of jobs in industry, as rewards for industry-serving actions; and the development of social-psychological incentives—camaraderie, golf games and other good times, the good opinion of important men in industry—as rewards for sympathetic association with industries and official support of their interests.[56]

The commissions' espousal of reform does not by itself prove that theories of capture were incorrect; the commissions may earlier have been biased in favor of the regulated industries, for the reasons adduced. But if so, such a bias was not inherent. It depended on political circumstances. Sources independent of the regulated industries could supply information about regulatory policy. Presidents and other actors purporting to speak for the general interest could devote attention to the performance of regulatory agencies. Presidents could give weight to policy goals in making regulatory appointments. Economic or social-psychological incentives proffered by industry to act on its behalf could be offset by the incentives of rival political forces purporting to serve the common good. Better jobs, prestige, or the approval of important people could be attained by acting in ways contrary to industry interests. Indeed, we believe that the commissions' receptivity to reform is to be accounted for largely by the development of a set of environmental circumstances such as we have just described. Capture theories, whether right or wrong under earlier circumstances, were inapplicable and irrelevant under the new ones.[57] When surrounding institutions began to encourage procompetitive reform, nothing in the commissions' relations with industry blocked or significantly slowed it.

56. For a summary, see Paul J. Quirk, *Industry Influence in Federal Regulatory Agencies* (Princeton University Press, 1981), chap. 1.

57. Ibid., chap. 6, casts doubt on their validity generally. For a revision of economists' views that regulatory agencies necessarily respond primarily to well-represented special interests, see Roger G. Noll and Bruce M. Owen, *The Political Economy of Deregulation: Interest Groups in the Regulatory Process* (American Enterprise Institute for Public Policy Research, 1983), chap. 9.

At the very least, then, it is fair to infer from our cases that industry influences operating on the commissions without mediation by the president or Congress (lobbying, the control of information, social relationships between officials and industry executives, and officials' subsequent employment by industries) are all less important than influences that operate by political mediation (for example, the use of appointments and public praise or criticism in legislative hearings and other forums).

If capture theories failed to predict how the regulatory commissions would behave under pressure to revise their policies, so too did theories that posited maintenance and enhancement as dominant organizational drives. Under criticism, all of the commissions proved willing to surrender important functions, partly because the criticism was so severe and concerted, as well as sufficiently backed by sanctions, that they were deprived of the will to resist, but also because the attachment of leaders to the organizations and their missions was in general weak or nonexistent.

It turned out that chairmen, though installed as heads of the commissions, might have little or no concern about the maintenance or enhancement of those organizations in the long run. While it is undoubtedly true that political executives usually adopt organizational maintenance as a central objective, it is nevertheless a contingent objective, dependent on political strategies and definitions of political success, rather than one that organizations can reliably impose by socializing leaders, who may care above all about promoting favored policies or their own careers, perhaps conceiving of the two as linked. Insofar as they do have goals for the organization, these goals may have to do mainly with its reputation for performance and achievement during their tenure.

In our cases, prevalent ideas had a powerful and direct influence on the behavior of the chairmen. Individuals were attracted to the chairman's office because they believed in procompetitive deregulation and saw a chance to achieve it; or they were attracted to procompetitive deregulation because they held the chairman's office at a time when that was the only new, exciting, and important goal the office could be used to achieve; or, even if they were regulatory traditionalists, they made tactical concessions to the reigning views about policy.

Support for reform from the staffs was, if anything, more at variance with one's expectations than that from the commission chairmen. Commission staff were more diverse than is generally assumed of bureaucrats. They were in particular less parochial and less consistently committed to the survival or growth of their organization. One reason for this open-mindedness may be the recent rise of professional policy analysis, using widely accepted standards of argument and criteria for choice, and of citizen-oriented watchdog organizations, both of which rival bureaucratic ideologies as a source of guidance and lend support to latent dissidents. Probably much more important, though, is that staff members, as disciplined bureaucrats, respond to duly constituted leadership, a disposition based both on ambition and duty. The amount of cooperation elicited by reformist leaders from incumbent staff, in combination with recruitment of new staff for key positions, was sufficient to sustain important procompetitive reforms in each commission. One must use caution, however, in extending the implications of this to other governmental organizations, since distinctive features of economic regulation were also pertinent. Sweeping reform might have been difficult if deregulation, as a generalized grant of permission to private parties, had not been essentially self-executing.

Enough support for procompetitive reform came from within the staffs that it became hard sometimes to tell in what direction influence ran. Within each commission, the chairman influenced members and staff, but to a lesser extent they also influenced him and one another. If diagrammed, this process would show arrows pointing in all directions, with some variations among different agencies. Thus in the FCC the staff—which was dominated by newcomers—probably had more influence on the chairman than vice versa, whereas in the ICC it was the other way around. The CAB was an intermediate case and a uniquely complicated one, given the anomalous presence of an early and extreme deregulator within the staff. Everyone involved tended to move toward a more procompetitive deregulatory position as these interactions occurred, and those who would not move fast enough tended to be left behind, deprived of influence and even sometimes of office. Kahn moved beyond what Robson had done and faster than he initially expected to. In the ICC, "the rate of change was more than anybody dreamed possible," a veteran administrative law judge told us. "O'Neal as chairman got the momentum for change really accelerating," and then O'Neal too "became passé" as new procompetitive members were added, including Gaskins as chairman.[58] In the FCC, the final decision in the Computer II inquiry in the spring of 1980 was far more deregulatory than the tentative decision taken only a year before under a different Common Carrier Bureau chief.

58. Interview, Robert Glennon, December 9, 1980.

When change is in the air, no one knows with any precision what will constrain which actors or how far change will go. Under such circumstances, officeholders play a kind of leapfrog, each one outdoing the other in a series of small jumps, until a limit is reached. The game of leapfrog may be driven by collective excitement and enthusiasm, with the players competing to see who will be first to attain some preconceived line of finish; or, more plausibly, in view of the risks and uncertainties of policy change, it may be thought of as a way in which political actors use each other to test, and thus also expand, the limits of the politically feasible. For the system of policymaking as a whole or for a part of it like the commissions, this leapfrogging facilitates innovation; it may be the principal way in which large innovations occur. In our cases, elements of the commissions all made proposals or took actions that they reasonably considered bold, only to find that others in the commissions lent support or went even further, and that no politically decisive resistance developed. Finding this encouraged them to go further still.

What we have been describing is plainly a dynamic process in which influence is reciprocal. External pressures caused the commissions to act or at least largely created the need and opportunity for action. Within them there followed a rapid series of interactions among chairmen, members, and staffs that culminated in important procompetitive reforms. And, in turn, the commissions' actions gave further encouragement to outsiders, as we will proceed to show. In all three of our cases, the commissions' actions on behalf of procompetitive deregulation were a spur to Congress.

CHAPTER FOUR

The Strength of the Reform Forces in Congress

CUSTOMARILY, in American government, major new policies are first set forth in statutes enacted by Congress; then in due course administrative agencies carry them out. In the case of airlines, trucking and telecommunications deregulation, however, this sequence was largely reversed. The commissions took the first formal steps toward procompetitive deregulation without new statutory instructions and proceeded to elaborate them with ever-increasing boldness. Serious legislative activity, beyond merely investigatory hearings, came later.

When it finally did act, Congress was under no obligation to endorse what the commissions had been doing, and in fact there was reason to doubt that it would do so. Congress could be expected to be less responsive than presidents and commissions to economists' arguments based on broad considerations of efficiency and less willing to override the strenuous objections of regulated industries and their employees.[1] Nevertheless, in each case Congress did eventually endorse reform. This chapter deals primarily with the political strength of the reform forces in Congress, and the following one, completing our account of the legislative developments, examines how the industry opposition proved in the end unexpectedly weak.

Reform Victories

Until Congress confirmed them by legislation, or at least made clear its intention to do so, reforms put into effect by the commissions had to be

1. Congress often is assumed to be far more responsive than the president to particularistic interests. See especially David R. Mayhew, *Congress: The Electoral Connection* (Yale University Press, 1974); and Morris P. Fiorina, *Congress: Keystone of the Washington Establishment* (Yale University Press, 1977).

viewed as provisional. Having shown an extraordinary freedom from the past, reform-oriented commissions could not control the future, because their decisions were subject to reversal by several means.

Some of the key commission decisions had been appealed by the regulated industries to the federal courts. In reaching those decisions, the commissions had assumed generous notions of administrative discretion and overturned long-standing statutory interpretations; judicial approval could not be assumed. Indeed, in the case of the CAB's policy of multiple permissive entry, the chairman estimated that the likelihood of approval was only "about fifty-fifty."[2]

In addition, the commissions themselves might eventually change policies once again, this time restoring regulatory constraints.[3] Future commissioners, selected by a president less committed to competition than Ford or Carter, might reconsider the new policies or find ways to weaken them in implementation. In historical perspective, such a reversal would represent a return to normal for the commissions. Finally, the new procompetitive policies could be nullified or drastically altered by Congress, which could enact new statutes clearly requiring restraints on competition. Each of the affected industries sought reversals or limitations of procompetitive deregulation from Congress, either by promoting legislation of its own or by trying to amend bills sponsored by reformers.

Instead of permitting or imposing any reversal, Congress accepted substantially all of what the commissions had done and in one case—the airlines—even extended it. For each industry Congress either enacted a measure that was markedly procompetitive or showed a clear intention eventually to do so. In the Airline Deregulation Act of 1978, Congress ordered an end to all economic regulation of the airlines after a short transition period, and, in view of this, an end to the CAB itself.[4] The Motor Carrier Act, enacted in 1980, was more compromised and moderate, but it still established liberal standards for entry, abolished many

2. "Economically Speaking," transcript of a Public Broadcasting Service television program, July 1978, provided to the authors by Delta Airlines. The Justice Department considered reforms of trucking regulation by the ICC to be threatened with judicial reversal (letter, Donald J. Flexner, deputy assistant attorney general, Antitrust Division, to John J. Fearnsides, deputy under secretary of transportation, December 7, 1978). The FCC's Computer II decision deregulating "enhanced services" depended on an obviously challengeable doctrine that it could assert jurisdiction—satisfying the conditions for AT&T's participation in those services under a 1956 consent decree—while forbearing to actually regulate.

3. See the remarks of Senator James Pearson in support of the airline bill, *Congressional Record* (April 19, 1978), pp. 10649-51.

4. On the adoption of the airline bill, see Bradley Behrman, "Civil Aeronautics Board," in James Q. Wilson, ed., *The Politics of Regulation* (Basic Books, 1980), chap. 3.

anticompetitive operating restrictions on trucking firms, eliminated any significant constraint on competitive price-cutting, and narrowed the antitrust immunity for collective rate proposals enough, according to the industry, to negate it entirely.

Only in telecommunications did Congress, despite several years of nearly continuous effort, fail to pass a reform bill. A number of difficult issues, most outstandingly the restructuring of AT&T, obstructed a final resolution, but Congress did reach a thoroughly procompetitive consensus on the issues. By late 1979 and thereafter it was presumed in every telecommunications bill seriously proposed that no segment of the industry would remain a protected monopoly, reserved to AT&T and the independent telephone companies participating in its network. And it was further presumed that controls on entry, pricing, and service would be drastically reduced and in any event would not be used to limit competition. Though lacking formal adoption, by 1980 this consensus was guiding administrative and judicial decisions and the development of the industry, and it represented the most sweeping, economically significant policy change in any of our cases.

In each case, as we will show in chapter 5, these clear procompetitive outcomes resulted in large part from an eventual decline in industry resistance. Nevertheless, the acceptance of reform in Congress did not occur simply by default. Even in the face of firm industry resistance, Congress in varying degrees demonstrated a willingness to support procompetitive policies. This was most apparent at early and intermediate stages of the legislative process, when the reformers confronted the industries in key tests of power and emerged successful. If there had not been such successes, the industry retreat would almost certainly have never occurred.

Of such victories, those in the telecommunications cases were the least decisive, since instead of significant steps toward procompetitive legislation they primarily involved Congress's refusing to prohibit competition. Having abandoned hope that the FCC might reconsider the basic policy of competition, AT&T in 1976 and 1977 led an effort to restrict competition by statute. Titled the "Consumer Communications Reform Act," the proposed bill was disparaged by opponents as "the Bell bill," but besides AT&T it was supported by the independent telephone companies, which had helped draft it, and in its broad purposes by the Communications Workers of America. The bill would have prohibited "duplication"—that is, competition—in transmission services and imposed the prohibitive burden of state-by-state regulation in terminal equipment.

In promoting the bill in Congress, AT&T and its allies mounted an intense publicity and lobbying campaign and used arguments that were well designed to alarm the legislators—such as the claim that residential rates would increase drastically under competition. Bringing to bear the advantages of enormous size, AT&T solicited grass-roots support from its three-quarters of a million employees and several million shareowners. The pressure on Congress was intense, and in 1976 the bill gained almost 200 cosponsors in the House and Senate, many of whom called for speedy action.

Congress did not pass the Consumer Communications Reform Act (CCRA) or seriously consider it, and in itself that was an important victory for the advocates of procompetitive reform. Instead of acting rapidly, the communications subcommittees in both houses began extensive hearings, the purpose of which was not to consider possible action on the bill but only to explore the general subject of competition in telecommunications. At the same time, about twenty House members and a handful of senators cosponsored a procompetitive resolution as an alternative statement of congressional policy. By late 1977 Congress had clearly rejected the bill. Asked about its status by a reporter, House Communications Subcommittee chairman Lionel Van Deerlin replied rhetorically, "Does anybody in this room not believe that the Bell bill is dead?"[5] Later, when subcommittee leaders in both houses got around to drafting telecommunications bills, it was even more clear that AT&T had failed to define the congressional agenda: the bills, bearing no resemblance to the CCRA, addressed the policy of competition in order to confirm it.

In the airline case, by contrast, the political strength of the reform movement carried it much further toward procompetitive legislation even while the industry opposition was largely intact. When Senator Edward Kennedy first broached the subject of deregulating the airlines during investigative hearings early in 1975, a unified industry was violently opposed. The Air Transport Association warned that the excellent performance of the nation's air transportation system "would be seriously compromised, if not lost, through deregulation." United Airlines predicted that "carrier profits would surely vanish."[6] By the time Senator Howard Cannon and the Aviation Subcommittee took up the subject in the spring of 1976, there had been only one partial defection. United,

---

5. *Telecommunications Reports,* April 4, 1977.
6. *Oversight of Civil Aeronautics Board Practices and Procedures,* Hearings before the Subcommittee on Administrative Practice and Procedure of the Senate Committee on the Judiciary, 94 Cong. 1 sess. (Government Printing Office, 1975), vol. 1, pp. 100, 631.

which was the largest of the carriers and felt it was not receiving a fair share of new route assignments from the CAB, had given deregulation a qualified endorsement. However, most members of the industry did not relent until more than two years later, in the last stages of the legislative process (see chapter 5).

Because of intense industry opposition, the committee markups on airline deregulation were contentious and unpredictable in both houses. The Senate committee, which began markups late in 1977, required eighteen meetings to report a bill; in the House, which began several months later but still required roughly as long, markups were suspended for seven weeks after a substitute measure providing for hardly any deregulation was almost adopted. Handing the industry clear defeats, the committees in both houses eventually reported bills that provided for a large amount of deregulation. As opposition began to fade, especially by the time the House acted, both bills were further strengthened on the respective floors.

In trucking deregulation the ability of the reform advocates to prevail over industry opposition was greater than in telecommunications and less than in airlines. In the Senate this ability was sufficient to pass a strong bill. The trucking industry, there is no doubt, was a powerful source of opposition. A large, economically important industry, it also was widely dispersed among states and congressional districts, and it shared with its major labor union, the Teamsters, a profound aversion to deregulation. When the Senate Commerce Committee introduced a strongly procompetitive trucking bill in January 1980, the industry was determined to have it rewritten. "Our industry is often described as possessing great political muscle and clout," said the American Trucking Association (ATA) in a mailing to its members just before Senate markups. "If we are serious about defeating deregulation, then now is the time to prove our strength."[7]

Although there were a number of close votes in the sharply divided committee, the attempted proof fell short. The committee approved a bill that, according to the next ATA mailing, "cuts the heart out of regulation." And indeed, the Congressional Budget Office, in estimating the effect of the bill on inflation, judged that it would approximate total deregulation. In the face of another strenuous lobbying effort by the in-

7. Bennett C. Whitlock, president of American Trucking Association, "To All Persons Interested in the Survival of the Motor Carrier Industry," February 22, 1980.

dustry, the whole Senate passed the bill without significant amendment, on a final vote of 70 to 20.[8]

In the House, reformers could not win such decisive victory. Jurisdiction was in the Committee on Public Works and Transportation—a client-oriented committee whose Surface Transportation Subcommittee, responsible for highway programs, had a strong affinity with the trucking industry. "Traditionally, the committee was not exactly corrupt," a reformer observed, "but highly responsive to private interests." On trucking regulation, a newly acquired jurisdiction, the subcommittee was more attentive to the industry than the Senate Commerce Committee or, probably, the majority of the House. In the end, subcommittee chairman James J. Howard, Democrat of New Jersey, refused to take any trucking bill into markup until agreement on a compromise measure had been reached by the Carter administration, the Senate leaders, and the industry.

In none of the cases did the preliminary victories or political strength of the reformers fully account for the policy changes that Congress enacted or accepted. The behavior of the affected industries later in the process was also important. Only in the airline case would Congress probably have enacted a deregulation bill regardless of the industry opposition; and Congress would not have adopted total deregulation of the airlines if the industry opposition had not largely dissipated by the end of the debate. In trucking, the attitude of the House committee made it unlikely that Congress would pass a reform bill that did not have the industry's consent. In telecommunications, observers agreed, AT&T's power would have made passage of a reform bill or achievement of consensus without the company's consent clearly impossible.

Nevertheless, the reform forces' strength in Congress was manifestly crucial. It meant that Congress would not act to restore anticompetitive regulation, as the telecommunications and trucking industries overtly proposed. By enabling reformers to make legislative progress on bills of their own, it altered perceptions of what would constitute a reasonable compromise and raised the risks of unrelenting obstructionism. And it

8. Ibid., March 14, 1980; and Congressional Budget Office, *Inflation Impact Statement, Motor Carrier Reform Act of 1980, S.2245,* March 26, 1980, p. 3. The vote on passage was not a test of support for deregulation; on the Senate floor, the industry, for reasons to be discussed, concentrated its lobbying effort on amendments and did not oppose passage of the bill.

demonstrated that any bill, in order to pass, would have to be without doubt reformist and procompetitive. These circumstances helped precipitate the industries' subsequent retreat.

In the rest of this chapter we try to identify the sources of the reformers' political strength in Congress and, as a secondary theme, differences in this strength among the cases. To do so, we first consider the behavior of a numerically small but important category of congressmen—leaders of committees and subcommittees in charge of the issues. We then discuss the sources of broader congressional support for procompetitive reform—features of reform and of its advocacy that were especially important in persuading members who were not leaders.

Leadership for Reform

Just as the reform effort was joined energetically by leaders of the regulatory commissions even when nothing in their prior convictions or experience pushed particularly in that direction, much the same thing happened in Congress. Congressional leaders in the controversies over airlines, trucking, and telecommunications—chairmen and ranking minority members of relevant committees or subcommittees, as well as those who led without the benefit of such positions—almost without exception supported reform. In contrast, the opposition conspicuously lacked well-positioned, aggressive spokesmen. This resulted in a great advantage for the reform forces in leadership and advocacy; and it is to be explained, we argue, by the special incentives and perspectives leadership entails.

In their decisions on legislation, members of Congress pursue several distinct goals: implementation of their ideologies or conceptions of the public interest; favorable opinion among salient groups—congressional colleagues, the Washington political community, and sometimes the national media and general public; and—perhaps preeminently, when it is thought to be at stake—reelection.[9] In pursuing reelection, moreover, members can emphasize several strategies in varying degrees: protecting state or district economic interests; catering to well-organized groups that

9. For generally similar notions of congressional goals, see Richard F. Fenno, Jr., *Congressmen in Committees* (Little, Brown, 1973); John W. Kingdon, *Congressmen's Voting Decisions,* 2d ed. (Harper and Row, 1981); and Kingdon, "Models of Legislative Voting," *Journal of Politics,* vol. 39 (August 1977), pp. 563-95.

can provide electoral assistance, such as in financing campaigns; and developing a record that will appeal generally to the voters.[10] Sometimes the different goals conflict, as may the alternative means to reelection. When they do, the choices members make, consciously or not, shape their responses to legislation.

Although they differ in many ways, members who are in positions of leadership on a given issue face distinctive pressures, opportunities, and responsibilities that very often will affect their choices. Leadership on an issue is mainly the result of formal roles in Congress's structure, especially the committee system. Sometimes members can also become leaders by taking it upon themselves to offer proposals or strongly advocate controversial positions. To the extent that a congressman finds or places himself in such a position, two related conditions follow, both of them likely to affect his response: his actions will be more consequential to the outcome; and because they will be more consequential, they will also be more widely observed. Leaders on an issue will be more prone to act on their conceptions of the public interest, because it is more irresponsible for those in a position of power to do otherwise. They will be more prone to use the issue to gain the respect of colleagues and other elites, because their behavior is more closely watched. And with regard to reelection, for the same reason, they will direct their appeals to broader, even though less attentive, audiences within their constituencies. Compared with other congressmen, leaders will have diminished regard for the wishes of organized interest groups and sometimes even for the economic interests of their states or districts.

This is not to say that committee leaders will have no regard for such interests or that they will respond uniformly to the incentives of leadership. On committees that habitually serve particular clients, to be sure, leaders will generally participate in the clientele relationship. Even on such committees, however, the leaders will be more exposed than other members to observation and criticism and thus, when visible conflicts arise, more disposed to accommodate broadly based demands.

Generally differences between leaders and other members are confounded by crosscutting conflicts of party, ideology, or interest group loyalties and do not become readily apparent. The differences were evident, however, in the cases at hand. The leading sources of pertinent

10. This diversity of available strategies is often neglected in attempts to explain congressional behavior as rational reelection seeking.

guidance concerning the public interest—liberal consumerism, laissez-faire conservatism, and economic analysis, the latter conceived as ideologically neutral—were in substantial (and unusual) agreement, all favoring procompetitive reform. For members disposed to make policy judgments independently, this was directly important. It also meant that political elites and the media would tend to approve of actions taken to promote reform, as would probably the general public, to the extent of its awareness. On the other hand, the organized groups that were intensely concerned were predominantly on the other side and also spanned the partisan cleavages. In defending regulation the regulated firms were joined by their unions, with both giving the issues highest priority.

Thus almost regardless of differences in party, ideology, or interest group affiliations, members faced equivalent choices. Support for reform was more likely if members based electoral calculations on broader segments of opinion as opposed to interest groups, if they discounted electoral calculations in order to reach judgments independently, or if they were importantly concerned to impress colleagues, the media, or political elites. It was the leaders on each issue who were most inclined to make these choices.

In each of the three cases, the leaders of the committees or subcommittees that handled the issue supported reform—at least enough not to appear as active opponents, but in most cases very strongly. The airline deregulation bill was cosponsored in the Senate by Aviation Subcommittee chairman Howard Cannon and ranking minority member James B. Pearson, Republican of Kansas. The corresponding House subcommittee, which was part of Public Works and Transportation, first took up a strong deregulation bill that the chairman, Glenn M. Anderson, Democrat of California, had drafted without involving the Republican minority. With several of the other Republicans, the ranking member, Gene Snyder of Kentucky, introduced an alternative bill that, although much more cautious, was also clearly procompetitive. Eventually the two leaders, joined in sponsorship by several other subcommittee members, collaborated on a bipartisan measure that was reported by the committee and passed by the House.

On trucking deregulation the Senate bill was again sponsored by Cannon, who was by then chairman of the full Commerce Committee, joined by ranking minority member Bob Packwood, Republican of Oregon. An articulate, independent-minded, economic conservative, Packwood was a more avid deregulator than Cannon and less inclined to accommodate the industry. The bill the two leaders agreed on was very procompetitive, and they worked in concert to move it through the Senate. The House leaders on trucking, who initially were more protective toward the industry, are discussed below.

In telecommunications, the support of committee leaders for procompetitive reform was all but uniform in both houses despite turnover in personnel. One senior Democratic member of the Senate subcommittee— Vance Hartke of Indiana, in line to become chairman in the next Congress—was a cosponsor of the anticompetitive CCRA in 1976, when the defense of FCC policy in Congress had barely begun. Attacked during his reelection campaign as a servant of AT&T, Hartke soon said he was reserving judgment on the merits of the bill. As it happened, he lost the election. With Ernest F. Hollings, Democrat of South Carolina, as chairman instead, the subcommittee held hearings in 1977 that were predominantly favorable to competition.[11] And in the Ninety-sixth and Ninety-seventh Congresses, subcommittee and full committee leaders of both parties—Hollings, full committee chairmen Cannon and Packwood, and senior Republicans Barry Goldwater of Arizona and Harrison H. Schmitt of New Mexico—brought forth a long series of proposals endorsing competition.

In the House, subcommittee chairman Lionel Van Deerlin and ranking minority member Louis Frey of Florida resisted the CCRA, held hearings favorable to competition like their Senate counterparts, and went further to promise a bill of their own—a procompetitive "rewrite" of the communications act. Van Deerlin cosponsored procompetitive bills with Frey, with Frey's successor as ranking minority member, James M. Collins of Texas, and at one point in 1980 with every other member of the subcommittee. Van Deerlin was succeeded in 1981 by Timothy E. Wirth, Democrat of Colorado, the earliest strong defender of telecommunications competition in Congress and a frequent opponent of AT&T.

Edward Kennedy and Other Activists

One can identify the incentives that produced this leadership support, and distinguish two somewhat different forms of it, by comparing Sena-

11. *Domestic Telecommunications Common Carrier Policies,* Hearings before the Subcommittee on Communications of the Senate Committee on Commerce, Science, and Transportation, 95 Cong. 1 sess. (GPO, 1977), pts. 1 and 2.

tors Cannon and Kennedy—the two main congressional figures in the reform effort. Kennedy's role resulted from his personal political stature, and possibly his presidential aspirations, combined with the constraints imposed by his committee assignments. The combination led him to serve the cause of procompetitive reform in a distinctive role as an initiator, publicist, and advocate.

Looking in 1974 for a project to undertake with his Subcommittee on Administrative Practice and Procedure, Kennedy noticeably lacked a significant record of legislative achievement. Because of his presidential potential and the high visibility on which it was based, he could draw attention to almost any issue he chose to pursue. He had both a need and an ability to initiate reform. On the advice of a staff consultant who took the unconventional view that airline regulation was ripe for reform, Kennedy approved an investigation. The resulting well-publicized hearings, highlighting Kennedy's strong statements and questioning of witnesses, created airline deregulation as an issue.[12]

Four years later, as the airline bill was about to be passed by the Senate, Kennedy was beginning an investigation of regulation in the trucking industry in an ultimately successful effort to repeat the achievement.[13] Perhaps surprisingly, the trucking deregulation effort was not impaired by the often bitter rivalry that developed between Kennedy and President Jimmy Carter, the leading sponsors of the measure, during the campaign for the 1980 presidential nomination. The bill was important to both candidates, and through carefully maintained staff contacts in the heat of the campaign they continued collaborating on its behalf.[14] Like Carter, Kennedy claimed credit in the campaign for the reform movement—calling himself "the father of deregulation."

Despite his influence and visibility, Kennedy's committee assignments imposed limits on his participation. Although his Judiciary subcommittee chairmanships gave him entrée to the subject of airline and trucking deregulation through investigations and oversight, it was Commerce that had primary jurisdiction over deregulation bills, and Kennedy was often deprived of involvement in legislative decisions. His own bills, never used

12. In addition to the sources cited in chap. 2, see Stephen Breyer, "Airline Deregulation and the Kennedy Report," prepared for the American Enterprise Institute for Public Policy Research, November 1978.

13. Interview, Philip Bakes, general counsel, CAB, September 18, 1979.

14. Interview, Rick Neustadt, associate director, White House Domestic Policy Staff, January 11, 1981.

as vehicles for action, served mainly to attract notice and create pressure for reform. In 1976 Kennedy and Cannon cosponsored an airline bill, the significance of which was mainly to indicate that Cannon and the Commerce Committee intended to act. When Cannon opened serious legislative hearings the following year, the bill under consideration was cosponsored with the subcommittee ranking member rather than Kennedy. On trucking, the Carter administration joined Kennedy in sponsoring the first major deregulation bill, a sweeping, uncompromising measure never expected to be enacted.

His own bills left out of consideration, Kennedy nevertheless exerted a continuing, almost palpable influence on the deregulation debate. Identified by the press as a leading advocate, he made strong public statements on behalf of reform. He commented on each stage of the legislative process, praising steps toward reform while calling for the resulting measures to be further strengthened, and he personally lobbied congressional friends, including members of the other chamber. Only when the bills came up for floor consideration in the Senate could he participate directly. On the airline bill, he offered an amendment to increase competitive entry by shifting the burden of proof in the CAB proceedings, and the Senate adopted it. On trucking, as floor debate approached, Kennedy's staff gave the impression that he would propose to abolish all antitrust immunity for the industry. Although he did not—he was away campaigning for president on the day of debate—the threat forced the industry to devote unproductive lobbying efforts to defeating it. Thus Kennedy's involvement was most direct and effective at the beginning of the legislative process and at the very end.

A similar form of leadership was provided by members of the legislative committees who, although lacking the power of a chairman or ranking member, advocated reform and sponsored amendments to strengthen bills. On the airline and trucking bills, Alan E. Ertel, Democrat of Pennsylvania, a junior member of the House Public Works and Transportation Committee, proposed strengthening amendments both in committee and on the floor. Timothy Wirth, a second-term member in 1976, was the most outspoken congressional critic of the campaign against competition waged by AT&T; thereafter, he remained one of Bell's main opponents as he moved up in seniority, becoming the chairman of the subcommittee in 1981. In the Senate both Harrison Schmitt and Adlai Stevenson III, Democrat of Illinois, worked to expand the scope of exemptions to trucking regulation. On the whole, such committee activists could not claim to be serving distinctive interests of their constituencies. But they could hope to be compensated for potential loss of interest group support by receiving personal credit for reform achievements. Stevenson, for example, was praised for sponsoring a successful committee amendment on trucking in a glowing editorial in the *Chicago Tribune*.[15] Because the logic of this role required demonstrating a difference from the committee mainstream, these activists assumed a relatively extreme posture, resisting compromise. Not always fussy about specifics, they sometimes asked the White House to provide strengthening amendments that it was prepared to support.[16] Some of the activists' amendments were adopted; and even in defeat, they added to the pressures favoring reform.

Howard Cannon

In sharp contrast with Kennedy and most of the activists, Howard Cannon was an unlikely reformer. Neither especially articulate nor well known outside the Senate, Cannon had not been prominent in debate on national issues in the mid-1970s, and he was considered friendly to the industry and labor clientele groups of the Commerce Committee. At least careless in relations with them, he was regarded as corruptible by leading Teamsters, who sought to guarantee his opposition to trucking deregulation by offering a bribe.[17] Cannon was initially skeptical of deregulation,

15. *Chicago Tribune*, April 27, 1980.

16. Interview, John Plebani, administrative assistant to Alan Ertel, July 16, 1980.

17. On February 6, 1980, a week after the introduction of his bill, the press reported that the FBI was investigating Cannon and several high-ranking Teamsters Union officials and associates to determine whether the senator had been illegally influenced in his handling of the issue. Cannon himself was never indicted, but in December 1982 Teamster president Roy L. Williams, Alan M. Dorfman, and three others were convicted of conspiracy to commit bribery and related charges. On our reading of the evidence reported in the press, Cannon probably did not understand that the Teamster officials intended to offer him a bribe, which he could easily have misunderstood because their conversations with him were exceedingly vague. The alleged payoff to Cannon was not to be cash but a large real estate transaction that he could have considered legitimate, and that would have benefited a group of his neighbors in Nevada as well as himself. (*Washington Post*, December 16, 1982.) If he did accept a bribe to block trucking deregulation, he clearly reneged. Of several participants in the trucking deregulation controversy whom we interviewed on the subject, none found in Cannon's behavior credible reason to suspect his guilt. What is more likely, they suggested, is that after he learned of the investigation, Cannon felt constrained to support deregulation even more uncompromisingly than he would have otherwise. In the judgment of several well-positioned observers, Cannon did not know of the investigation until the day the press reported it, when his strongly deregulatory bill already had been introduced. The most apparent effect of the episode was electoral. Running for reelection in 1982, Cannon was burdened by adverse publicity from the pending trial and, although not previously thought to be vulnerable, was defeated by a narrow margin in the general election.

in regard to both its political feasibility and the substantive merits, but soon enough became thoroughly committed: he managed the airline and trucking bills in committee and on the floor, negotiated firmly on both bills with the more cautious House, and from 1978 to 1982 helped lead those in the Senate who favored procompetitive policies and structural reform in telecommunications.[18]

Cannon's actions, by no means the result of a crusading disposition, were a response to the conditions of committee leadership, which worked in several ways to induce his support. Like any chairman, Cannon felt compelled to defend his committee's jurisdiction and prestige, which were threatened on airline and trucking deregulation by Kennedy's initiatives based in a rival committee. To protect the committee's prerogatives, Cannon had to dispel suspicion (encouraged by Kennedy and his supporters and given general currency by the press) that Commerce would abjectly defer to the regulated interests and obstruct reform. "This committee is completely open-minded on the basic issue of deregulation," Cannon said in floor debate on the referral of a trucking bill that Kennedy had framed as an antitrust proposal and sought to consider in the Judiciary Committee. "We have a very fine record on regulatory issues, and it is grossly unfair to be accused of delaying or sabotaging proposals for change." As he opened the committee's hearings, Cannon asserted that the issue would be decided on the merits; and he warned the industry not to use certain favorite arguments that he pronounced lame.[19]

Beyond defending the committee against loss of prestige, some believed Cannon wanted to build an impressive record of legislative achievement to mark his stewardship—much as his predecessor, Warren G. Magnuson, Democrat of Washington, had done in the area of consumer protection. The enactment of a series of laws deregulating major industries would indeed be an impressive record.[20]

An additional influence leading Cannon to adopt reform was exerted by the committee staff. According to a disenchanted industry lobbyist,

18. Cannon was viewed as a potential obstacle to reform in the early stages of debate on both airlines and trucking. Interview, Gerald Ford, March 14, 1983; and Neustadt interview.

19. *Congressional Record* (February 7, 1979), pp. 2006–7. On the tension between Cannon and Kennedy early in the airline debate, see Rochelle Jones and Peter Woll, *The Private World of Congress* (Free Press, 1979), pp. 56–75. Jones and Woll offer a useful interpretation of congressional motives, similar in some respects to the interpretation offered here.

20. Interview, Bill Mattea, legislative director, office of Senator Adlai Stevenson, July 14, 1980.

Cannon had become captive to a committee staff dominated by aggressive free-market zealots who insinuated their beliefs into the committee's bills.[21] Clearly, some of the staff—such as Will Ris, a young lawyer who came to the committee after learning procompetitive principles at the CAB—had definite predispositions to favor reform. Rather than being a staff that captured Cannon, however, this was a staff that Cannon had deliberately created. For a committee to maintain stature in the contemporary Congress, its staff must be talented and experienced, have substantive and political expertise, and not be too clearly identified with interest groups concerned with the committee's business.[22] For the Commerce Committee in the late 1970s, this almost inevitably meant a staff that advocated procompetitive reform. Responsible for the reputation of the committee as an institution, Cannon assembled such a staff.

Finally, Cannon's role as a committee leader did not merely create pressures that competed with his desire to be reelected—it also altered his electoral stakes. His position magnified the rewards of supporting reform and, at the same time, reduced the costs. Cannon told us that his role in the deregulation of airlines and trucking had helped him acquire an image as an opponent of unnecessary government regulation—an image very appealing, he noted, to voters in Nevada.[23] In getting this image across, of course, it was crucial that Cannon had done more than simply vote for deregulation. As chairman, he also had sponsored the bills, presided over their consideration in committee, and managed them on the Senate floor; they were, in a substantial and very visible way, a personal achievement. At the same time, the chairmanship protected Cannon to some extent from retaliation. Asked in 1980 whether the ATA would contribute to his 1982 reelection campaign, an official of the association did not expect to exact punishment: "We'll remind him a bit about what he did to us, but we'll probably support him."[24] In the interim, Cannon would have chances to repair hard feelings, and without assurance of success the industry could not lightly oppose a committee chairman.

The position of chairman also encouraged in Cannon a certain style of leadership. In contrast with Kennedy's role of initiating and publicizing

21. Interview, George Meade, lobbyist, American Trucking Association, January 23, 1981.

22. On the recent professionalization of congressional committee staffs, see Arthur Maass, *Congress and the Common Good* (Basic Books, 1983), p. 110.

23. Interview, Senator Howard Cannon, February 26, 1981.

24. Meade interview. According to Federal Election Commission reports, the ATA's political action committee gave Cannon's 1982 reelection campaign $3,000.

issues, Cannon's role was to shape feasible proposals, build confidence in their soundness, and negotiate with groups and other senators for necessary support. Whereas Kennedy's hearings, designed to get attention, had been orchestrated and accusatory in tone, Cannon's hearings, designed to build consensus, were moderate in tone and conspicuously fair. On both airlines and trucking, Cannon started out asking skeptical, probing questions of both reformers and opponents, carefully concealing his own opinion. This, he said, was primarily to demonstrate to the committee that he intended to be appropriately cautious. In drafting bills, Cannon instructed staff to meet with industry representatives and "satisfy their legitimate demands."[25] Although concessions were made, none was thought essential by the staff, and the result was to facilitate passage of bills. "It's so important around here to be able to say that a bill is moderate, that it's a compromise," a staff member explained. The concessions permitted this to be said even though opponents did not consider them nearly sufficient.[26]

By no means, however, was Cannon a neutral mediator, indifferent to what a bill said so long as it passed. His bills were ambitiously reformist and procompetitive and thus strained the willingness of the Senate to concur. His trucking bill, released early in 1980, was "surprisingly good," judged a White House aide, and would be "a major victory for the president if it passes intact."[27] In markups and on the floor, Cannon stood firm against nearly all weakening amendments and often joined in support of strengthening ones. Although he assuredly wanted to pass bills, Cannon obviously could also see that their content, that is, whether they were viewed as substantial reforms, would reflect on his leadership.

Presidential Support

In two of the cases, the incentives accompanying positions of committee leadership were reinforced by strong presidential support for reform. The Carter administration gave first the airline bill and later the trucking

25. Cannon interview. See Cannon's questioning of various witnesses in *Economic Regulation of the Trucking Industry,* Hearings before the Committee on Commerce, Science, and Transportation, U.S. Senate, 96 Cong. 1 sess. (GPO, 1979). See also Linda E. Demkovich, "The Cautious Approach of Cannon's Commerce Committee," *National Journal,* vol. 10 (May 27, 1978), pp. 846–50.

26. Interview, Will Ris, Senate Commerce Committee, majority staff, February 26, 1981.

27. White House memoranda, Rick Neustadt to Stuart Eizenstat, January 30, 1980; and to Dan Tate and Bob Schule, January 31, 1980.

bill high priority in its legislative program. Congressional testimony was delivered by cabinet-level officials—Transportation Department secretaries Brock Adams and Neil Goldschmidt, Council of Economic Advisers chairman Charles L. Schultze, and inflation adviser Alfred E. Kahn—who also visited individual members of Congress to promote the bills. Personally enthusiastic about them, Carter highlighted the deregulation bills in major speeches, issued statements prodding Congress to act, and, somewhat uncharacteristically, also lobbied key individual members by telephone or in meetings at the White House.[28] The evidence that the president himself cared about the bills and was willing to invest heavily in the effort to pass them made reform more attractive to committee leaders.

Nevertheless, the leaders' support was by no means merely a reflection of presidential influence; possible bases of that influence, such as party loyalty, the president's ability to rally the public, and deference to the office, seem to have played a minor role. The bipartisan character of that support suggests a modest role for party loyalty, and by the time the trucking bill was considered, in 1979 and 1980, Carter had lost popularity. On telecommunications, perhaps the most politically perilous issue, the president was a minor factor. The Ford administration drew back from initial criticism of the Bell bill and, as we describe in the following chapter, Carter stayed out of the telecommunications debate until a de facto resolution of the central issues had been reached, afterwards staking out a position that showed due regard for the interests of AT&T. On the whole, as much as presidents elicited support from committee leaders, those leaders prompted earlier or more overt support from the president. Ford's proposal of an airline bill, as mentioned in chapter 2, was finally precipitated by the need for the administration to testify in Kennedy's hearings. Similarly, the Carter administration, after a period of delay and equivocation, decided to move forward on trucking when Kennedy was about to offer his own deregulation bill in the spring of 1979.[29] Carter's eventual support for telecommunications legislation, like his earlier support for the airline bill, was a case of adopting bills that had already made progress in Congress without his assistance.

---

28. For a description of the Carter administration's exceptionally heavy and well-organized lobbying effort on behalf of the trucking bill, see Dorothy L. Robyn, "Braking the Special Interests: The Political Battle for Trucking Deregulation" (Ph.D. dissertation, University of California–Berkeley, 1983), pp. 354–61. The same kind of effort had been made on the airline bill.

29. Ibid., p. 68.

Leadership against Reform

In contrast with the abundant and committed leadership supporting reform, congressional leadership for the opposition was scarce and hesitant. In each case, the industries had difficulty recruiting well-placed congressional spokesmen and maintaining their allegiance. The main representatives of the opposition were, with few exceptions, more junior members of the legislative committees or senior members who did not hold positions of leadership or were not members of the relevant committee. Instead of forcefully defending regulatory limits on competition, they preferred to obscure their positions in debate and sought to avoid confrontation.

The pressures on anti-reform leaders, and their resulting lack of resolve, were evident in the consideration of trucking deregulation by the House Surface Transportation Subcommittee, whose leadership initially was disposed to resist reform. Like many members of the subcommittee, the leading figures—chairman James Howard, ranking minority member Bud Shuster of Pennsylvania, and William H. Harsha, Republican of Ohio, the ranking member of the full committee—had strong ties with the trucking industry. In the deregulation controversy, Howard often worked with the ATA in devising a strategy, and according to a White House memorandum, there was "no daylight" between the industry and the two Republicans.[30] If the subcommittee leaders had insisted on a restrictive bill, pushing it through the House as the administration feared, a much weaker measure might have emerged in the end from the conference committee. The subcommittee leaders did not so insist, however, because they had no taste for the kind of open confrontation with the reformers it would have required.

Chairman Howard especially had no taste for it. From the start, the trucking deregulation controversy had made him uncomfortable. A consensus seeker accustomed to harmonious relationships with interest groups, Howard also was said to be concerned about his lack of expertise on regulatory issues. Wanting neither to define his own position nor to be criticized, Howard found himself in a political quandary. When the industry complained early in 1979 about independent action by the ICC, he

---

30. Neustadt interview. ATA president Bennett Whitlock considered Howard, Harsha, and Shuster—as well as full committee chairman Harold ("Bizz") Johnson, Democrat of California, who was not active on trucking—to be "friends" of the industry. Transcript, ATA executive committee meeting, February 16, 1977.

wrote to chairman A. Daniel O'Neal demanding an end to it. But O'Neal claimed the authority to continue, and Howard lamely conceded the point. "Oh . . . okay," was his reply, as parodied by a Teamster lobbyist. The ATA viewed the episode as a disaster.[31]

Early in 1980 Howard introduced a trucking bill and held hearings on it. Although presented as a reform measure, it had been carefully negotiated with the trucking industry, and the *New York Times* described it in an editorial as "so limp that even opponents of deregulation tacitly support it," a criticism picked up by an important newspaper in Howard's district. Howard did not hide his distress over these editorials, which he correctly assumed to have been stimulated by the White House. He complained that deregulation advocates had ignored the liberalizing features of his bill, and his press secretary vainly sought endorsements from supporters of reform.[32]

After the Senate passed the Cannon-Packwood bill, the pressure on Howard intensified. His plans were the subject of speculation and conflicting reports in the press. He was invited, along with full committee chairman Harold Johnson, to the White House for a session of personal lobbying by the president, who pressed him to take a strong bill into markup. And he was concerned, some supposed, that if he proceeded with a restrictive bill he would have to defend it openly in the conference committee—debating against Senate conferees who would be better staffed and better prepared and would be arguing the easier case. Finally, it was clear by then, in the early summer of 1980, that Howard faced a serious reelection challenge by a popular, consumer-oriented Republican; such an opponent might have found trucking deregulation an effective issue if Howard had openly opposed it.

Under conflicting pressures, Howard had difficulty deciding what to do—and for several weeks he did nothing. At one point he intimated, preposterously, that he might take a bill totally deregulating the industry into markup, with regulatory provisions to be added as amendments. Although intended to force the administration to admit the need for mod-

31. Howard was perceived by participants on both sides of the deregulation controversy as wanting to avoid conflict. Interviews, Bartley O'Hara, legislative counsel, Teamsters Union, January 27, 1981, and Stanton P. Sender, transportation counsel, Sears, Roebuck, January 1981; and ATA executive committee transcripts, October 7, 1979.

32. *New York Times,* March 9, 1980; and interview, Frank Swain, legislative counsel, National Federation of Independent Business, January 16, 1981.

eration, it was a half-baked idea that only frightened the industry's sub-committee supporters, who did not care to vote repeatedly for amendments restoring regulation.[33] In the end, Howard refused to act until handed an agreement that would bind the industry, the administration, and the Senate sponsors to all the provisions of a compromise bill. To make sure his industry friends made concessions, he affirmed that the ICC could continue administrative deregulation if no bill was passed. The resulting bill—only marginally different from the very procompetitive Senate version—quickly was passed by the House, accepted without a conference by the Senate, and signed by the president into law.

As part of the agreement, the Carter White House had promised to "spread the credit" for trucking deregulation to include Howard, Harsha, and Shuster—ignoring their lengthy but cautious, and ultimately abandoned, effort to obstruct it. The administration kept the promise. And Howard pointed to the achievement of deregulating the trucking industry in his successful campaign for reelection. The subcommittee leaders had not effectively protected the industry, but had quite effectively protected themselves.

Outside of House action in trucking, opposition groups had to rely for leadership on members who were even less disposed to resist reform openly or less well positioned to do so effectively. Senate opposition to trucking deregulation was led by two senators who, as chairmen of other major committees, were not thoroughly engaged in Commerce Committee work. Warren Magnuson, who had given up the chairmanship of Commerce in order to become chairman of Appropriations, used a former Teamster as an aide and sponsored the union's principal amendments. By 1980 Magnuson was enfeebled by age and ill health. He attended trucking hearings and markups only intermittently, requiring assistance to enter and leave the committee room, and delivered rambling speeches against deregulation in a weak voice. Budget Committee chairman Ernest F. Hollings, also a Commerce Committee leader on telecommunications, was the main, and only reliable, spokesman for the trucking industry. Although the ATA thought that it had lined up another senator to speak for

---

33. Howard's strategy was described to us by, among others, Jack Schenendorf, House Public Works and Transportation Committee, minority staff, interview, July 14, 1980. To avoid calling for limits on deregulation, the White House ignored the proposal: Neustadt interview. The industry and subcommittee Republicans strongly opposed the idea and Howard dropped it.

its major amendment on the Senate floor, none did and Hollings bore the entire burden. "I got pretty lonesome out there," he later complained.[34]

On airlines also, Magnuson, then still chairman of the Commerce Committee, had not been enthusiastic about deregulation. His main method of hindering its progress, however, was to let full committee markup sessions drag on tediously, which, although annoying, did not pose a crucial obstacle. On the Senate floor Magnuson voted against the leading proposal to limit airline freedom of entry—a proposal whose main Democratic advocate, George McGovern of South Dakota, was not a member of the committee. Some of the airline industry officials opposing reform regarded Elliott H. Levitas of Georgia as the member of the House whose thinking most resembled their own.[35] The fourth-ranking Democrat on the Aviation Subcommittee, Levitas publicly was much less forthright than they were in opposing deregulation, ostensibly objecting to reform bills mainly on grounds of scope and timing. It was partly Levitas's complicated, ambiguous strategy, we will argue in chapter 5, that ultimately helped lead to the most radical provisions in the final bill.

In telecommunications, congressional leadership against procompetitive reform was, if anything, even weaker. No leader of the Communications Subcommittee in either house advocated passage of the Bell bill, nor in the subsequent Ninety-sixth or Ninety-seventh Congress was any prominent leader consistently aligned with AT&T. In part, this may have indicated that Bell, with its elaborate capacity for lobbying, had less need of congressional spokesmen than other industries. But it also indicated the unattractiveness of Bell's position on competition to congressional leaders.

The ability to attract the commitment of enthusiastic advocates and committee leaders served the cause of deregulation and procompetitive reform in several ways. Leaders and advocates formulated proposals, drew attention to them in the media and Congress, and argued forcefully for their adoption. Perhaps as important, they controlled the timing and presentation of issues for decision. In telecommunications, in fact, the leaders' main accomplishment was the negative exercise of this control— the withholding of action on the Bell bill and formation of their own agenda. As we will show in chapter 5, the resulting several years' delay in

34. Meade interview; and *Journal of Commerce,* April 16, 1980.

35. Interview, James P. Bass, vice-president for governmental affairs, American Airlines, September 14, 1981.

legislative action was a major cause of the thoroughly procompetitive eventual outcome. On airlines and trucking—where many members might have preferred watered-down reforms that would eliminate the need for hard choices—leaders forced them to vote openly on strong measures vigorously opposed by the industries. All these services were mostly unavailable to the opposing groups, which could create a good deal of congressional resistance to reform, but could not recruit prominent, well-placed members of Congress to lead the effort.

Reform Advocacy in Congress

Support from presidents and committee leaders would have been futile, of course, if the case for procompetitive reform had not also been salient and convincing to the rest of Congress. It had to be persuasive, in other words, in view of ordinary members' methods of using information and criteria for choice. Differing in some degree from those of other policymakers, those methods and criteria—and thus the congressional perspective on the issues—posed potentially serious obstacles to support for reform.

First, having to make hurried decisions on numerous unrelated issues, most congressmen could be expected to become only superficially acquainted with the arguments and evidence in the debate. In most senators' offices, for example, the Commerce Committee's report accompanying the trucking deregulation bill probably would not be read even by a legislative assistant, a committee staff member believed at the time.[36] In general the relevant research, expert opinion, and ideological beliefs— the influences in the realm of ideas—converged quite unequivocally in favor of reform. The problem for the reformers was that the members of Congress—unavoidably inattentive, and distracted by conflicting rhetoric and lobbying by the industries—might not fully perceive this.

Second, members of Congress had to be concerned not only with how reform would affect the national economy but also with its narrower distributive effects. It is the individual senator and representative, in the

---

36. Interviews, Cindy Douglass, Senate Commerce Committee, minority staff, April 4, 1980; and Peter Trask, legislative assistant to Senator Daniel Inouye, April 9, 1980. On the limited use by congressmen of reading as a source of information, see Kingdon, *Congressmen's Voting Decisions,* chap. 8.

U.S. governmental scheme, who is charged with looking out for particular regional or local interests and whose political survival may depend on doing so.[37] Each of the regulated industries alleged that a change to a freer competitive order would do harm to certain vulnerable groups or geographic areas. In each case the main prospective victims were said to be small cities and towns and rural areas—economically vulnerable yet politically well represented places. In telecommunications, residential customers, as opposed to businesses, also were said to be threatened. These issues of distribution might be set aside by a president, expecting to be held accountable for the whole economy, or a regulatory commission, perhaps not accountable at all; and they were essentially irrelevant to economists. But congressmen could be counted on to weigh them heavily.

Finally, unlike presidents or even committee leaders, most congressmen knew that their decisions for or against reform would be relatively invisible. None of the issues were markedly salient or extensively covered by the press, and in any case, each congressman was but one among many; they could not expect their actions to be observed by a significant part of the general public. Industry and labor groups, on the other hand, would monitor the votes, publicize them to their members, and perhaps choose to remember them in the next election.[38] In this situation, it might be easy to defer to the organized groups that opposed reform and unrewarding and potentially dangerous to deny them.

Airlines and Trucking

In order to succeed, reform advocacy had to neutralize or overcome these potential sources of resistance inherent in a congressional perspective. In airlines and trucking, the reformers found pertinent and reasonably effective means for dealing with each of the obstacles. On the whole, the obstacles to support for reform seem to have been roughly as important for rank-and-file members of the legislative committees as for the rest of the full House and Senate. The two categories of congressmen showed

37. For a study of members' geographic concerns and their consequences for policy, see R. Douglas Arnold, *Congress and the Bureaucracy: A Theory of Influence* (Yale University Press, 1979).

38. For an example of this monitoring, see "Deregulation: Catastrophe Now Looms Unless Teamsters Act," *The International Teamster,* April 1980, pp. 8–9.

no consistent differences in support for reform, and we do not distinguish between them in the analysis.[39]

CUES ON THE MERITS. Whether congressmen attended carefully to the particulars of policy debate was made less critical, in airlines and trucking, by the nature of deregulation advocacy. The argument for reform had a simple, intuitive character and was sanctioned by a pattern of endorsements—providing cues that made it easy for congressmen to be persuaded on the merits without investing much effort in making an assessment.

At the foundation of deregulation advocacy in Congress, though not directly its most persuasive feature, was the advice that derived from economic theory and research and was offered, in person or in print, by professional economists. As we have noted, academic criticism of airline regulation was based on a substantial body of empirical economic research that was well developed before the reform movement began. The strength of this research resulted partly from the simplicity of the airline industry, which made it comprehensible, and the availability of data on fares and service from the CAB. Using this research, the Kennedy subcommittee produced a report in 1975 that an airline analyst for a major stock brokerage company found distressing. The arguments for deregulation were "sound" and likely to be persuasive, he told his clients in a newsletter, and this he considered bad news for the industry.[40]

The trucking industry was far more difficult to study—for example, its published rates numbered literally in the billions—and had received less scholarly attention over the years. But as trucking reform became part of the political agenda, a roughly comparable body of research accumulated, some of it sponsored by the Department of Transportation and other agencies promoting reform; and like the airline literature it strongly supported deregulation. Economists, of course, would have condemned price and entry regulation in airlines and trucking, like any other "workably

39. There were floor amendments with significant support, both to strengthen bills and to weaken them. If either group of congressmen had been substantially more supportive of reform, the floor amendments should have had a predominant direction.

40. *Civil Aeronautics Board Practices and Procedures,* Committee Print, Subcommittee on Administrative Practice and Procedure of the Senate Committee on the Judiciary, 94 Cong. 1 sess. (GPO, 1975). This staff study presents a thorough summary of the economic literature critical of airline regulation that was available at the time. Oppenheimer and Company, research meeting notes, July 28, 1975 (by Bert Fingerhut).

competitive" industry, on theoretical grounds alone. Research was devoted less to judging whether regulation was desirable in these industries than to estimating the economic losses resulting from it.[41]

Such confidence would not automatically transfer, however, from members of the economics profession to members of Congress. Congressmen easily enough could fail to absorb technical arguments, empirical findings, and policy recommendations buried in academic books and articles and lengthy government documents. Even if aware of them, congressmen could doubt their reliability when contradicted by the judgment of experienced, practical people in the industries. Thus the intuitive character of the reform arguments and the pattern of endorsements assumed great importance.

Unlike much economics, the main arguments and evidence in support of deregulation were not abstruse or inaccessible; they could be presented simply and effectively in layman's language. The most vivid evidence involved straightforward comparisons between regulated and unregulated markets in the two industries. Regarding airlines, reformers pointed to the major intrastate markets in Texas and California (Dallas-Houston and San Francisco–Los Angeles) in which fares, free from regulation by the CAB, were 50 to 60 percent lower than those in CAB-regulated, interstate markets that were otherwise similar.[42] In trucking, parallel evidence came from an experiment that had been conveniently arranged by a federal judge. In the 1950s, a court decision caused trucking rates for poultry and poultry products to be suddenly deregulated under an expanded agricultural exception. According to a study by the Department of Agriculture, freight charges for those commodities quickly declined by roughly 33 percent.[43] Even if these simple comparisons were not necessarily the most rigorous, reliable evidence, they had the advantage for use in Congress of being readily grasped by the layman.

The theoretical premises of the argument for reform were already part of the common understanding of how businesses and markets behave. Key arguments could be made, as in a Carter administration letter on

41. A review of the literature, emphasizing the estimated costs of regulation, was prepared by the Council on Wage and Price Stability: see W. Bruce Allen and Edward B. Hymson, "The Interstate Commerce Commission's Staff Analysis of the Costs and Benefits of Surface Transportation Regulation," *Economic Regulation of the Trucking Industry*, Hearings, pt. 2, pp. 404–17.

42. *CAB Practices and Procedures*, Committee Print, p. 41.

43. *Congressional Record* (April 15, 1980), p. 7797.

trucking, merely by posing rhetorical questions: "Can anyone reasonably question that the object of a truck rate bureau meeting is to produce a rate that is higher than it would be if market conditions prevailed?" As a result of fewer restrictions on entry, the letter went on, "existing motor carriers would be forced by the market place to behave more competitively, knowing that an attempt to raise rates above a competitive level would draw an influx of additional service from new and existing firms. The net result of freer entry would be to force prices down to normal competitive levels whenever any attempt might be made to elevate them."[44] The arguments on airlines were essentially the same.

Moreover, the arguments were reinforced and in a sense corroborated by a revealing pattern of endorsements. Coming from extraordinarily diverse sources, these endorsements demonstrated that the case for deregulation, in no way sectarian, was persuasive from a wide range of perspectives. Prominently featured, of course, were economists themselves. Testimony in support of airline and trucking deregulation was given by economists employed in various institutional settings—universities, Washington-based "think tanks," and economic advisory agencies in the government. Two of the leading think tanks, the Brookings Institution and the American Enterprise Institute for Public Policy Research (AEI), were even thought by some to have "sponsored" deregulation, as it was put by a Senate aide. Staff agencies, such as the Council of Economic Advisers (CEA) and the Council on Wage and Price Stability (COWPS), also institutionalized the economic perspective and, with studies and testimony, added to the endorsements. On the other hand, prominent economists who opposed deregulation could not be found; deregulation was, in effect, a recommendation of the economics profession as such.

In addition, endorsements came from government agencies that had a wide range of functional and representational responsibilities and were not dominated by economists. Reform advocates in Congress displayed statements of support from the cabinet departments most directly concerned with the issues: Transportation; Justice, whose Antitrust Division was concerned with competition; and Agriculture, whose clients crucially depended on transportation. In one case, this unity was partly a matter of White House discipline. Carter's first secretary of transportation, Brock Adams, a former congressman with long-standing ties to the transporta-

44. Letter from Secretary of Transportation Neil Goldschmidt to Senator Howard Cannon, *Congressional Record* (April 15, 1980), pp. 7777–79.

tion industries, initially opposed both airline and trucking deregulation within the administration; and although he worked hard on behalf of both bills after losing the internal debate, his earlier position was well known. Otherwise executive branch support—including that of Neil Goldschmidt, who succeeded Adams in 1980—was either spontaneous or readily forthcoming.

Congress's own nonpartisan staff agencies—the General Accounting Office and the Congressional Budget Office—added their support, as did the Federal Trade Commission, an independent agency concerned with competition. Most striking, because it meant attacking their own functions, both the CAB and the ICC favored deregulation and their chairmen lobbied for the bills. Almost as among economists, there was a consensus in favor of deregulation among the pertinent agencies of government, even though their concerns and interests differed in many respects.

One more comparably diverse set of endorsements came from sources representing neither the economics profession nor the government. Interest group support for deregulation was organized in an ad hoc coalition that formed in 1977 to lobby for airline deregulation and stayed together, with a few changes in membership, to work on trucking. The coalition included an array of ideological and public interest groups that covered most of the political spectrum—from the Ralph Nader–affiliated Transportation Consumer Action Project (T-CAP) to the centrist Common Cause and the American Conservative Union. It included relatively encompassing economic groups such as the National Association of Manufacturers (NAM), the American Farm Bureau Federation, and the National Federation of Independent Business (NFIB), the largest national association of small businesses. There was also a handful of trade associations and individual firms, including Sears, Roebuck, whose Washington office helped organize the coalition.

The significance of this organized support did not lie in the tangible political resources—lobbyists, money, and votes—brought to bear; those resources were far from compelling. Its significance, in accordance with the character and motivation of the groups, was primarily symbolic. Even on trucking deregulation, with the larger economic stakes of the two issues, interest group support for reform was described by a Senate aide as "nebulous." Except for the small, specialized Nader group, trucking was not a matter of the highest priority for the ideological or public interest groups, nor was it a "bread and butter" issue for the economic groups, all of which had other matters of more vital concern.[45] Since agricultural products were already exempt from trucking regulation, the Farm Bureau mainly sought some modest amendments expanding the exemption. The NAM and NFIB, both large and politically important organizations, participated largely because of the enthusiasm of their staffs; their members, few of whom were exercised about trucking regulation, lent passive support on ideological as much as economic grounds.[46] Except for a handful, the hundreds of large American corporations and industry-specific trade associations, the principal spokesmen for the interests of business, were conspicuous by their absence.

Nevertheless, the pattern of interest group support indicated the status and character of the substantive debate. Consisting of diverse, broadly based groups and lacking comparable opposition, the coalition demonstrated once more the degree to which widely shared interests and values converged in support of reform. The coalition recognized this function and sought to enhance it in its method of lobbying. Most often, the coalition made its lobbying visits to congressional offices in teams that included representatives of both liberal and conservative groups as well as of business. Instead of an ordinary application of interest group power, this was a form of political theater.[47] It dramatized the compatibility of airline and trucking deregulation with the interests of large economic sectors and prevailing conceptions of the public interest—demonstrating that the opposition was truly a "special" interest. The coalition received assistance in the demonstration from newspaper editors, institutionalized opponents of interests that are seen as special. Virtually all of the nation's larger newspapers, for example, editorialized in favor of trucking deregu-

45. Mattea interview. Another Senate aide observed that groups in favor of trucking deregulation, unlike the industry and the Teamsters, "did not see it as a life-and-death issue." Interview, Suzelle Smith, legislative assistant to Senator Howell Heflin, Democrat of Alabama, April 10, 1980. Certainly none were concerned to the degree of the Teamsters Union, which told its members, "There are no words left to describe the enormity of the devastation that will result, should this legislation become law." "Deregulation Is Just Around the Corner," *The International Teamster,* June 1980, p. 10.

46. Frank Swain, legislative counsel for the National Federation of Independent Business, said his participation was "the most fun I ever had as a lobbyist." The NFIB's involvement began because of a survey of members initiated by the staff. Interview, January 16, 1981.

47. Interview, Ann McBride, lobbyist, Common Cause, January 26, 1981; and Sender interview. On the theory and methods of Common Cause's lobbying, see Andrew S. McFarland, *Common Cause: Lobbying in the Public Interest* (Chatham House, 1984).

lation, many of them repeatedly. The coalition members and other reform advocates kept track of the editorial support, some of which they also stimulated, to be able to cite it in their lobbying.[48]

Airline and trucking industry representatives, on the other hand, were unable to present arguments that were nearly as well supported or endorsements nearly as credible. To be sure, in opposing reform they made numerous assertions: that under deregulation firms would flock to the "most lucrative" markets, leaving others with inadequate service; that unrestrained competition would bring "chaos" and "instability"; and that it would permit large firms to overcome smaller ones, eventually leading to extreme concentration. The most plausible and effective objection, discussed below in more detail, was that deregulation would harm small communities and rural areas.

On all of these claims, the reformers and their economist allies were prepared with cogent rebuttals. Compared with the main reform arguments, the rebuttals tended to be more complex and less intuitive; they held, for example, that any market that could support service would continue to attract it in the long run, and that "chaos," if that meant bankruptcies and service realignments, need not be harmful to the general public. Pressed to describe the patterns of service that would prevail in a deregulated airline industry, Alfred Kahn replied, paradoxically, that "the superiority of open markets . . . lies in the fact that the optimum outcome *cannot be predicted.*" On many of the points, the rebuttals, even if not intuitive, could be presented on grounds of economic theory as virtually certain. And sometimes the industries' case was hard to argue in the first place. The trucking industry withheld an expected push for a floor amendment on antitrust immunity, a lobbyist said, partly because it would have been difficult to explain "the need for price-fixing" to the senators.[49]

More apparent than the difficulties of their arguments was the fact that the opponents lacked credible witnesses to defend their claims. Econo-

48. Sears kept a file of the many favorable and the very few unfavorable editorials on trucking deregulation in hundreds of newspapers across the country. Before House committee action, the Carter administration's trucking task force reported that it had sent materials to and telephoned editorial writers "at some 35 newspapers in key districts, most of whom said they'd give us good editorials this week." White House memorandum, Ronald Lewis to Stu Eizenstat, May 5, 1980.

49. *Aviation Regulatory Reform,* Hearing before the Subcommittee on Aviation of the House Committee on Public Works and Transportation, 95 Cong. 2 sess. (GPO, 1978), p. 584; and Meade interview.

mists who would argue against deregulation evidently could not be found. Although the opponents did present a few academics as expert witnesses, they were mostly professors of business administration who did not have national reputations. In the 1978 hearings on trucking before the Kennedy subcommittee, the industry offered the testimony of a paid consultant. Senator Howard M. Metzenbaum, Democrat of Ohio, producing a copy of the consultant's original proposal, indignantly pointed out that he had essentially promised his study would support regulation before he was hired. Later, in an elaborate statement of its position before the Senate floor debate, the industry gave prominent attention to a purported critique of trucking deregulation by a Stanford University economist. Cited without facts of publication, the source turned out to be a commentary in the *Los Angeles Times* that was more cautionary than critical and described no research.[50]

In summarizing the evidence, the administration could point to "an almost total absence of studies in defense of the current system" in comparison with "literally dozens of serious studies" supporting reform.[51] Unlike the reformers, as we have noted, the industry opponents found no substantial support from ideological or public interest groups, governmental agencies, or groups representing broad sectors of the economy.

SMALL-COMMUNITY SERVICE. The second threat to congressional support—the tendency of congressmen to protect particular geographic areas, sometimes at the expense of the nation as a whole—also was substantially vitiated. Both the airline and trucking industries, in their most effective argument, claimed that deregulation would do great harm to small communities and rural areas. Regulated firms, they said, had a "common carrier obligation" to provide service, binding even when it was not profitable to do so; with their sparse markets, small communities and rural areas were asserted to be the main beneficiaries. This arrangement was possible, the industries argued, only because regulation limited competition in the denser markets between larger cities, permitting higher than normal profits in them that made up the losses in sparser markets. Deregulation would bring this cross-subsidization to an end, and less

50. *Oversight of Freight Rate Competition in the Motor Carrier Industry*, Hearings before the Subcommittee on Antitrust and Monopoly of the Senate Committee on the Judiciary, 95 Cong. 2 sess., vol. 3 (GPO, 1975), pp. 1286–87; and *Motor Carrier Reform Act of 1980*, S. Rept. 96–641, 96 Cong. 2 sess. (GPO, 1980), p. 35.

51. Goldschmidt letter to Cannon, *Congressional Record* (April 15, 1980), pp. 7778–79.

urbanized areas would suffer drastic price increases or losses of service. Members of Congress from rural areas, including several members of the Senate Commerce Committee, were especially concerned. "Deregulation could easily come to mean abandonment of poorer or less profitable routes," Senator Larry Pressler, Democrat of South Dakota, warned. "If so, South Dakota and other rural states could suffer."[52]

If the reformers had tried to overpower Congress's concern for small communities, quite likely they would have failed. Deferring to it instead, they largely satisfied this concern through a combination of research, analysis, and policy adjustment. Deregulation advocates were able to argue that the presumed benefits of regulation for small communities were, for the most part, pious fictions. Their argument owed little to academic economics. As a matter of both intellectual tradition and normative outlook, regulatory economists had mostly ignored the differing effects of regulation on different areas or groups, addressing instead broad questions of efficiency and overall performance.[53] For pertinent analysis, the reform advocates had to look to others—primarily themselves. Studies of the small-community service problem were conducted or initiated in several places: the Senate Judiciary and Commerce committees, the ICC and CAB, and especially the Department of Transportation, in which a regulatory analysis group in the Office of the Secretary coordinated deregulation research for the executive branch. Altogether the reformers accumulated several separate studies of small-community service for each of the industries.[54]

52. See the statement of C. E. Meyer, Jr., president of TransWorld Airlines, in *Regulatory Reform in Air Transportation*, Hearings before the Subcommittee on Aviation of the Senate Committee on Commerce, Science, and Transportation, 95 Cong. 1 sess. (GPO, 1977), pt. 1, p. 470; American Trucking Associations, "The Case for Economic Regulation of the Motor Carrier Industry," *Economic Regulation of the Trucking Industry*, Hearings, pt. 1, pp. 209–10; and *Motor Carrier Reform Act of 1980*, S. Rept. 96–641, p. 71.

53. George C. Eads, "The Demise of Cross-Subsidy in U.S. Domestic Air Transportation: Reasons and Implications," *Canadian Transportation Commission Research Seminar Series* (Fall 1977), pp. 35–54.

54. The CAB staff presented the reformers' case concerning small-community airline service in a paper entitled "Five Truths About Subsidized Small Community Air Service," in *Aviation Regulatory Reform*, Hearings before the Subcommittee on Aviation of the House Committee on Public Works and Transportation, 95 Cong. 2 sess. (GPO, 1978), pp. 665–719. On trucking, see Congressional Budget Office, Natural Resources and Commerce Division, "The Impact of Trucking Deregulation on Small Communities: A Review of Recent Studies," Staff Working Paper, February 1980.

The studies demonstrated that no common carrier obligation to provide unprofitable service had been seriously enforced in either industry. For years the CAB had permitted airlines easily and routinely to delete routes from their certificates if they wished; thus in a recent period of ten years, more than seventy communities had lost all certificated airline service. Although trucking firms also could give up authorities, more commonly they avoided providing service without surrendering the right to do so. Some companies theoretically serving a community were not even listed in its telephone directory, and the ICC almost never had penalized nonperformance. The presence of any genuine cross-subsidization was challenged by the reformers. Said the administration: "There are two kinds of trucking service to small communities: profitable and nonexistent."[55]

Further, the reformers argued, it was precisely in the sparse, economically marginal markets of small communities that firms most needed flexibility to provide service and that regulatory rigidities were especially harmful. In many small cities, for example, airline service had labored under regulations that discouraged the use of smaller aircraft, which could profitably make frequent flights with fewer passengers. A small shipper in a rural area might have to make casual or spontaneous arrangements for trucking service because more regular, elaborate service would not be supportable; regulation, often as not, would complicate the arrangements. In short, even if some cross-subsidization existed, it was more than offset by regulatory impediments to service; and deregulation, rather than harming airline and trucking services in small communities, would actually improve them.

Often designed and carried out in haste by consultants or staff, the small-community service studies were not scientifically rigorous, but they addressed congressional concerns as concretely as possible. During the Kennedy investigation, United Airlines produced a list of seventy-five route segments that it claimed to be serving unprofitably. By discussing the list with the company and examining its accounts, the staff was able to show that United already had suspended service on some of the seg-

55. *Amending the Federal Aviation Act of 1958*, S. Rept. 95-631, 95 Cong. 2 sess. (GPO, 1978); Denis A. Breen and Benjamin J. Allen, "Motor Carrier Obligations and the Provision of Motor Carrier Service to Small Communities," U.S. Department of Transportation, July 1979; and Statement of Secretary of Transportation Brock Adams, *Economic Regulation of the Trucking Industry*, Hearings, pt. 2, p. 433.

ments, and many of the others were being served profitably, either to position aircraft or as feeder routes that generated traffic on longer segments. Only twenty-nine of the segments, accounting for 0.5 percent of United's business, "might be viewed as the beneficiaries of cross-subsidy." With the alternatives of commuter airlines and modest public subsidies, the staff concluded, "It is nearly inconceivable that service to any community would be totally eliminated."[56]

In trucking, reform advocates arranged a series of surveys of shippers in small communities that were designed overtly for congressional consumption. As the Senate Commerce Committee took up the issue, the Department of Transportation offered to survey shippers in two communities in any state represented on the committee, at the request of the respective senator. In a sampling procedure they could hardly question, the senators themselves chose the communities. Shippers who were surveyed mostly took a dim view of regulated trucking service and reported that, to a great extent, they avoided relying on it. In one New Mexico community, selected for Senator Schmitt by the ATA, it turned out that no regulated company was providing service—an embarrassment the association sought to dismiss by blaming it on an irresponsible carrier. The senator, already leaning toward support for deregulation, was moved to become a vigorous advocate.[57]

The reformers also sought to assure Congress about small-community service by incorporating provisions in bills. This was most useful in the airline case, in which the industry's manageable size and complexity made possible actual guarantees. The airline bill provided that every city served by the certificated airlines would continue to receive at least "minimum, essential service" for ten years. In order to withdraw from a city, a carrier would have to give 180 days' prior notice, and a federal subsidy would be used, if necessary, to attract a replacement. Offering a certainty, even if limited and temporary, that did not exist under regulation, the small-community provisions had little to do with free markets. The reformers could accept the deviation because they expected the subsidies to

56. *CAB Practices and Procedures,* Committee Print, pp. 65–68.

57. Several of the committee members asked for the surveys. For a list of the studies and others concerned with small-community trucking service, see *Congressional Record* (April 15, 1980), pp. 7788–89. Interview, Steve Beck, legislative assistant, Harrison Schmitt, July 15, 1980.

be infrequent and small and they considered the program essential to enactment of the bill.[58]

With its vast number of service points and many distinct varieties of service, the trucking industry did not lend itself to guarantees. Nevertheless, to achieve some of the same political purpose, the Cannon-Packwood bill contained a special provision easing entry and increasing flexibility for small-community service. As deregulation opponents pointed out, this was to ensure against harm from deregulation by pushing deregulation even farther. Even so, the provision gave small communities a modest advantage and at least the appearance of favored treatment.

The greatest embarrassment to the reformers' strategy on small communities occurred in the debate on trucking but involved, ironically, the behavior of airlines. For several months after the passage of the Airline Deregulation Act, the industry performed beyond expectation: stimulated by a strong recovery of the general economy, ridership expanded, and even with low fares, profits rose to record levels. Advocates of trucking deregulation pointed to the airlines to show what deregulation could accomplish. "By every standard of economic measurement . . . the results of airline deregulation have been phenomenal," Senator Kennedy informed the Commerce Committee, citing an estimate that one year's savings to consumers would approach $2.5 billion. "Significant reductions in the structure of federal regulation of the trucking industry are likely to produce even greater savings." He went on to explain the "important similarities" of the two industries.[59]

But as airlines restructured routes, problems soon developed and raised doubts about the reliability of the reformers' assurances. A number of small cities and even some larger ones, such as Bakersfield, California, and Charleston, South Carolina, experienced sharp reductions of airline service or were notified that a major carrier intended to withdraw. Airline deregulation once again became controversial and some congressmen openly regretted having voted for it. Senator Hollings, who was person-

58. Eizenstat interview.

59. *Economic Regulation of the Trucking Industry,* Hearings, pt. 1, p. 7. Even though fares were low, airline profits rose because of the dramatic increase in ridership. As Behrman points out, airline profits in the third quarter of 1978 exceeded annual profits in all but five previous years. Behrman, "Civil Aeronautics Board," pp. 416–17.

ally inconvenienced on weekend trips to Charleston, proclaimed himself to be "a born-again regulator." Opponents of trucking deregulation were quick to exploit the dissatisfaction. In a full-page advertisement in the *Washington Post,* the industry ridiculed deregulation, portrayed as the "Red Baron," for allegedly shooting down air service in twenty-five cities. An aide to another senator who felt his state had been harmed judged before Senate floor action that "the worst thing that ever happened to trucking deregulation was airline deregulation."[60]

Responding elaborately, the reformers gave each congressman a compilation of CAB data on service to and from all of the more than 400 interstate airport cities, organized by state. Although the results varied considerably among cities, the study indicated that service had improved, on the average, even at the smallest category of airports.[61] The reformers argued that most of the complaints were premature, since replacements would be found before departing carriers actually left, and that the reductions in service in some places represented only problems of transition.

In the end, supporters of trucking deregulation were more likely to stress the differences between the two industries than the similarities they had stressed earlier.[62] Comparisons aside, they had given members of Congress ample grounds for rejecting contentions about the benefits of regulation for small communities. Thus in both the airline and trucking cases, as the bills were being considered, cogent arguments and evidence were produced to suggest that small communities would not suffer under deregulation, but would actually benefit.

ANONYMITY AND SALIENCE. The third and final obstacle to congressional support—the relative anonymity of rank-and-file members—was mitigated, although not wholly removed, by effective rhetoric. Seizing upon opportunities that good fortune made available, the reformers linked deregulation of airlines and trucking to two issues then of intense concern to the general public: inflation and big government. "One of my Administration's major goals is to free the American people from the burden of over-regulation," President Carter said in asking Congress to reform airline regulation. He went on to say that airline regulation stifles

60. The industry advertisement, and the detailed rebuttal by the CAB, are described in the *Washington Post,* March 11, 1980. Smith interview.

61. "CAB Report on Airline Service, Fares, Traffic, Load Factors and Market Shares," October 1979.

62. *Congressional Record* (June 19, 1980), p. 15579.

competition, discourages innovation, and "has denied consumers lower fares where they are possible." Opening the floor debate on the trucking bill, Senator Cannon used similar themes. "It is a rare opportunity," he said, "for the Senate to be able to do something more than merely pay lip service to reducing Government regulation and do something concrete to fight inflation."[63]

Each of these themes, highly salient in the period of the debate, was a powerful tool of political persuasion. In the late 1970s the public was extremely concerned about inflation, and congressmen of both parties wanted to build records for fighting it. Although it was also highly salient, the big government theme was associated with conservative ideology and hence was to some extent partisan. In lobbying party colleagues on the trucking bill, Senator Packwood pointed out that Republicans, professing belief in limited government, would be hypocritical to set aside that belief just because the trucking industry wanted protection from competition. Conversely, a Senate Democrat, arguing against the bill in private discussion with fellow liberals, warned that voting for it would seem to endorse the trend toward abandoning governmental activism. Yet even here the partisan difference was muted, since in this period most Democrats as well as Republicans wanted credit for reducing government.[64]

These themes were stressed and seemed to work even though the effects of airline and trucking deregulation on inflation and government's intrusiveness were so modest as to be essentially symbolic. Air fares in their entirety represented less than 0.5 percent of the consumer price index; for deregulation to reduce inflation noticeably, it would have had to make airline service virtually free. The trucking industry was much larger, but its supporters could claim, for example, that trucking service contributed only a few cents to the price of a can of peas.[65] Nor was economic regulation of airlines or trucking what people who worried

63. "Airline Industry Regulation," Message to the Congress, March 4, 1977, *Public Papers of the President: Jimmy Carter, 1977*, bk. 1 (GPO, 1977), p. 277; and *Congressional Record* (April 15, 1980), p. 7777.

64. A survey in 1979 found that, when asked about federal regulation of business in general, 46 percent of the public wanted less, 22 percent more, and 25 percent the same amount there is now. Louis Harris and Associates, "Public Attitudes toward Competition in the Telecommunications Industry," prepared for AT&T, July 1979, p. 5. Interview, Will Ris, July 16, 1980; and interview with a legislative assistant to a Democratic senator.

65. James W. Callison, "The Airline Reform Movement—Is It Deregulation or Re-regulation?" speech delivered to the American Society of Women Accountants, Atlanta, Georgia, May 9, 1978, p. 10.

about "excessive government regulation" normally had in mind. That worry had been prompted by the growth of so-called social regulation—sweeping, costly, and often controversial governmental interventions dealing with such matters as environmental quality, occupational safety and health, and employment discrimination. Airline and trucking regulation, neither recently created nor considered onerous by the regulated industries, were little noticed by the general public.

For the rhetorical purposes at hand, however, such loose connections were quite sufficient. They were in particular strong enough that the themes of inflation and big government could be used convincingly to advocate or defend deregulation, or criticize opposition to it, before the general public.

Placed in a rhetorical context that gave them salience, the deregulation bills promised to receive substantial news coverage when Congress acted and, moreover, to provide material usable by members or their opponents in election campaigns. In the 1980 campaign, in fact, several senators who had voted for trucking deregulation made use of the issue in seeking reelection. Often in response to questions about inflation or big government, they would mention trucking deregulation as one of several issues on which they had taken constructive action.[66] In other words, the veil of anonymity of rank-and-file members of Congress was, to a degree, pierced. In voting on airline and trucking deregulation, members of Congress were not required, and were not able, to assume their actions would go unnoticed.

THE EFFECTIVENESS OF REFORM ADVOCACY. By piecing together available evidence, some of the actual effects of deregulation advocacy can be roughly assessed. The trucking case, where we have help from contemporaneous interviews in addition to voting patterns in the Senate, is especially revealing. Despite all the effort to establish broadly based support, the reformers could not quite match the electoral pressures brought to bear against deregulation by the Teamsters and the industry. Rather, as a lobbyist with the ad hoc coalition estimated, they managed to make the

66. To find out what, if any, role trucking deregulation played in the election, we did brief phone interviews in November and December 1980 with staff who had worked in the reelection campaigns of twelve senators. We asked whether the senator's position on trucking had been raised in the campaign and—if so—how and with what effect. Because a compromise had been reached before floor action in the House, a similar inquiry there would not have been useful.

Table 4-1. *Senate Voting on Passage of the Motor Carrier Reform Bill in 1980, by Type of State*

Type of state[a]	For	Against
Rural	19	12
Moderately urban	26	6
Urban	25	2
Total	70	20

Source: Authors' calculations, based on voting data from *Congressional Quarterly Weekly Report*, vol. 38 (April 19, 1980), p. 1062.

a. States are classified by the percentage of their populations living in places with populations under 2,500, according to the 1970 U.S. census, with divisions as follows: 0–24 percent, urban; 25–39 percent, moderately urban; and 40–100 percent, rural.

issue "a close call" for most congressmen, one with important political costs and benefits on both sides; he suggested that this had permitted them to act more freely on their opinions of the merits.[67] Broadly speaking, this assessment was probably correct. The Senate defeated weakening floor amendments—56 to 34 on entry, 47 to 39 on the exemption of processed food—and then passed the resulting bill 70 to 20. On final passage, deregulation won the approval of majorities in both parties—34 to 18 among Democrats and, despite benefits for a president of the opposite party, 36 to 2 among Republicans. If the balance of political inducements had not seemed close, but instead had massively opposed reform, these votes presumably would have been impossible.

In the effort to allay fears about small-community service, trucking deregulation advocates largely, but not entirely, succeeded. Senators from the most rural one-third of the states voted to pass the trucking bill by a ratio of more than 3 to 2—a substantial majority, even though smaller proportionately than in the rest of the Senate (table 4-1). That some resistance remained was not surprising. The problems with airline service in small communities, transitional or not, obviously weakened the reformers' case. Moreover, regardless of evidence, the industry's claims about cross-subsidized service gave rural senators the most convenient rationale to oppose reform. Under the circumstances, the support obtained from rural senators suggests that the reformers' research, arguments, and special measures on small-community service were indeed effective.

67. Sender interview.

Table 4-2. *Senate Voting on Amendments to and Passage of the Motor Carrier Reform Bill in 1980, by Reelection Status and Party*[a]

Reelection status and party	Processed foods amendment[b]		Entry standard amendment[c]		Small-community entry amendment[d]		Final passage	
	For	Against	For	Against	For	Against	For	Against
Running	8	19	10	16	7	19	18	8
	(30)	(70)	(38)	(62)	(27)	(73)	(69)	(31)
Democrat	4	16	5	14	3	16	11	8
	(20)	(80)	(26)	(74)	(16)	(84)	(58)	(42)
Republican	4	3	5	2	4	3	7	0
	(57)	(43)	(71)	(29)	(57)	(43)	(100)	(0)
Not running	40	21	46	18	30	33	52	12
	(66)	(34)	(72)	(28)	(48)	(52)	(81)	(19)
Democrat	18	14	19	14	13	19	23	10
	(56)	(44)	(58)	(42)	(41)	(59)	(70)	(30)
Republican	22	7	27	4	17	14	29	2
	(76)	(24)	(87)	(13)	(55)	(45)	(94)	(6)
Total	48	40	56	34	37	52	70	20
	(55)	(45)	(62)	(38)	(42)	(58)	(78)	(22)

Source: Authors' calculations, based on voting data from *Congressional Quarterly Weekly Report,* vol. 38 (April 19, 1980), p. 1062.

a. The voting data include those who were paired for and against each measure. Votes on amendments, all three of which were defeated, are coded so that a vote "for" indicates support for deregulation. Numbers in parentheses are percentages of the raw totals in each category.

b. Offered by Ernest F. Hollings, Democrat of South Carolina; would have eliminated an expanded agricultural exemption.

c. Offered by Warren G. Magnuson, Democrat of Washington; would have imposed a more restrictive test on applications for entry.

d. Offered by Harrison H. Schmitt, Republican of New Mexico; would have eliminated the requirement to meet a test of public convenience and necessity as it applied to applications to provide service to small communities.

Even if it was close, the balance of political pressures was not equal or too close to call: if they were giving primary consideration to their prospects for reelection, most senators apparently still saw an advantage in opposing reform on the key votes. This was evident in the actions of those senators for whom electoral concerns were most immediate. On each of the three floor amendments (one of which would have strengthened the bill), senators who were running for reelection in 1980 voted against deregulation markedly more often than those who either did not have to run or had chosen to retire (table 4-2). For example, on the industry-sponsored amendment to keep processed foods under regulation, the vote decided by the narrowest margin, senators who were not running rejected the industry position by about 2 to 1 (40 to 21); those who had a reelection campaign impending gave their support just as heavily (19 to 8). The same tendency appeared on the other amendments and was evident within each party considered separately.[68]

It is not likely that senators who were running for reelection differed from others in judging which votes were, on balance, electorally preferable. Rather, the difference, we suppose, was that for senators not immediately at risk, the political cost of supporting reform would diminish before the next election and thus was a matter of less importance.

Only on the final vote, it seems, did the strongest political pressures favor deregulation. As the vote most visible and understandable to the general public, it would have been under any circumstances the hardest one on which to oppose reform. In addition, for strategic reasons the industry concentrated its lobbying on amendments and, while certainly not endorsing the bill, did not attempt to defeat it on final passage. With the choice thus simplified, even senators who were up for reelection voted in favor of passage by the large margin of 18 to 8.

For the whole set of votes, it seems, the politically safest approach for senators was apparently a mixed one. A senator could show deference to the interest groups by voting against deregulation on, say, at least two of the three amendments, yet avoid criticism as a reform opponent by voting to pass the bill. Twenty-two senators did just that. In a meeting afterwards, ATA president Bennett Whitlock said that it was only the thirty senators who voted against the industry on every roll call with whom he intended to "get even."[69]

There seem to have been several reasons many senators did not heed the strongest electoral inducements, but rather voted for trucking deregulation even on amendments. Some took an untypical view of the electoral effects. In the opinion of Senator Stevenson (who, in any case, was retir-

68. For another analysis of Senate roll call voting on trucking deregulation, with findings consistent with ours, see John P. Frendreis and Richard W. Waterman, "PAC Contributions and Legislative Behavior: Senate Voting on Trucking Deregulation," paper prepared for the 1983 annual meeting of the Midwest Political Science Association. Concerned mainly with estimating the effect of ATA campaign contributions on Senate voting, an issue we do not specifically address, the authors conclude that this effect was substantial. That conclusion, although entirely plausible to us, cannot be established by their regression analysis. An unknown and potentially large part of the measured relationship between contributions and votes would represent a causal effect in the opposite direction: the ATA undoubtedly contributed to the campaigns of senators who would have supported its position on deregulation anyway.

69. Transcripts, ATA executive committee meeting, May 28, 1980.

ing from the Senate), those effects would depend on the senator's other positions and methods of campaigning. If one took the stance of serving "public" instead of "private" interests, acted that way consistently, and then "marketed" the image to the voters, even positions strongly opposed by organized interests, like support for trucking deregulation, would bring political rewards.[70] Other senators may have been influenced mainly by the committee leaders (both Democratic and Republican) or by the president, preferring to be thought cooperative even if it meant incurring political costs. Finally, and we think crucially, some senators voted for deregulation largely because they were convinced of its merits. Said one senator to a colleague before casting a vote to strengthen the bill: "I know I'm going to take heat for this. But, damn it, it's right."[71]

On the airline bill, many of the influences and voting patterns were similar—except that, since the industry and labor opposition was weaker and more divided and the issue was somewhat more visible to consumers, airline deregulation was easier to support. Senators who were running for reelection in 1978 also withheld support more often than others, but the difference was inconsequential: on the main attempt to weaken the bill, 71 percent of those who were running supported deregulation, compared with 76 percent of those who were not.[72] As was true in trucking, the political balance was more favorable for reform on final passage, permitting overwhelming approval, 92 to 8. And, again as in trucking, most of the concern about small-community service was apparently satisfied. On the two significant floor amendments senators from urban and moderately urban states voted for stronger deregulation by margins of about 4 to 1; those from rural states voted for it by a smaller but still solid margin of 2 to 1 (table 4-3).

Telecommunications

The great difficulty with which Congress came to accept procompetitive policies in telecommunications over a period of several years can be

70. Interview, former Senator Adlai Stevenson III, January 22, 1981.
71. Mattea interview. As an aide to Senator Stevenson, who was active in the debate, Mattea had access to the Senate floor. Numerous participants we interviewed on the subject assumed that senators' judgments of the merits and willingness to disregard some electoral cost were important influences on the vote.
72. The amendment, sponsored by Senators George McGovern and Barry Goldwater, would have restricted the automatic entry program that was a central deregulatory feature of the bill.

Table 4-3. *Senate Voting on Amendments to the Airline Deregulation Act of 1978, by Type of State*

Type of state[c]	Automatic entry amendment[a]		Entry burden amendment[b]	
	For	Against	For	Against
Rural	23	12	22	12
Moderately urban	27	5	22	9
Urban	21	7	24	2
Total	71	24	68	23

Source: Author's calculations, based on voting data from *Congressional Quarterly Almanac*, vol. 34 (1978), p. 22-S.

a. Sponsored by Barry Goldwater and George McGovern; would have limited the scope of a free-entry provision in the committee's bill, but was defeated. It is coded here so that a vote "for" indicates support for deregulation.

b. Sponsored by Edward Kennedy and passed; placed the burden of proof in entry cases on those opposing, rather than those making, applications for new route assignments.

c. See note a, table 4-1.

understood by contrast with the airlines and trucking cases. In part, legislative action on reform was deterred by the daunting political resources of AT&T, the independents, and the communications unions—a well-connected group, vastly superior even to the trucking industry in size and employment. But just as important, the obstacles to rank-and-file support were more intractable in telecommunications, compared with airlines and trucking, because the reform advocacy did not have comparable strengths for persuasion in Congress.

In contrast with the clarity and consensus of academic opinion regarding airlines and trucking, there was uncertainty among independent experts regarding the advantages and appropriate scope of competition in telecommunications. In one area, terminal equipment, competition admitted by the FCC had produced obvious, important benefits. The so-called interconnect companies had generated an outpouring of useful new products, ranging from improved on-premises switching equipment to computers that conversed over telephone lines. To offer the immense variety of these technologically advanced products would have been beyond the innovative capacity of a single firm—especially a regulated monopoly. In long distance transmission, on the other hand, the benefit of competition was open to doubt. Because AT&T's long distance rates were elevated in order to subsidize rural and residential service, competitors enjoyed an artificial advantage in price. Even with rates lower than Bell's, the competitors could have higher real costs and thus, using resources less efficiently, represent a loss to the economy. The magnitude of this phenomenon, called "cream skimming" by its critics, was debated hotly and indecisively—with any clear resolution of the issue precluded mostly because Bell's accounting system was incapable of identifying the separate costs of its various services.[73]

Academic and governmental analysts of telecommunications policy were ready in the mid-1970s to condemn the drastic restrictions on competition proposed in the Bell bill, but they were not ready to give competition unlimited scope, nor even to say with any precision or agreement how far competition should be permitted to go. Confused themselves, analysts could not convey clear cues to policymakers.[74]

The telecommunications case was also unlike that of airlines or trucking in that Congress's concerns about the distributive effects of procompetitive reform could not easily be relieved. The groups allegedly receiving cross-subsidies included—besides rural users—residential customers (as opposed to business) and local callers (as opposed to long distance). At least some of the purported shifting of burdens clearly existed, having been facilitated by monopoly and encouraged by state public utility commissions, which resisted increases in local rates. The growth of competition threatened to upset these long-standing arrangements, ultimately reorienting the industry's rate structures and causing noticeable increases for rural and residential customers.

Implicit in this prospect were huge political risks, which in fact brought the congressional career of House Communications Subcommittee chairman Lionel Van Deerlin to a sudden end. In a Republican party mailing sent to his entire district the week before the 1980 election, Van Deerlin was charged with sponsoring a bill that would cause residential rates to increase 400 percent. Even though the charge was spurious and was quickly repudiated by the California official quoted in the mailing, Van Deerlin rapidly lost an apparent lead and was narrowly defeated in the election.

In telecommunications bills, Congress was inclined to exert control over changes in the structure of rates, replacing cross-subsidies with new sources of revenue or very gradually phasing them out. It could not agree,

73. For a thorough review of the issues, see Gerald M. Brock, *The Telecommunications Industry: The Dynamics of Market Structure* (Harvard University Press, 1981).

74. For an example of uncertainty on the part of one generally devoted to competition, see Alfred Kahn's testimony in *Competition in the Telecommunications Industry,* Hearings before the Communications Subcommittee of the House Committee on Interstate and Foreign Commerce, 94 Cong. 2 sess. (GPO, 1976), p. 976. In 1981 Kahn speculated that competition in intercity transmission might be harmful to static efficiency but nonetheless beneficial overall because it would encourage innovation. *Telecommunications Competition and Deregulation Act of 1981,* Hearings before the Senate Committee on Commerce, Science, and Transportation, 97 Cong. 1 sess. (GPO, 1981), pp. 152–83.

however, on the methods of doing so. Besides using intricate financial arrangements with special governmental bodies to administer them, the proposed mechanisms involved very large amounts of money. Conflict over them had several dimensions—urban versus rural, residential versus business users, federal versus state, and established firms versus the new competitors—and was further complicated by the preference of many reformers to eliminate most of the subsidies relatively soon. In over five years of deliberations, no durable consensus emerged, and the problem of adverse effects of competition on particular groups remained a serious obstacle to action by Congress.[75]

Finally, procompetitive reform in telecommunications was deficient in rhetorical themes that could make it salient and appealing for broader audiences. The themes that had given force to reform advocacy in airlines and trucking were, by contrast, problematic or confused in their application to telecommunications. With probable increases in residential rates, the most direct communications expense for the general public, it would have been imprudent to portray bills expanding telecommunications competition as measures to fight inflation. Competition was being advocated in order to aid innovation and improve services, especially for business users, as much as to reduce prices.

Other issues in telecommunications policy also constrained and complicated reform advocacy. Of greatest importance, any telecommunications reform bill had to address the conditions under which AT&T itself would operate in competitive markets, a formidable problem unique to the case (see chapter 5). The long distance and terminal equipment competitors, fearful of AT&T's continuing market power, demanded structural measures to reduce the threat to competition. Ideally, they wanted a governmentally imposed divestiture, severing all relationships between Bell's competitive and monopoly services. Bell denied the need for any modification of its structure. From 1978 until the historic antitrust settlement of 1982, when it finally accepted divestiture, AT&T resisted even more moderate structural proposals, yielding ground only very gradually in the congressional debate.

Designed as compromises, reform bills discussed in Congress generally called for the creation in one or another form of "separate subsidiaries" for AT&T's competitive operations. But none of the structural proposals were acceptable to both AT&T and its competitors. Because of the struc-

75. See Michael Wines, "The Rate Game," *National Journal,* vol. 15 (August 20, 1983), pp. 1720–26.

tural issue, it was impossible to portray telecommunications reform as a way to reduce the intrusiveness of government: even a requirement for a separate subsidiary was no inconsiderable intervention.

Lacking rhetorical means to make procompetitive reform appealing and vivid to the public, congressional leaders in telecommunications, compared with those in other areas, labored in obscurity. Representative Tim Wirth, one of the most prominent, had not been seriously harmed by having an adversary relationship with AT&T, an aide judged in 1981; but he had paid a price for devoting much of his time to the telecommunications issue, which despite its importance did not help him attract notice or build popularity.[76] Compared with Wirth, of course, members of Congress who were not leaders on the issue would have found using it to appeal to a broad constituency even less rewarding.

Even if AT&T and its allies, the communications workers and independent telephone companies, had controlled only ordinary political resources, to advocate procompetitive telecommunications policies in Congress would have been a forbidding task. Bell's exceptional access and lobbying capability magnified the obstacles and it was taken for granted that the company could block any telecommunications bill it decided to oppose.[77] In both Houses, telecommunications leaders made this capability a premise of their strategy, refusing to put procompetitive proposals up for a vote, even in subcommittee, until Bell had agreed to them. From 1976, when Bell started the legislative debate with its own measure, until 1980, when the House Commerce Committee adopted a procompetitive bill with the company's consent, overt congressional support for telecommunications competition was limited almost entirely to the leaders and a few activist members of the committees involved. Strong procompetitive bills were proposed and discussed, but the main concrete accomplishment was in preventing action to reverse reform.

Conclusion

Congress responded to procompetitive policies of the commissions by lending support. Although the strength of this support varied among

76. Interview, David Aylward, chief counsel, House Subcommittee on Telecommunications, Consumer Protection, and Finance, September 17, 1981.

77. Pickard Wagner, AT&T's Washington spokesman, thought an insignificant or watered-down telecommunications bill might pass without the company's support, but not an important one. Interview, August 29, 1981. Former AT&T chairman John de Butts disagreed, saying that "the power of big business is a myth." Interview, May 29, 1981.

the cases, it was sufficient in each for the reformers to win important legislative victories even while industry opposition remained intense—the defeat of the Bell bill and formation of a procompetitive telecommunications agenda in the House and Senate, passage of a strong trucking bill by the Senate, and major steps in both houses toward substantial deregulation of the airlines. These victories and the political strength that made them possible were crucial to the eventual success of reform. In addition, we argue, they reveal important, yet often unrecognized, influences and capacities in the behavior of Congress.

According to an influential line of academic analysis, Congress has little intrinsic capacity to serve broad or diffuse interests of the nation as a whole. Rather, as a consequence of its structure and the incentives of members, Congress's central impulse is to distribute "particularized benefits" to specific localities and organized interest groups.[78] The premise of this analysis, often stated quite baldly, is that members of Congress in their legislative behavior are motivated by the single goal of winning reelection. Policy views and ideologies, proclaimed as deep commitments, in fact are used merely as instruments to achieve that purpose. This assumption about members' goals is defended, though indirectly, by several observations: that the congressional life, with its glamour, travel, and amenities, is intrinsically attractive; that even if a member genuinely wishes to serve the public, getting reelected is the first requirement; and that in a competitive political world, members who do not primarily seek reelection may not be around long enough, in large enough numbers, to matter much in the institution. To the objection that many members of Congress have safe seats and do not need to devote themselves single-mindedly to reelection, it is answered that safe seats only show how assiduously those members have pursued electoral support. Besides, fewer seats appear safe when viewed over the course of several elections, and fewer still look safe to the members—who may act as if they are not safe even when they are.[79]

Further stipulated in the analysis is the behavior that members of

78. Mayhew, *Congress: The Electoral Connection;* and Fiorina, *Congress: Keystone of the Washington Establishment.* Of the two, Mayhew's analysis seems to leave more room for response to diffuse interests. For contrasting views see William K. Muir, Jr., *Legislature: California's School of Politics* (University of Chicago Press, 1982); and Maass, *Congress and the Common Good.*

79. Thomas E. Mann, *Unsafe at Any Margin: Interpreting Congressional Elections* (American Enterprise Institute for Public Policy Research, 1978).

Congress seek to perform because it serves their reelection. In regard to legislation, the electoral rewards come from working on behalf of organized interest groups or seeking tangible benefits, such as grants and projects, for one's district or state; only in these ways can a member of Congress bestow benefits on groups capable of recognizing the effort and rewarding it with support. On the other hand, the argument holds, a member gains little electoral support by attending to broad national interests or trying to implement an ideology because, as surveys show, few voters base choices in congressional elections on specific policy issues or, except on issues of unusual salience, even are aware of what congressmen do. Members can satisfy the electorate's demand for commitment to broader purposes largely by rhetoric and symbolic gestures.[80] Moreover, the structure of Congress has been designed above all to assist in distributing the particularized benefits. The specialized committees and subcommittees assist by giving control over programs to the groups and geographic areas directly affected, which generally are well represented on the pertinent committees.

Thus the only politicians who have strong reasons to be concerned with broad interests of the entire nation are the president and sometimes, based on a notion of "collective responsibility," the congressional party leaders. It follows that the ability of the political system to respond to broadly based interests fundamentally depends on the degree to which those politicians control the Congress.[81]

No doubt this account of a Congress deeply and inherently prone to particularism has a substantial measure of validity, but as a general or comprehensive account, it is quite misleading. By the support it gave procompetitive reform, Congress proved responsive to very diffuse interests of the general public and to beliefs, arguments, and values presumed to express these interests. Congress did this without much interest group

80. See Mayhew's discussion of "position taking." Listed as one of the principal reelection-seeking activities, position taking certainly includes rhetoric and gestures designed to appeal to large audiences; but it also includes casting roll call votes for the same purpose. As vote casting, position taking can account for congressional responses to broadly based concerns, and it corresponds to part of the argument we will develop. In Mayhew's discussion, most of the emphasis is on the other form, rhetoric and gestures, and there are suggestions that members can satisfy constituents without the necessity of genuine achievement. *Congress: The Electoral Connection,* pp. 61–73, 132–36.

81. For strong statements to this effect, see Morris P. Fiorina, "The Decline of Collective Responsibility in American Politics," *Daedalus,* vol. 109 (Summer 1980), pp. 25–45; and Fiorina, "The Presidency and the Contemporary Electoral System," in Michael Nelson, ed., *The Presidency and the Political System* (CQ Press, 1984), pp. 204–26.

support and often despite powerful and intense interest group opposition. And it did this on issues that, rather than being highly salient to the general public, were in fact relatively obscure, affecting, for example, trucking prices that most of the public never saw. The explanation of this responsiveness not only exposes the limitations of the particularistic view of Congress; it also helps identify some of the motives and mechanisms of action in Congress that this view fails to notice.

In choosing their positions on procompetitive reform, members of Congress were not only pursuing reelection. They were also acting on substantive policy judgments or opinions "on the merits," which led some to endorse reform even when the stronger electoral incentives argued against it. In seeking support, reformers relied heavily on the substantive persuasiveness of their arguments, cultivating it as a major resource by sponsoring research, presenting elaborate evidence, and gathering endorsements by appropriate experts. In interviews afterwards, reform advocates pointed to members' substantive opinions as a major explanation for support, attributing "courage" or "independence" to many who gave it. Members themselves also claimed these virtues. And, what is perhaps more convincing, the pattern of roll call votes confirms, at least in the case of trucking, that senators did indeed see support for reform as the riskier position electorally. Sufficient majorities supported it regardless.

Such evidence could perhaps be interpreted away if there were compelling theoretical grounds to do so, that is, if all the apparent attention to substantive issues in Congress seemed likely to be an elaborate disguise. On the contrary, the supposition that most congressmen seek only reelection lacks credibility, if only because it fails to consider plausibly why they want to be congressmen in the first place. Some of them, undoubtedly, care only for the perquisites of office. But at least for many, clearly, much of the attraction of serving in Congress is the opportunity to debate issues, form opinions, and make efficacious judgments on matters of public concern. Such activities hold interest and satisfaction for many persons—including, one suspects, many of the political scientists who dismiss such motives—and not the least for politicians. Exercising a certain amount of political independence and voting on the merits of issues is for such members part of the point of having the job.[82] This is not to

82. Muir aptly expresses a similar point: "The legislators needed to feel meaningful and valuable, to have a sense that they had done something that would endure. Put negatively, the personal incentive was to avoid not mattering." *Legislature: California's School of Politics,* p. 181.

say that congressmen will ignore political pressures or will often take large, avoidable electoral risks. Rather, with hundreds of interest groups affected by their votes—on most of which policy and electoral goals will conveniently mesh—large, or even clearly perceptible, risks are rarely required.

Furthermore, to the extent that congressmen feel the need to take electoral considerations into account, the organized groups intensely involved in an issue do not necessarily dominate the calculations. Even on these reform issues of low or moderate salience, the attitudes of ordinary voters had significant weight. Attaching the issues to widespread concerns about inflation and big government, the reformers succeeded in making them seem potentially relevant to those voters and eligible for use in political campaigns. In the end they felt they had established modest political inducements favoring reform; on the most visible votes, those on final passage of the airline and trucking bills, the inducements were strong enough to produce lopsided victories.

As they decide issues, members of Congress often profess to worry about the attitudes of typical voters. Conceivably, such members misconstrue their electoral risks—since, as surveys seem to imply, the voters rarely will notice what they decide. Or perhaps they doubt that voters will notice their decisions, but feel obliged to pretend otherwise. More likely, we think, the worries are genuine and sensible, and congressmen are concerned about issues' potential electoral effects that are too subtle and indirect to be measured in surveys.[83]

Such effects might occur in several ways. Voters may be influenced in their image of a congressman by his position on an issue, and yet at the time of an election (or a survey) may remember only the image and not the issue. Alternatively, issues may have their most important effects through opinion leaders—media figures, civic notables, and other informed individuals—whose political views, in their diversity, resemble those of the electorate as a whole. While paying considerable attention to issues themselves, opinion leaders may convey only much simpler evaluations to other voters. In a sense, an issue can be part of an electoral campaign even though it is rarely or never specifically mentioned. Although lacking sufficient salience of its own for electoral use, an issue can

83. For a similar argument, see R. Douglas Arnold, "The Logic of Congressional Action" (Princeton University, Department of Politics, 1984).

help justify and support a campaign theme that could not be used without such support.

Such effects will not often be large, compared with other forces in an election. But they can still make the attitudes of ordinary voters a major influence on the electoral incentives facing congressmen when they decide on a bill. The possible loss or gain of one voter in a hundred, well below the threshold for detection in a survey, would be viewed as a matter of extraordinary importance, and a small fraction of that could make the difference in a close election. Concerned daily with small gains and losses of political support, members of Congress will want to respond to voters at large and be able to explain their decisions to them, not just rarely, but routinely.[84] Interestingly, the intangibility of these influences means that congressmen have considerable freedom even in construing electoral constraints: a member who would prefer to support broad interests, for example, often can choose estimates of the diffuse electoral effects that will make this support seem politically sensible.

Finally, it is not only the president or congressional party leaders who take responsibility for broad, national interests. In the deregulation cases, committee and subcommittee leaders of both parties generally sought to serve diffuse constituencies, rather than organized groups, and thus adopted reform ideas. It was not, apparently, an idiosyncratic group of leaders. The consistency and bipartisanship resulted from the unusual dimensions of conflict on procompetitive reform—the ideological breadth of the reform movement competing with collaborative opposition by industry and labor. With conflicting group loyalties and ideologies removed as complicating factors, a common leadership approach oriented toward broadly based interests was able to emerge.

Committee leaders presumably have the same inclinations to act with a certain degree of independence as other members. But they also have distinctive incentives attached to their positions that reinforce those inclinations. These include the desire to win respect in Congress and in Washington for committee achievements; the sense of heightened responsibility and aspiration to statesmanship that often, though not always, comes with power; and personal electoral stakes that are not just counterbalanced, but actually altered, by leadership roles. Because they can capture

---

84. On the members' concern about being able to explain their votes, see Richard F. Fenno, Jr., *Home Style: House Members in Their Districts* (Little, Brown, 1978), chap. 5.

much of the attention and credit, committee leaders obtain greater rewards for pursuing broad goals; because interest groups cannot afford an attack against a committee leader that may not succeed, leaders have additional safety from retaliation.

The evidence of this chapter does not suggest that Congress's preference for broad "public" interests is firm and reliable. As we have stressed, procompetitive reform was in some respects an unusual issue. Presenting in the transportation cases a rare liberal-conservative coalition, an academic consensus, and intuitively persuasive arguments connected to problems of high public concern, reform policies were especially suited to elicit a congressional response oriented toward general interests and shaped by ideas. In the telecommunications case, which presented fewer of these features, such responsiveness was still in evidence but noticeably weaker. In many instances Congress does indeed take refuge in particularism. So too, however, does the president—especially if one takes into account not just leading policy initiatives, but all the actions and omissions of a president's administration. It is misleading to ignore the countervailing capacities in Congress or to pretend that the president and Congress act on impulses that are fundamentally different.

CHAPTER 5

The Industries' Retreat

THE political strength of the reform forces was sufficient to produce major legislative victories despite intense and unified opposition by the regulated industries. Nevertheless, that strength alone was not sufficient to account for the sweeping policy changes that Congress enacted into law, in the airline and trucking cases, or accepted without actually passing a bill, in telecommunications. It was also crucial that in each case the industry eventually modified its position, allowed its political effort to slacken, or both. This enabled Congress to fashion bills that were far more deregulatory and procompetitive than otherwise would have been possible.

In only one of the cases—the airlines—and then only in part, did the retreat result from a change of attitude toward procompetitive policies: for the most part, the industries did not surrender their abiding preferences for the traditional regulatory regimes. Instead, policy change by the commissions, and in telecommunications also by the courts, put each industry at a severe strategic disadvantage and tended to compel concessions. Under the circumstances, moreover, it proved unexpectedly difficult for the industries to act skillfully in the political process on behalf of their interests. The precise nature of the difficulties varied among the industries, depending on their form of political organization.

Airlines and Trucking

We will first consider together the cases of airlines and trucking. In both cases the respective commissions put sweeping deregulation into effect administratively, and their actions led before long to legislative results that were very favorable for reform. The telecommunications case—in which both the effects of administrative and judicial actions and the pattern of the established industry's retreat were far more complex—will be treated separately.

The Effects of Commission Action

Administrative deregulation by the CAB and the ICC drastically undermined the ability of the airline and trucking industries to hold firm against deregulation in Congress, and was, without a doubt, the major reason in both cases that their resistance declined. Nevertheless, this political effect of administrative deregulation was not anticipated at the outset. It was quite unclear whether such action, in the long run, would advance the cause of reform or limit its success. Deregulation by the commissions was viewed by reformers as "a two-edged sword" because it might relax some restrictions on competition but by doing so relieve the pressure for legislative reform.[1] Nor did the opponents ignore this possibility. Senator Barry Goldwater (whose free-market principles did not cover the airlines) seized on the CAB's early liberalizing actions to dispute the need for reform legislation. The changes already instituted, he argued in 1976, proved that the 1938 law was able to accommodate any genuine need for reform.[2] Later, when the ICC began to loosen the regulation of trucking, it was widely assumed that Chairman A. Daniel O'Neal wanted to undercut support for a bill.

Not until relatively late in the debate on trucking were the effects of administrative action on industry behavior clearly recognized and deliberately exploited by White House reformers. Although President Ford did seek through appointments and exhortation to encourage policy change by the commissions, his administration concentrated on the preparation of bills. After Alfred E. Kahn's leadership of the CAB demonstrated the possibilities of promoting legislative policy change through administrative action, Carter officials adopted that as a conscious strategy. With several vacancies on the ICC to be filled during 1979, a White House aide, Rick Neustadt, argued internally that it was largely the CAB's aggressiveness that had forced the airlines to make concessions and urged that

1. Interview, Stuart Eizenstat, assistant to the president for domestic policy, April 13, 1981. See on this point, and generally on the airline case, Bradley Behrman, "Civil Aeronautics Board," in James Q. Wilson, ed., *The Politics of Regulation* (Basic Books, 1980), chap. 3.

2. *Congressional Record* (April 19, 1978), pp. 10663–64.

strong supporters of deregulation be chosen for the ICC in order to obtain the same effect. Evidently persuaded, the president chose Darius Gaskins, Marcus Alexis, and Thomas Trantum—all avid deregulators—and elevated Gaskins to the chairmanship when O'Neal left.[3]

The loosening of regulatory controls by the commissions unexpectedly turned out to boost the prospects for reform legislation mainly because the changes they adopted were unexpectedly drastic. Administrative deregulation, gathering momentum as it proceeded, swept aside or deeply compromised the basic methods of regulatory control over entry and pricing in the industries. By the spring of 1978, the CAB not only was encouraging special discount fares but proposing to give the carriers freedom to cut any fare they wished by as much as 50 percent and to vitiate any practical significance of route assignments by granting authority, with no obligation to provide service, to every carrier applying for a route. ICC deregulation of trucking was roughly parallel, though about a year behind. On pricing the ICC created a similar zone of rate flexibility and voted to prohibit most rate proposals from being made collectively. It weakened entry restrictions through changes in regulations as well as by simply approving the preponderance of new applications. Before Congress assumed control of the subject in late 1979, the ICC had agreed on a procedure to make entry into whole segments of the industry completely free.

Such far-reaching administrative change undermined the strategic rationale of the industries' resistance and thus drove them to accept and even support reform legislation. In the first place, deregulation by the commissions forced the industries to operate in environments of debilitating uncertainty; by comparison, the stability potentially afforded by legislative action offered a distinct advantage. Administrative reform developed piecemeal, through a series of proceedings on particular regulations and individual cases, some of which (again piecemeal) might be modified or reversed by the courts. In the end, whatever policies endured

3. See Paul MacAvoy, "Regulatory Reform: How To Get There From Here," in W. S. Moore, ed., *Regulatory Reform: Highlights of a Conference on Government Regulation* (American Enterprise Institute for Public Policy Research, 1976), p. 13; Eizenstat interview; interview, Ronald Lewis, deputy adviser for regulatory affairs, Council on Wage and Price Stability, January 23, 1981; and White House memorandum, Rick Neustadt to Stu Eizenstat, October 18, 1979. For evidence of the Ford administration's awareness of the potential for administrative change, see Louis M. Kohlmeier, " 'Big Government' a Campaign Issue," *National Journal,* vol. 7 (November 1, 1975), p. 1520.

this process still could be upset by Congress. Because of the ICC's actions, said American Trucking Association president Bennett C. Whitlock, "the motor carrier industry is now operating under an intolerable burden of uncertainty. From one week to the next we do not know what the rules will be. This has resulted in an adverse effect on industry planning, our ability to obtain adequate financing, and our recruitment and retention of top management staff." An airline industry official, citing the difficulties of mapping routes and acquiring aircraft, said, "It was impossible to plan."[4]

Moreover, because of administrative action there was no longer a great deal of the traditional regulation left to defend. Deregulation was, in large part, a fait accompli. The reform forces' strength in Congress precluded a legislative reversal, while the possibility of a sharp turnaround in administrative policy was speculative and distant. Even strongly procompetitive legislation might merely ratify policies that were already in effect.

Finally, each of the increasingly bold commission actions tended to set a new baseline for congressional deliberations, so that legislation was needed if there were to be any reliable limits on how far or fast deregulation would proceed. Rather than vote to restore controls, even those only recently relaxed, Congress was more likely to keep up with the commissions by amending legislative proposals. In 1978, when the CAB created a larger zone of price flexibility than was provided in the pending airline bills, the legislative reformers incorporated the change. The Carter White House promised to block any trucking bill that would reverse reforms already achieved by the ICC. On trucking, concern about the tendency for issues to be foreclosed led eventually to a moratorium on further administrative deregulation for the purpose of allowing Congress to act. The respite, as the ICC and the committee chairmen in both houses agreed, was to be of only six months' duration.

In short, then, the deregulatory activism of the commissions gave the airline and trucking industries compelling reasons to prefer some sort of statutory result, to want that result to be reached quickly, and, if necessary, to accept broad procompetitive provisions in order to get it. By 1978 the airlines stopped trying to prevent passage of a deregulation bill; and when it appeared that the Ninety-fifth Congress might adjourn without

4. *Economic Regulation of the Trucking Industry,* Hearings before the Senate Committee on Commerce, Science, and Transportation, 96 Cong. 1 sess. (Government Printing Office, 1979), pt. 1, p. 80; and interview, Norman Philion, vice-president for governmental affairs, Air Transport Association, July 30, 1982.

completing action, the industry pleaded for it not to do so. In much the same way, the trucking association, though long opposed to reform legislation, eventually urged Senator Howard Cannon to act and considered it "a great victory" when he and his House counterpart, James Howard, announced a schedule for passage of a bill.[5]

While driving the industries to retreat, administrative deregulation did not pacify the reformers but instead excited their ambition. Despite the important gains, reformers argued, legislation was needed in order to avoid the uncertainties of judicial review and preclude the possibility of a later return to protectionism by the commissions. In any case, the dramatic, unexpectedly easy success of reform in the commissions undoubtedly whetted appetites in the White House and on the part of committee leaders for further, and more visible, successes in Congress. In the case of airline deregulation, CAB action also boosted support for legislation because the early results in fares and service were impressively favorable.

Deregulation by the commissions thus prevented the industries from exploiting the numerous opportunities to obstruct or delay congressional action that are often the crucial advantage for opponents of change. The threat of delay, used overtly by the White House in bargaining with the trucking industry, was, if anything, a weapon for reformers. Unable either to obstruct or to impose their will, the industries were forced to make concessions; and they consented to bills that they would have denounced a few months earlier as impossibly radical.

In the extent of the concessions, though, the cases differed. Whereas airline industry resistance to deregulation thoroughly collapsed, the trucking industry managed a strategic, well-disciplined, and limited retreat—a difference that was very evident in the resulting bills. In order to account for this contrast and more fully explain the policy outcomes, it is necessary to look more closely at the industries themselves and how they operated politically.

Political Disorganization in the Airline Industry

The airline industry's political resistance to deregulation eventually, in effect, ceased. When the Airline Deregulation Act finally cleared Congress in 1978, therefore, it seemed a product of a consensus that regula-

5. *Aviation Daily,* June 16, 1978; and interview, George Meade, American Trucking Association lobbyist, January 23, 1981.

tion should be abolished. "When I announced my support of airline deregulation soon after taking office," President Carter observed at the signing ceremony, "this bill had few friends. I'm happy to say that today it appears to have few enemies."[6]

This consensus, or at least lack of vocal opposition, was important not only for its effect on the airline bill itself, which otherwise would not have been so radical, but also for the significance of airline deregulation as a political precedent. The industry's eventual docile acceptance of the measure, after fervent opposition, seemed to dramatize the proposition that deregulation was an idea whose time had come. Perhaps it was such an idea, but this acceptance was caused more by the industry's political disorganization than by its being persuaded on the issues.

The airline industry's resistance to deregulation was likely to be both less imposing and less resolute than that of the truckers on economic grounds alone. Its size, number of employees, and structure made it less formidable politically. In the mid-1970s the scheduled airline industry included eleven trunk carriers, about eight relatively large regional, or local-service, carriers, and a number of smaller regionals. Only six of the trunks—United, Eastern, American, TWA, Delta, and Pan Am (which was primarily an international carrier)—were major corporate entities, and though together they had a 70 percent share of the airline passenger market, none had revenues, for example, on the scale of the fifty largest industrial corporations. The airline industry as a whole had only about one-third the revenues and one-fourth the employees of the regulated trucking industry, and unlike trucking it deployed its employees mainly at a small number of large installations. Not many congressmen were under direct constituency pressures to support the industry, and the Carter White House felt able to risk alienating it with relative equanimity.[7]

VIEWS OF REGULATION. Even before the CAB came under the influence of reformers, the workings of regulation left much to be desired from the airlines' viewpoint, and the shortcomings undoubtedly had some effect of weakening their resolve. Under regulation the airline industry operated as a cartel of sorts, but one that was highly imperfect. Largely

---

6. "Airline Deregulation Act of 1978," *Public Papers of the Presidents: Jimmy Carter, 1978,* bk. 2 (GPO, 1979), p. 1837. (Hereafter *Public Papers: Carter.*)

7. "The Fortune Directory of the 500 Largest U.S. Industrial Corporations," *Fortune,* May 1977, pp. 364–86; U.S. Bureau of the Census, *Statistical Abstract of the United States, 1981* (GPO, 1981), pp. 610–11; and Eizenstat interview.

prevented from competing against each other on price, the airlines nevertheless could, and aggressively did, compete in the quality of service—providing ever more palatable meals, handsomely dressed flight attendants, and, most important and expensive, the convenience of more frequent flights, even though planes were flying on the average almost half-empty. Efforts to control service rivalry through "capacity-limitation agreements" sponsored by the CAB proved to be more controversial than effective and eventually were abandoned by the board. At the same time, the CAB in the mid-1970s strongly constrained upward trends in airline fares. It refused to allow fare increases to support the burden of underutilized equipment and, in a stock analyst's judgment, had fare policies such that "you could never catch up to costs, especially in an inflationary environment."[8] Owing largely to "the existing regulatory structure and the manner in which the CAB has applied the rules," TWA's chairman testified in 1976, "the airline industry had the distinction of being the least profitable of any major industry surveyed by the Conference Board in 1975," with "earnings so poor as virtually to destroy its credit rating." Recognition of the need for some sort of reform, especially to reduce regulatory lag and raise fares, was widespread in the industry by the mid-1970s, having been discussed within the industry's national organization, the Air Transport Association (ATA), for several years.[9]

Even though dissatisfied with current results, the airline industry proved remarkably devoted to the continuation of regulation. TWA, which was so critical of the CAB for undermining industry profits, was if anything even more harsh in condemning "the proposal of the theorists that more competition would not only solve our economic problems but provide the public with better service at lower cost, thus enabling everyone to live happily ever after." Eastern Airlines President Frank Borman, among other airline spokesmen, was aware of the irony. After complaining about his company's condition and its treatment by the CAB, Borman conceded in 1977 legislative hearings that "it seems strange . . . to find

8. Oppenheimer and Company research meeting notes (by Bert Fingerhut), November 11, 1975; and, on the airlines' difficulties under regulation, see Behrman, "Civil Aeronautics Board."

9. *Regulatory Reform in Air Transportation,* Hearings before the Subcommittee on Aviation of the Senate Committee on Commerce, 94 Cong. 2 sess. (GPO, 1976), p. 650; and interview, Norman Philion, July 23, 1982. Both the airline and the trucking associations have the same initials, ATA. To avoid confusion we use the initials only when it is clear from the context which organization is being referred to.

myself arguing for continued government intervention in what might be a free market."[10]

One might suppose that in opposing deregulation airline managements were merely looking out for their personal interests and feared that skills suited to a regulated environment would become obsolete if competition shifted from the political arena to the marketplace. If so, this motive failed to reveal itself in any clear pattern of policy differences related to executives' backgrounds: the two chairmen during this period of United, the major carrier that first and most strongly endorsed deregulation, recently had come from an unregulated industry; but so had the president of American, one of the opponents that never fully relented.[11] The more important reasons for the airlines' defense of regulation were genuine corporate ones, as well as concerns—to all appearances also genuine—about service to the public.

In 1976, airline executives firmly and uniformly believed that, as the ATA argued in hearings before the Cannon subcommittee, the national airline system was "premised on the principle of route security." On this security, they argued, depended the willingness of the carriers to develop markets, the predictability of their equipment needs, and their ability to attract crucially needed investment capital.[12] Whatever the airlines' difficulties under current policies, deregulation was considered an even more serious threat, a view confirmed by others concerned with the financial condition of the industry. An airline analyst in a major brokerage firm, alarmed by deregulation proposals, held that "the potential fallout and impact on different companies is almost indefinable" and steered his clients away from the industry's securities. Eastern Airlines, stressing the anxieties of institutional investors, urged that Congress end discussion of proposals for free entry as rapidly as possible. Compared with the alternative, the industry preferred to give the CAB the benefit of a doubt. "Viewed over any reasonably extended period of history," Delta affirmed, "the CAB's administration of the statute has been good."[13]

---

10. *Regulatory Reform in Air Transportation,* Hearings, p. 649; and *Aviation Regulatory Reform,* Hearings before the Subcommittee on Aviation of the House Committee on Public Works and Transportation, 95 Cong. 1 sess. (GPO, 1978), pt. 2, p. 1713.

11. Richard Ferris and Edward Carlson of United both had worked in the hotel industry; Albert Casey of American had worked for the *Los Angeles Times* and came to the airline industry just before the deregulation debate began, in 1974.

12. *Regulatory Reform in Air Transportation,* Hearings, p. 1014.

13. Oppenheimer research meeting notes, February 10, 1975; *Regulatory Reform in Air Transportation,* Hearings, p. 585; and *Aviation Regulatory Reform,* Hearings, pt. 2, p. 1477.

Even the stunning success of CAB-induced discount fares, which helped airline ridership and industry profits reach record levels in 1977 and 1978, had no marked impact on the industry's thinking. Reformers found in those results evidence that lower, competitive fares could benefit the industry. But airline executives, experienced in the use of discounts, considered their effect on ridership to be unreliable and temporary. The discounts had coincided with a strong recovery of the general economy, to which the airlines industry is highly sensitive; and as one industry representative noted, the CAB had helped promote use of the fares through its efforts to claim credit.[14]

Through most of the four-year-long congressional debate over airline deregulation, most of the industry remained firmly, even bitterly, opposed. In the first round of Senate Commerce Committee hearings in 1976, there was no support for the proposed deregulation bills among the certificated carriers. Eighteen months later, when the Senate marked up a bill, a few of the airlines had defected, most notably United; but the other major domestic carriers still intensely opposed deregulation. The industry's opposition was not ineffective. After long, contentious markups, the committees in both houses reported bills that, while incorporating major reforms, also had important limitations. Neither bill totally eliminated regulatory control of entry or even reversed the burden of proof to favor the applicant; the automatic market entry program in the House bill, described as "experimental," was restricted and temporary. In the spring of 1978, CAB Chairman Kahn assured an industry opponent that Congress was "not about to give us a charter to go all the way, even gradually, to deregulation."[15]

What Kahn did not foresee, however, was that industry opposition would collapse—as the result of which the CAB received a charter to deregulate completely and rapidly. This collapse, far exceeding any strategically necessary retreat, occurred because political organization in the industry came unraveled.

POLITICAL INDIVIDUALISM. The Air Transport Association—whose twenty-four members in 1976 included almost all of the scheduled carriers in the United States—lacked the organizational strength and cohe-

14. Testimony of Eastern Airlines in *Regulatory Reform in Air Transportation,* Hearings, especially p. 1712; and interview, Lee Hydeman, attorney for Continental Airlines, September 15, 1981.

15. Alfred E. Kahn, letter to Lee Hydeman, March 3, 1978. The letter, immediately released, clearly was intended as a public statement.

siveness necessary to sustain a coordinated response. Although the ATA's officers were politically experienced and its staff competent and sizable, neither controlled the association—which instead was governed by an active board of directors consisting of the heads of most of the member firms. As a formal matter, association decisions could be taken through a majority vote of the board. In practice, however, no major decisions could be taken without the unanimous consent of at least the major airlines.[16] Part of the reason, undoubtedly, was that with dues assessed for each firm in relation to its revenues, the major airlines provided the bulk of the association's financial support.

Unanimity was hard to achieve because the airlines tended to form policy views independently and insist on them emphatically, an individualism that followed naturally from the industry's structure and the character of its regulatory environment. Each of the eleven trunk carriers was large enough to sustain its own capacity for political action, and their normal mode of political activity involved competitive endeavors as much as joint ones. Above all, the highly politicized and bitterly fought contest for route awards inevitably made them political rivals. The smaller trunk carriers resented the "big five," which dominated the market. There had been running disputes over the CAB's "route strengthening program," favoring smaller carriers, and the capacity-limitation agreements, which helped only a few large ones.[17]

The individual firms thus cultivated the habit of political self-reliance. Their leading executives made frequent visits to Washington, and nearly every firm was represented there by a corporate office as well as a law firm kept on retainer. Although the ATA made only trifling contributions to political campaigns, the individual firms gave substantially, sometimes exceeding the limits of the law.[18] Airline chief executives saw each other frequently and were generally on casual, friendly terms. But on neither matters of policy nor those of political strategy were they inclined to conform or defer. They had confidence in their own political judgments and did not assume their interests to be identical.[19]

16. Philion interview, July 30, 1982.

17. Interview, Fred Houghteling, July 7, 1982; and for a statement on behalf of the smaller trunk carriers, see Continental's testimony in *Aviation Regulatory Reform*, Hearings before the Subcommittee on Aviation of the House Committee on Public Works and Transportation, 95 Cong. 2 sess. (GPO, 1978), pp. 448–53.

18. Both Braniff and American admitted making large illegal corporate contributions to Richard Nixon's 1972 presidential campaign.

19. Philion interviews.

The airlines' difficulty in arriving at a common position was evident in the deregulation controversy even before sharp disagreements emerged. In the hearings before Kennedy's subcommittee in 1975, the airlines were fundamentally in agreement—all had complaints about the CAB, and yet all opposed deregulation. Nevertheless, their arguments and major concerns differed significantly. Some wanted only changes in administrative policy while others were prepared to support legislative amendments, mostly of a procedural nature. According to an analysis by the Department of Transportation, no two carriers took positions that were completely alike.[20] Apart from the opposition to any substantial deregulation, there was no clear industry position—no concrete counterproposal nor any clear refusal to contemplate a bill.

The internal difficulties became genuinely serious, however, when the largest carrier—United Airlines—opened a much more evident rift in the industry's position. The change in its stance was motivated, in part, by United's belief that it had been singled out because of its size for shabby treatment by the CAB; the company complained that it had received virtually no new route authority for eight years. Late in 1975, therefore, United announced that it "would welcome total deregulation." This announcement caused a sensation in the industry and among analysts of the industry's stocks, but its actual political import was hard to judge. The company did not endorse and in fact strongly criticized all of the important pending bills, and it warned that route security, that is, restricted entry, was of the "utmost importance" for maintaining service; its defection from the industry position, in other words, was avowedly selfish. Because of its current size and manifest intention to expand further, United's position lent credibility to fears that deregulation would concentrate the industry. Reformers in the Carter White House regarded United's support as a mixed blessing.[21]

The industry group that, under ATA sponsorship, sought a consensus

20. See, generally, *Oversight of Civil Aeronautics Board Practices and Procedures,* Hearings before the Subcommittee on Administrative Practice and Procedure of the Senate Committee on the Judiciary, 94 Cong. 1 sess. (GPO, 1975), vols. 1–3. The Transportation Department's analysis (untitled and undated) was designed to assist in tailoring reform advocacy to the particular airlines.

21. *Aviation Daily,* October 31, 1975, p. 329; Oppenheimer research meeting notes, November 10, 1975; *Regulatory Reform in Air Transportation,* Hearings, pp. 531–46; and interview, Mary McInnis, White House domestic policy staff, January 6, 1981. On the basis for United's complaint, see *Aviation Regulatory Reform,* Hearings, pt. 2, p. 1840, where an article on United is reprinted from *Forbes,* August 15, 1977.

on deregulation was the Task Force on Regulatory Reform, formed in 1975, which included representatives of several trunk airlines and a few large regionals. The members were primarily lawyers or governmental affairs specialists, and the group was chaired by a senior official of the ATA. By late 1976, the task force was prepared to recommend a carefully worked out legislative proposal for moderate regulatory reform. The group believed that the industry itself needed reform of the right kind and it also rendered a political judgment. Reporting in a memorandum for airline chief executives that congressional interest in reform legislation showed "signs of increasing," the task force predicted that Congress probably would enact legislation "at least along the lines suggested by Senator Cannon"; and it concluded that "a positive, unified industry position will substantially increase chances of assuring the best possible legislative result, and help avoid the adoption of extreme or unacceptable proposals."[22]

The staff realized that this judgment, like most political estimates, was debatable in that supporting legislation would not necessarily guarantee the industry any control over the outcome. Even so, some joint strategy was obviously needed: "The financial community . . . wonders why the airline industry can't get its house in order to deal more effectively with what investors and creditors believe to be the most serious threat the airlines face."[23] As the 1977 Senate hearings approached, the ATA staff worked feverishly and the airline chief executives assembled twice in the hope of finding a common position.[24]

Despite all the effort, no common position could be found. The airlines had no difficulty agreeing that the current Senate proposals—the Kennedy-Cannon bill, and one sponsored by Senator James Pearson—would be "highly destructive" and should be opposed. On other issues—whether to endorse any deregulation and, if so, what kind—discord prevailed. Surprisingly, it was not United Airlines, the most unorthodox firm, that forced negotiations to be abandoned. To United, like the ATA staff, presenting a common position was essential for the industry to be able to influence the legislation. Despite reservations, it pronounced the task force recommendations generally acceptable and offered to negotiate further. Delta Airlines, as one of the strongest opponents of deregulation,

22. ATA staff memorandum, November 22, 1976.
23. ATA staff working paper, February 18, 1977.
24. Philion interview, July 30, 1982.

would have preferred a harder line but also was willing to live with the task force report.[25]

When discussion broke off, it was mainly because several firms, including National and American, remained adamant. They were neither sanguine about limited deregulation nor willing to defer on questions of strategy. They did not agree that legislation was inevitable; even if it was, they held, concessions should be made at a later stage. And even among the holdouts there were differing objections to the task force proposals.[26] What the last chief executives' meeting had demonstrated, one participant concluded, was that there was "no consensus at all," and that further efforts to reach agreement would be futile.[27]

Thus, before the key legislative hearings had begun, the airlines had lost any semblance of political coordination. The association, unable to address the central issues in the debate, testified on lesser issues about which the airlines agreed and otherwise stayed out of the way. On several occasions efforts were made to coordinate positions within smaller groups of like-minded carriers. Delta helped organize several of the more steadfast deregulation opponents for a brief time, and a lawyer for Continental managed to arrange a few small meetings. None of the organizing efforts outside of the ATA led to lasting collaboration or had concrete results. Even in smaller, more homogeneous groups strongly opposed to deregulation, airlines refused to set aside differences over specific issues or political strategy. Throughout 1977 and 1978, in the crucial phases of congressional action, each airline spoke only for itself if it spoke at all.[28]

THE COLLAPSE OF RESISTANCE. Pursued in this way, of course, the airlines' opposition to deregulation could not be fully effective; more impor-

25. Addendum to agenda for ATA board of directors meeting of March 3, 1977; ATA memorandum, Norman Philion, March 4, 1977; and memorandum, Philion to the ATA Task Force on Regulatory Reform, January 5, 1977.

26. Philion interview, July 30, 1982; and memorandum, Philion to the ATA Task Force on Regulatory Reform, February 18, 1977.

27. Letter to the ATA staff from Harvey Wexler, vice-president for governmental affairs, Continental Airlines, December 14, 1976.

28. Statement of Paul R. Ignatius, president, Air Transport Association, *Regulatory Reform in Air Transportation,* Hearings, 95 Cong. 1 sess. (GPO, 1977), pt. 4, pp. 1671–84. The association had not testified in twelve previous days of this series of hearings. Interviews, James Callison, general counsel, Delta Airlines, August 18, 1982; and Lee Hydeman, attorney for Continental, September 15, 1981. The small regional carriers, though belonging to the ATA, also had an organization of their own, the Association of Local Transport Airlines (ALTA). ALTA opposed deregulation while seeking preferential treatment for small carriers in deregulation bills. A small-scale organization, it was not a major participant in the debate.

tant, it could not even be maintained. Without discipline or coordination the airlines were prey to the Carter administration's strategy to divide and conquer. The director of the deregulation effort for the White House made it clear that only airlines that cooperated by endorsing deregulation and working for a bill could expect their concerns to be accommodated in its provisions. The most blatant accommodation was, in fact, a straightforward purchase of support. To win over Frontier Airlines, an important regional carrier, the administration amended its proposals governing subsidy for small-community service in the company's favor. A model of efficiency, the amendment was worth a few million dollars to Frontier but affected no other airline—and came to be known, unabashedly, as the "Frontier amendment." Even though rather openly bought, Frontier's support proved that a small airline could support reform, which helped to rebut predictions that deregulation would concentrate the industry. The reformers were delighted to add an endorsement by a small airline to the earlier endorsement by United, and thus considered the deal a bargain.[29]

For other companies a possible inducement, though harder to calculate, was concern that intransigent opponents might be subtly penalized in the assignment of routes by the CAB or, for international routes, by the president. The reformers could not overtly hold out that inducement. But there was some suspicion that United was rewarded for supporting deregulation when the White House gave it authority for service between Seattle and Japan, and at least one strong opponent, Western Airlines, apparently bowed to the force of this consideration. Although Western denied that this explained its abrupt reversal when it first testified in favor of deregulation in 1978, the concern about routes was later freely admitted: "During the legislative process," explained the man who had then headed the company, "we realized we were paying too heavy a price in being opposed to it. Our route awards—domestic and international— dried up. So we changed sides."[30] The industry's labor unions, also strongly opposed to reform, did not change sides. But they too looked eventually to narrower interests of their own, working mainly for provisions to protect employees whom deregulation might displace.

In the main, however, airline opposition faded for reasons that were more diffuse: as the reform effort gathered momentum, in part through

29. McInnis interview; and interview, Will Ris, majority staff, Senate Commerce Committee, September 11, 1981.

30. *Aviation Regulatory Reform,* Hearings, 95 Cong. 2 sess., pp. 267–68; and John Newhouse, "A Sporty Game," *New Yorker,* June 14, 1982, p. 63.

airline defections, the remaining firms saw their efforts as probably hopeless; they grew weary of controversy, of being in a visible confrontation
with the president, or of the effort and expense of lobbying; and in some
cases they came very late to be persuaded on the merits, or at least to
have doubts. In a few firms, key executives argued among themselves,
making it difficult to take any position at all.[31] When, for any of these
reasons, a firm was inclined to change its position or stop taking part in
the debate, no effective peer pressure or organizational discipline bolstered its commitment.

The industry's retreat was unplanned, random, and sometimes precipitous. At the 1978 House hearings, the carriers who had kept up the opposition the year before were thoroughly disorganized. In addition to
Western, Continental gave the committee bill its qualified endorsement,
while several other airlines—American, Eastern, TWA, Northwest Orient,
and Braniff—failed to put in appearances. Too late to appear in the
record, Braniff wrote to say it could accept the House bill; by then, it
apparently was already plotting a vast expansion of its route system under deregulation that eventually led to the company's bankruptcy. American's president sent a peevish letter whose only clear message was that he
resented certain patronizing implications in the reformers' rhetoric. The
letter endorsed no bill, but later American endorsed the CAB's radical
proposal for multiple, permissive entry. Among the trunk carriers, only
Delta, which was expected to do well under deregulation, appeared at the
hearing and strongly opposed it.[32]

Since industry concessions were not made collectively or offered con-
tingently—indeed, were often not even explicit—the reformers had no
need to respond with concessions of their own. They responded instead
by strengthening proposals. Floor amendments were adopted in both
houses reversing the burden of proof in entry cases so as to favor applicants instead of opponents. In the House the amendment was sponsored,
without White House assistance, by a junior member of the Public Works
Committee, who succeeded largely because active opposition was negligi-
ble.[33] At the conference committee stage, with industry quiescence only

31. Ris interview; and interview, James P. Bass, vice-president for governmental affairs,
American Airlines, September 14, 1981.

32. *Aviation Week,* March 20, 1978; and *Aviation Regulatory Reform,* Hearings, 95 Cong.
2 sess., pp. 558–59.

33. Interviews, John Plebani, administrative assistant to Representative Alan Ertel, July
16, 1980; and Charles Zeigler, House Aviation Subcommittee, majority staff, July 15, 1980.

deeper, the reformers went even further. Rather than fashioning what could fairly be called a compromise between the House and Senate versions, the conference combined and reformulated some of the stronger provisions of both bills, arriving at a result more thoroughgoing than either of them.

The collapse of the industry's resistance accounts for most of the radicalism of the airline bill. Yet even this collapse would not have led to rapid and total deregulation if not for the presence in the House bill of a "sunset" provision calling for the eventual abolition of the CAB—a provision whose original purpose, ironically, was not evidently to promote reform. Except for Ralph Nader, who raised the idea in 1975, political advocates of airline reform did not call for complete deregulation or abolishing the CAB until just before those decisions were actually reached. Such notions were considered so extreme as to appear irresponsible, and the reformers took pains to reject them explicitly. Alfred Kahn, after praising a House bill in the final hearings as "a move in the direction of deregulation," added that "I am not suggesting we go all the way."[34]

A sunset provision for the CAB was first introduced in Congress, not by an avid reform advocate, but by Elliott H. Levitas, Democrat of Georgia, who included it in a measure that he promoted in the 1977 House hearings and in one that he offered as a substitute bill, briefly adopted, in the Aviation Subcommittee markups in 1978. Levitas pursued an independent approach of some complexity. In the hearings he took a predominantly negative stance toward deregulation, especially in any rapid form, and his bill called for little deregulation, apart from abolishing the agency after seven years. Levitas argued for his bill in two contrasting ways: to airline executives opposed to deregulation, he stressed the modesty of the near-term measures and explained that the sunset provision would only force Congress to reevaluate the subject before the sunset date; the unstated implication was that Congress could repeal the provision and there might never be much deregulation. On the other hand, Levitas also touted the bill as "the only true deregulation proposal" before the Congress, since it was the only one that could do away entirely with regulation. Later, having further complicated his position during committee debate on an amendment, Levitas received a compliment for his agility: "My colleague has the ability to be on three sides of any given issue," observed another member. "And I respect that ability."[35]

34. *Aviation Regulatory Reform,* Hearings, 95 Cong. 2 sess., p. 145.
35. *Aviation Regulatory Reform,* Hearings, pt. 2, pp. 1710–11.

That Levitas's sunset proposal found its way into a compromise committee bill and survived the deliberations of the House was mostly a testimony to its political ambiguity. The main spokesmen for reform were skeptical of the proposal's sincerity. "The only way in which a sunset declaration can succeed," Chairman Kahn argued in the final House hearings, "is if the industry takes it seriously, and begins to prepare for that event with the definite understanding that it will come to pass." With Congress still hesitant about deregulation, Kahn did not believe a sunset provision would be taken seriously, and he feared that its inclusion in a bill would be an excuse for postponing genuine reform. Privately, the reformers presumed it was merely a diversionary tactic and would be quietly dropped at a convenient time. Neither was strong support for sunset forthcoming from the airlines. Eventually, some carriers did want a sunset provision, so as not to be left with a CAB concocting unwanted forms of regulation; but others did not and none of them invested effort in lobbying for it.[36]

Although no one but Levitas strongly supported sunset, no one strenuously opposed it either, and the House committee leaders kept the measure in the bill while sometimes almost pretending it did not exist. In the lengthy introduction to the committee report, the sunset provision was not mentioned. The committee, it said, "has by no means concluded that total deregulation is desirable," but only that it was time for "a moderate, controlled release of some regulatory fetters." Summarizing the bill on the House floor, committee chairman Harold T. ("Bizz") Johnson, Democrat of California, observed that sunset could "permit complete deregulation" if Congress found it warranted with experience under the act—omitting to mention that, in order to reach that result, no congressional action would be required.[37] The provision was not debated by the whole House, which easily passed the bill.

When conference committee negotiations to reconcile the House and Senate bills began in October, swift and complete deregulation of the airlines was a feature of neither one. Defending their version, the conferees from the Senate, led by Cannon, argued for broader and more immediate deregulation and for preserving the CAB, which they believed would have significant remaining functions even if rate and entry regula-

36. *Aviation Regulatory Reform,* Hearings, 95 Cong. 2 sess., pp. 120–21; and interview, Will Ris, July 16, 1980. Mimi Cutler, of Nader's Aviation Consumer Action Project, pronounced the House sunset proposal a "farce." *New York Times,* April 24, 1978.

37. *Air Service Improvement Act of 1978,* H. Rept. 95–1211, 95 Cong. 2 sess. (GPO, 1978), p. 4; and *Congressional Record* (September 14, 1978), p. 29528.

tion was drastically reduced. The House delegation, which included Levitas, wanted on the contrary to keep sunset but make the deregulatory provisions more modest and some of them, in fact, temporary. By then active political pressure from the airlines to limit deregulation essentially had ended, and the Senate conferees, seizing the opportunity to strengthen the bill, proposed a way of trading off the issues that would have seemed preposterous if the resistance had continued. Drawing from the Senate bill, the Senate conferees proposed strong near-term provisions. Drawing from the House bill, they made them temporary—to be superseded, however, by another notion attributable with some irony to the House, that of abolishing regulation. Under no real pressure to do otherwise, the House conferees grudgingly agreed.[38]

Having decided that economic regulation of airlines would be phased out by the end of 1982, and that two years later the CAB would cease to exist, the conference committee marked the change in the bill's spirit by replacing the cautious term "regulatory reform" in its title with the now more accurate "deregulation." The congressional decision to deregulate completely had been reached not in several years, as the House committee chairman had suggested it might be—but in a matter of days.[39]

Organizational Strength in the Trucking Industry

Speaking to a trucking industry audience as the debate on trucking deregulation entered the legislative phase, a Delta executive summarized the lesson of the airline case. "Where was our industry during all of this?" he asked, after recounting the passage of the bill. "Well, we were all over the lot, and as a consequence we were ultimately divided and conquered." This had happened, he went on to explain, even though virtually all of the carriers opposed deregulation in the beginning.[40] The trucking industry, in contrast, remained remarkably unified throughout the deregulation debate, retreating under control and no farther than required by its strategic position. The lesson of the airlines was not lost on the trucking industry;

38. Proceedings, Senate Committee on Commerce, Science, and Transportation and House Committee on Public Works and Transportation, Joint House-Senate Conference on Deregulation of Airlines, September 29, October 5–6, 1978.

39. As provided in the bill, the CAB closed its doors on January 1, 1985.

40. James W. Callison, senior vice president–general counsel, Delta Airlines, "Deregulation—An Airline's Perspective," speech delivered to United Van Lines 33rd International Convention, Scottsdale, Arizona, November 9, 1979.

the more fundamental sources of unity, however, were in its organization and structure.

One might have supposed that the trucking industry would be incapable of effective political organization. With about 16,000 regulated firms, only a few of which, such as Roadway and Consolidated Freight, were large corporate entities, its fragmented structure might have seemed an insuperable obstacle. Moreover, trucking firms were diverse, not only in size, but in the nature of their operations and in the importance they attached to various aspects of regulation. The large-shipment segment of the industry, for example, was somewhat competitive with respect to rates, regardless of regulation, because its shippers could operate their own trucks if rates offered by common carriers were too high. This segment was mostly concerned about regulation of entry. Small-shipment carriers had large networks of routes and owned warehouses for breaking down and reconsolidating shipments. They believed that this would afford them substantial protection from new competitors even if regulatory barriers to entry were relaxed; on the other hand, because the users of their services could not easily avoid relying on common carriers, minimum rate regulation and antitrust immunity were effective and well worth fighting for.

It occurred early to trucking reform advocates that these divisions might be exploited. The Ford administration's trucking bill, although never aggressively promoted, had been designed to divide the industry by offering special "goodies" to some of the segments. A similar strategy was advanced by Carter's Transportation Department, which proposed a bill with especially liberal entry standards for large-shipment carriers. Later, ICC chairman Darius Gaskins promoted the idea that trucking executives should not "blindly follow a collective strategy," but should look out for the interests of their own firms. As Congress was moving toward legislative action, there were rumors that some large companies were in fact wavering and might try to cut deals of their own.[41] However plausible they may have seemed, efforts to divide the industry did not succeed. The

41. The leadership of the American Trucking Association recognized the Ford administration strategy: transcript, American Trucking Association executive committee meeting, February 18, 1976, p. 53. The Carter Justice Department opposed the Transportation Department's similar strategy: memorandum to John J. Fearnsides, deputy under secretary of transportation from Donald J. Flexner, deputy assistant attorney general, Antitrust Division, Department of Justice, November 24, 1978. Speech by Gaskins to the Regular Route Common Carriers Conference, *Traffic World,* February 11, 1980.

industry maintained a high level of intensity and cohesiveness, and its national organization, the American Trucking Association, kept its political efforts under firm control.

The organizational strength of the trucking industry was based partly on underlying habits of trust and cooperation shaped by its operating methods and regulation. Since a large fraction of all shipments were "interlined"—transferred, often with a choice of collaborators, by one carrier to another—trucking firms depended on each other to proffer business. A more intense form of collaboration occurred in the deliberation of rate bureaus, in which trucking companies agreed, under antitrust immunity, on collective rates to be filed with the ICC and on whether to protest independent rates filed by individual carriers. Often greatly important to a company's success, rate bureau decisions were made through discussion, bargaining, and voting by the member firms; participants were expected to set aside business rivalry in favor of fairness and to have regard for each other's interests. The effect, according to an ATA executive, was noticeable: "If you can sit down and talk price with your competitors, even if you may be calling them sons-of-bitches and disagreeing frequently, you have something like a fraternity. It gives a kind of coherence to the industry."[42]

THE ATA STRUCTURE. Probably more important than these operating practices as a source of the trucking industry's unity, however, was the nature of its political organization, that is, the structure and methods of the ATA. In contrast with the airlines, significantly, neither individual trucking firms nor even segments of the industry could exercise a veto over ATA policies, which therefore were sometimes adopted over impassioned dissent. The absence of effective veto power reflected at least partly the industry's size and diversity: to require unanimity in such an industry would have made action in pursuit of its common interests routinely impossible.

To manage conflict among segments of the industry having different interests, the ATA had developed elaborate institutional arrangements. Each of twelve distinct segments had a separate conference within the

---

42. Interview, Richard Hinchfield, executive director, Regular Common Carrier Conference, American Trucking Association, September 16, 1981. For an explanation of rate bureau operations, with a similar analysis but critical conclusions, see Motor Carrier Ratemaking Study Commission, *Collective Ratemaking in the Trucking Industry: A Report to the President and Congress of the United States* (Washington, D.C.: The Commission, 1983), pp. 87–133.

association, each with its own officers and staff. A conference was entitled to appeal decisions to the association's executive committee and, in cases of irreconcilable conflict, to enunciate its own policies publicly. One of them, the Tank Truck Carrier Conference, early in 1979 pressed for industry sponsorship of an extremely anticompetitive bill to reverse reform further than the leadership thought advisable. Two of the others—the Private Carrier Conference and the Contract Carrier Conference—felt burdened by aspects of regulation. Having divided loyalties, their officers attended strategy sessions of the reformers as well as the industry and had to observe an honor system to avoid breaches of confidentiality.[43] By permitting diverse concerns to be expressed within the association and even outside it, the conference framework vented pressures that might have imperiled cohesion; by keeping diverse groups together in a single organization, it preserved opportunities to resolve differences by bargaining.

The trucking industry's fragmented economic structure may have made establishing and maintaining the organization more difficult, but given that those problems had been solved, it enhanced the ATA's political authority within the industry.[44] Individual firms, even the largest, could not rival the ATA in political weight: "It was the ATA," a conference executive noted, "that had eight or ten lobbyists and all the political contacts." Its staff considered the ATA the only significant spokesman for the trucking industry and felt confident that Congress also recognized the status.[45] Potential defectors from ATA positions would have little to gain, so doubtful was their ability to be effective.

In the deregulation controversy, therefore, the trucking industry managed to avoid being weakened by division. The conferences with significantly diverging views reached compromises within the association or confined dissent to narrow issues. The Private Carrier Conference, which might have sought broad freedom to carry goods for hire on backhauls or in slack periods, instead focused on "intercorporate hauling" (that is, compensated services among corporate affiliates); it accepted a compro-

43. Letter, Tank Truck Carrier Conference to ATA Sound Transportation Regulation—Our National Goal Committee, April 4, 1979; and interview, Thomas A. Callaghan, Jr., managing director, Contract Carrier Conference, September 17, 1981.

44. On the problems of organizational formation and maintenance, see James Q. Wilson, *Political Organizations* (Basic Books, 1973); Mancur Olson, *The Logic of Collective Action* (Harvard University Press, 1965); and Terry Moe, *The Organization of Interests* (University of Chicago Press, 1980).

45. Callaghan interview; and Meade interview.

mise, worked out within the association, permitting such services but only for wholly owned subsidiaries. The Contract Carrier Conference lobbied against certain restrictions on contract operations but otherwise deferred to the ATA. What was more remarkable, though, was that no regulated firms openly endorsed deregulation or struck a separate agreement with the reformers. If any firm did, neither Senator Cannon nor ATA executives knew of it.[46] Presumably some among the 16,000 regulated trucking companies expected to flourish in an unregulated environment, but none acted on this expectation in the political process.

THE TEAMSTERS. The most important failure of solidarity among opponents of trucking deregulation was divergences between the ATA and the Teamsters Union, not so much on policy as on strategy and tactics. The Teamsters opposed deregulation, if anything, more strongly than the industry, but the two groups, while keeping each other informed of plans, did little to coordinate their political efforts. Having the normal tensions between management and labor, officials of the two groups avoided appearing too close to each other, if only to maintain the confidence of their respective constituencies. In addition, the industry kept a distance from the Teamsters because of the union's blunt style and shady reputation, which, in the opinion of ATA president Bennett C. Whitlock, made their support a two-edged sword.[47]

The Teamsters' forte was in being direct. In committee hearings they opposed deregulation, not only as the industry did, by challenging it from the point of view of the public interest, but also by asserting their own interests in drivers' wages and job security: "We oppose vigorously tam-

46. Interview, Howard Cannon, February 26, 1981; Hinchfield interview; Callaghan interview; and Daniel Machalba, "Trucking Association, Powerful for Decades, Has a Load of Trouble," *Wall Street Journal,* February 21, 1984. Without substantiation, Machalba says of this period: "The staunch proregulation stand of the ATA split the membership. . . . So when ATA tried to present a united front on Capitol Hill, some members lobbied on their own for opposite results." The White House had hoped this would occur but it never did: "We made a real effort in the fall of 1979 to split the industry," said Rick Neustadt in our interview with him. "We basically got nowhere." By the mid-1980s, as Machalba accurately reports, the ATA and the industry encountered serious internal difficulties—the result partly of differences over how long to persist in defending regulatory restraints rapidly being phased out under the 1980 act, and partly of criticism of the ATA's performance on other issues. ATA president Bennett C. Whitlock resigned in 1984. As these later developments make evident, there are limits to the duration and intensity of internal disagreement that organizational arrangements can overcome.

47. Lobbyists for the two organizations gave similar accounts of their relationship: Meade interview; interview, Bartley O'Hara, legislative counsel, Teamsters Union, January 27, 1981; and ATA executive committee transcripts, January 27, 1981.

pering with the most efficient transportation system in the world because it would destroy most of the companies from which our members and their families derive their livelihoods."[48] To underline the seriousness of these stakes, the Teamsters brought a group of truck drivers to observe the committee markups. Wearing royal blue union windbreakers in an audience mostly wearing business suits, the drivers stood out prominently as they glared at the committee members. The Teamsters' methods were sometimes embarrassing to the ATA. In one instance described by an ATA official, a Teamster lobbyist, in his presence, pointedly told a congressman the number of Teamsters in his district. The ATA preferred not to be associated with this overly direct threat, which only angered the congressman. Most certainly, the ATA preferred not to be associated with the attempt to bribe Senator Cannon.[49]

A tough, uncompromising approach on deregulation was for the Teamsters a matter of both their attitude on the issue and their personal style. The principal Teamster lobbyist on deregulation was not smooth or affable in the manner of lobbyists, and appeared at legislative proceedings with clothing and hair in need of arranging. His opening words to us on the subject of deregulation, shortly after passage of the trucking bill by the House, were a scatological expletive. As a result of deregulation by the ICC, he then explained, drivers whom he knew well were being laid off. Teamster lobbying on deregulation functioned primarily to demonstrate the union's seriousness, anger, and disposition to retaliate politically. Its posture on the issues, correspondingly, was inflexible; unlike the ATA, the Teamsters Union did not consistently concede the need for a bill to resolve the issues, and it sought weakening amendments, such as a Senate floor amendment on entry, even when the effort was quite hopeless. Because the Teamsters were even less compromising than the ATA, lack of coordination between them did not cause resistance to crumble, although it probably in some degree diminished the opponents' bargaining power. The reformers might have offered larger concessions for the consent of both industry and labor than for that of the industry alone.

POLITICAL SKILL. Besides unity, at least on the management side, the ATA gave the trucking industry the advantage of politically astute leadership. Formally, the ATA's decisions on legislation were the responsibility

---

48. *Economic Regulation of the Trucking Industry,* Hearings, pt. 2, p. 517.
49. Meade interview. On the bribery attempt, see chap. 4.

of a large elected executive committee, with representatives of all segments of the trucking industry. In practice, the committee, which met only three times a year, was elaborately briefed by the officers and staff and relied on their advice in political matters, on which few committee members claimed expertise. Insofar as the committee gave instructions on political strategy, it was understood that the staff should exercise discretion in actually following them.[50] ATA positions and strategy were shaped largely by the staff and especially by the president, Bennett Whitlock, who closely supervised the association's lobbying.

Whitlock, moreover, was suited to the task. Well-connected in Congress, a friend since college of Senator Ernest Hollings, Whitlock was a shrewd tactician and analyst of the institution. In 1976, when Representative James Howard was considering holding hearings on trucking regulation in order to protect his subcommittee's recently acquired jurisdiction, Whitlock skillfully intervened. From his perspective, Howard was well intentioned and the Surface Transportation Subcommittee quite reliable, but Whitlock feared the unpredictability of hearings and the publicity they could give to deregulation. However, Whitlock did not simply oppose the hearings. Appreciating the institutional problems, he worked with Howard to try to find other, more innocuous ways for the subcommittee to exercise authority.[51] Along with others on the staff, Whitlock provided tactical skill and a detailed knowledge of how Congress works. In addition to organizational unity and discipline, therefore, the ATA gave the trucking industry the political sophistication necessary to put organizational strength to effective use. And the industry avoided each of two dangerous extremes—excessive militance, which could have been counterproductive, and disorganized, precipitous retreat.

For the entire five years of the deregulation debate, the ATA had to calculate opportunities realistically, adjust strategy to changing circumstances, and yet at the same time nurture and express intense opposition. Beginning shortly after the Ford administration announced in 1975 that it planned to seek deregulation of trucking, the ATA mounted a vigorous lobbying and public relations campaign to defend regulation. Led by the STRONG committee, a group of trucking executives whose acronym stood for Sound Transportation Regulation—Our National Goal, the campaign was addressed to the transportation and business communities

50. Meade interview.
51. ATA executive committee transcripts, June 17, 1976.

and, to a lesser extent, the general public. For assistance the ATA hired a leading public relations firm, Hill and Knowlton, spending over $2 million for its services in 1979.

At the same time, the ATA also played a restraining role. In response to the ICC's deregulatory actions under Chairman O'Neal, state trucking associations, individual firms, and one of the ATA's conferences demanded that the industry go beyond rhetoric and take action, that is, draft legislation to reverse the ICC's decisions and get it passed. In 1978 the ATA began drafting an industry bill, a process that involved lengthy bargaining among the association's several constituencies. The bargaining, not surprisingly, produced an openly anticompetitive measure, essentially a catalogue of the industry's wishes, which was approved as ATA policy. To press for action on such a bill would have been reckless and potentially harmful to the industry's cause. In the prevailing climate of opinion, the ATA proposal was unlikely to be taken seriously; it would merely encourage Congress to act, with a bill that would be far less acceptable to the industry as a possible result. Using their discretion, the ATA leaders found a way to avoid the risk. Within the association, they expressed strong determination to promote the bill and get it passed, but in dealing with Congress, they delayed for several months in even having it introduced. Eventually, Representative Howard and full committee chairman "Bizz" Johnson introduced it without fanfare, "by request." With no one investing effort in promoting it, the bill died quietly in committee.[52]

Within a few months, having finally become convinced of the need for legislation, the ATA treated the industry bill as a harmless irrelevance. Without offering public concessions, the ATA staff made itself available to Congress for negotiations and worked behind the scenes with Howard and his staff, helping him develop another bill. The result, though still largely anticompetitive, was far less ambitious than the industry bill in reversing deregulation and appeared sufficiently moderate for Howard to adopt as his own proposal.[53]

52. Called the Motor Carrier Regulatory Improvement Act of 1979, the bill was introduced June 18, 1979, four months after the executive committee meeting that approved it, and a day before the next meeting. Although the ATA defended its provisions in Senate hearings in June 1979, it was not then advocating legislative action. *Economic Regulation of the Trucking Industry,* Hearings, pt. 2, pp. 489–517.

53. H.R. 6418 was introduced in February 1980. The trucking bill ultimately enacted, formally an amendment in the nature of a substitute for this bill, had the same number but otherwise did not much resemble it.

In the Senate, where majorities both in the Commerce Committee and on the floor supported deregulation, the ATA used calculated self-restraint to limit damage and keep it reversible. Having been disappointed in the Cannon-Packwood bill when it was introduced in January 1980, then further disappointed in committee markup, the ATA faced hard choices concerning amendments and strategy for the Senate floor. While only a few senators were willing to oppose deregulation across the board, there were a number of senators willing to do so on one or a few amendments and thus "give something" to the industry and the Teamsters.[54] To put such support to use, the industry had to concentrate on a few requests that those senators would find palatable, not dissipate the support in losing efforts on several issues. Moreover, if the industry was likely to lose a contested vote on the Senate floor, the best course was to avoid the contest. The House was expected to pass a less procompetitive bill, and the conference committee would be more likely to adopt the House provisions if in doing so it did not have to reverse explicit votes of the full Senate.

The ATA thus passed up the opportunity to contest the bill's two most fundamental issues on the Senate floor. It did not support the Teamsters' effort to amend the bill's liberal entry standards, which the industry had vigorously resisted in committee. Nor did it push for an amendment to preserve antitrust immunity for collective rate making—an issue crucial for large trucking companies, on which an ATA-sponsored amendment had failed in committee by a single vote. Instead, the ATA concentrated on two narrower issues, each important to a part of the industry—an exemption for processed foods and a measure easing entry in small communities. Even its position on these issues did not define the industry's minimum demands for an acceptable bill. Committed to the enactment of some bill and counting on the House for better treatment, the ATA did not ask for the bill's defeat, no matter the outcome on amendments.

Despite the deeply compromised objectives, the ATA organized a lobbying effort on a massive scale. Several hundred trucking executives, answering the call, came to Washington for the final days before Senate floor action. Impressively coordinated, delegations from each state camped outside the offices of their respective senators, conveying the industry's views at every opportunity and regularly phoning ATA headquarters for instructions.

54. Meade interview; and Lewis interview.

When the Senate had acted, defeating all significant amendments and approving the bill, attention shifted to the House. Because Howard did not strongly back the industry position, as he had been expected to do, but instead delayed markups and insisted on an overall compromise, the process changed to one of private bargaining among the Carter administration, the Senate leaders (Cannon and Packwood), and the industry—with the House subcommittee staff in the role of mediator. Although the loss of Howard's firm support weakened its position, the ATA nevertheless bargained hard. In a series of difficult meetings, dragged out despite the threat of Congress adjourning without a bill and hence of resumed deregulation by the ICC, the ATA insisted on a number of changes in the bill as passed by the Senate. The Senate leaders and the White House, which carefully explained its decision to groups that supported reform, reluctantly accepted several of the changes.

When the bill that had been agreed to by the White House, the Senate, the House committee leadership, and the trucking industry was discussed in markup in the House, a few of the committee members professed to be annoyed that their decisions had been foreclosed. The bill, as one of them groused, in effect had already been passed by the House, reconciled with the Senate version, and signed into law by the president—all before the House subcommittee had had a chance to vote.

The ATA claimed to be reasonably satisfied with the bill, reporting to the membership that although it "is not everything the industry wants and contains some things we'd rather not have, it does preserve the basic concept and principles of economic regulation."[55] The ATA's self-serving assessment aside, precisely how much traditional economic regulation was preserved by the bill was hard to judge. Price regulation was rendered all but irrelevant by a generous zone of rate-making flexibility. Entry regulation was relaxed in various ways, for example, by the removal of many restrictions in operating certificates. More to the industry's liking, however, the general standard for entry, although more liberal than previous law, was kept somewhat vague—so it was at least possible that a future ICC could use it restrictively. And some current ICC initiatives to expand entry freedom radically in selected parts of the industry were expressly prohibited. Most distressing to the largest firms, the bill sharply

55. Letter from Bennett C. Whitlock, Jr., president of the ATA, to "All of Those Who Are Interested in the Survival of the Trucking Industry," May 28, 1980. This referred to the bill as approved by the House committee; it was enacted into law without significant amendment.

restricted antitrust immunity for collective rate making. But this was to occur only after four years had elapsed and a special study commission had examined the issue, and the industry held out hope for passage of a new bill reversing the decision on collective rate making before the deadline. Viewed from an earlier perspective, the bill was a clear and even dramatic defeat for the industry. Yet, by delaying change and creating some possibilities for preventing or reversing it, the bill was not a total defeat.[56]

The Carter administration, the reformers in the Senate, and the leaders of the ICC could claim success far more easily and enthusiastically. They attributed their success in large part to the decline of trucking industry opposition. That opposition had undergone a phased and calculated narrowing, which first produced consensus that some bill was needed and finally permitted a strong bill to pass. The reformers did not, in view of this, question the ATA's unity and effectiveness or its political skill, but explained the result by the weakness of the industry's position. "I cannot fault their strategy," a White House lobbyist later said.

Telecommunications

The response of AT&T and the independent telephone companies to administrative reform differed in obvious ways from that of the airline and trucking industries. The telephone industry's effort to reverse administrative policies permitting competition was far more ambitious and aggressive, and it threatened the survival of those policies far more gravely. Only in the telephone case were industry concessions—either on substantive issues or at least on the need for a bill—not sufficient to facilitate relatively prompt congressional action. Nevertheless, a broadly similar pattern of retreat still occurred. AT&T and the independents eventually accepted strongly procompetitive policies; and it was this acceptance, and not any ability of reformers to push such policies through Congress, that guaranteed a procompetitive outcome. As in the airline and trucking

56. The industry's hopes regarding antitrust immunity were disappointed. The study commission, led by Senator Packwood, endorsed the restrictions on antitrust immunity, and no serious attempt was made in Congress to keep them from going into effect, on schedule, in 1984. Motor Carrier Ratemaking Study Commission, *Collective Ratemaking in the Trucking Industry.*

cases, this retreat represented the political effects of action by the regulatory commission, supplemented in this instance by events in the judicial arena; and its timing, character, and ultimate extent were shaped importantly by the nature of political organization in the industry.

The Attempt to Reverse Competition

There were some grounds to expect, in the early and middle 1970s, that Bell and the independents could be reconciled without undue stress to the new competition. In 1971 AT&T chairman H. I. Romnes acknowledged that in "some aspects of the company's business"—such as intercity private line service and terminal equipment—"competition makes sense."[57] Unlike the airline or trucking industries, the telephone industry was subject to strict public utility regulation with an administered rate of return; thus, in theory, competition might be a matter of indifference to the stockholders. Romnes's successor, John de Butts, seized on this idea in order to claim that his opposition to competition "was not for the purpose of protecting the profits of the American Telephone and Telegraph Company." Even its continued growth was not at issue, since the dramatic, technologically driven growth of the entire telecommunications market greatly exceeded the incursions of the new competitors.[58]

Failing such acceptance, one might have expected the industry to oppose competition effectively, with an organized and skillful political effort. In addition to the sheer magnitude of its political resources, their concentration in the control of a single firm was a presumptive advantage. In the mid-1970s AT&T accounted for roughly 80 percent of the telephone industry, measured by assets, revenues, or employees.[59] Through the presidents and other executives of the operating companies, who bore the main responsibility for lobbying, the company had an elaborate net-

57. Quoted in Alvin von Auw, *Heritage and Destiny: Reflections on the Bell System in Transition* (Praeger, 1983), p. 160.

58. *Competition in the Telecommunications Industry,* Hearings before the Communications Subcommittee of the House Committee on Interstate and Foreign Commerce, 94 Cong. 2 sess. (GPO, 1977), p. 11. In 1983 MCI, AT&T's largest long distance competitor, was expected to control only 5 percent of that expanding market by 1988. Brian O'Reilly, "More Than Cheap Talk Propels MCI," *Fortune,* January 24, 1983, p. 69.

59. Standard & Poor's *Industry Surveys: Telephone: Basic Analysis,* August 8, 1974, p. T.9; also U.S. Bureau of the Census, *Statistical Abstract of the United States: 1978* (GPO, 1978), pp. 587–88.

work of political contacts. "If I say something to a congressman," found a House subcommittee counsel, "the next day Bell is asking the chairman why I said it."[60] In making political decisions, AT&T consulted with the independent telephone companies through the United States Independent Telephone Association (USITA) and such major firms as General Telephone and Centel, but the locus of responsibility and leadership was clear. The telephone industry thus was immune to the internal difficulties of less concentrated industries: it neither could be badly split, like the airlines; nor could it come under pressure from a militant membership, like the leaders of the American Trucking Association.

In fact, however, AT&T and the independents in the mid-1970s neither accepted competition nor negotiated skillfully. They sought by a bold and ambitious legislative campaign very nearly to restore monopoly. Uncompromising in substance and aggressive in tactics, the campaign was counterproductive, blundering away any chance to limit the expansion of competition. The political centralization of the industry, proving to be a mixed blessing, helped cause this response. A few years later, with a change of leadership and strategy, the industry adopted a more effective political approach, but by then the issue of competition had to be conceded.

Pleadings of disinterest notwithstanding, the industry's resistance to competition was partly a matter of economics. The markets that were becoming competitive under the FCC policies of the late 1960s and early 1970s—principally those in terminal equipment, private line service, and data communications—also happened to be the most rapidly growing and lucrative segments of the industry.[61] In traditional markets, especially for local residential service, rates of return permitted in theory were often, in effect, forbidden in practice, as state utility commissions refused to match increases in costs with corresponding increases in rates.[62] For the

60. Interview, David Aylward, chief counsel, House Subcommittee on Telecommunications, Consumer Protection, and Finance, September 17, 1981.

61. For a detailed treatment of Bell's interests and responses to competition and technological change, see Gerald M. Brock, *The Telecommunications Industry: The Dynamics of Market Structure* (Harvard University Press, 1981), chaps. 7–9.

62. The worst of Bell's problems with state regulators were in California. See *Wall Street Journal,* March 10, 1981. See also Paul W. MacAvoy, *The Regulated Industries and the Economy* (Norton, 1979). A perceptive account of the California commission is given in Douglas Anderson, *Regulatory Politics and Electric Utilities* (Boston: Auburn House, 1981); for a valuable multistate comparative analysis, see William T. Gormley, Jr., *The Politics of Public Utility Regulation* (University of Pittsburgh Press, 1983).

independents, especially those serving rural areas, the main threat of competition was the possible loss of cross-subsidies from the "separations and settlements" process; for AT&T there was a danger of having to maintain these subsidies while losing the protected markets from which to draw them. With such economic interests at stake in the debate, it was not surprising that Bell, in opening its campaign against competition, solicited support from the company's shareholders.[63]

THE IDEOLOGY OF THE TELEPHONE INDUSTRY. The industry did care about more than securing profits; a distinctive industry ideology was at least as important in shaping its behavior. Like airline and trucking officials, telephone industry officials believed in the traditional regulatory regime as beneficial for the general public. With some support in the legal sources—especially the 1934 communications act and a 1956 consent decree with the Department of Justice that restricted Bell to providing regulated communications services—they thought of the industry as a publicly chartered monopoly, duly constrained and rendered accountable. Probably most important, however, they held a special conception of the industry—one that claimed an exceptional character and social role and was endowed with moral value.

Almost from the start, AT&T had found it necessary to be something other than an ordinary profit-seeking enterprise. Early in the century AT&T was headed by Theodore Vail, a visionary leader who had resigned from the company in protest of what he considered shortsighted management and later had been brought back as president to implement his beliefs. Vail believed that the company's potential for monopolistic abuse, if not somehow controlled, would ultimately result in nationalization. Thus, to make its private operation legitimate, he promulgated the edifying doctrine that "our business is service"—establishing it as a premise for internal management and indoctrination, not merely public relations.[64] In managing the network, AT&T emphasized quality and expansion of service more than near-term financial returns, and when its leaders assessed the threat of competition in the early 1970s, they wor-

63. *Washington Star,* April 1, 1976. "Separations and settlements" refers to the procedures and methods by which, before AT&T's divestiture of the local Bell operating companies, long distance revenues were shared among AT&T Long Lines, the operating companies, and the independent telephone companies—all of which provided facilities used in the service.

64. Peter F. Drucker, "Managing the Public Service Institution," *Public Interest,* no. 33 (Fall 1973), pp. 53–54; and von Auw, *Heritage and Destiny,* pp. 62, 262.

ried, as much as anything, for the customers' well-being. Their main fear, as revealed in notes of high-level meetings that were made public years later in litigation, was that competition would "burden the general users of telephone service."[65]

Vail also established a policy of cooperating with regulatory bodies, whose success he deemed essential for the firm's survival. Until the era of competition, regulatory harmony was easy to maintain because scale economies and technological change continually drove costs downward, and the companies themselves initiated rate decreases.[66] But the industry's cooperation with government went beyond this to participating, in effect, in the design and implementation of an ambitious social program.

With only loose supervision and some financial assistance from government, AT&T and the independents collaborated in the objective, mandated by the communications act, of providing "universal service at reasonable, affordable rates." In part, this mandate reflected the political power of rural areas, where costs of service could be exorbitant; it also embodied an egalitarian sentiment and the ideal of a nation linked by the most natural and immediate means of communication, the human voice. For the industry, pursuing this ideal involved the sharing of responsibility, revenue, and risk among firms in the industry, accomplished by financial transfers built into the terms of separations and settlements. On AT&T's part, it led to rate averaging on interstate long distance calls. More than merely cooperating with regulation, this was assuming quasi-governmental functions, responsibilities, and indeed prerogatives: bestowing subsidies and imposing taxes on behalf of national goals. And monopoly was as much a premise for this role as it is for government.

Because the industry operated under regulated rates of return, to assume this role did not necessarily require financial sacrifice. Another Bell doctrine of long standing taught that "to serve well, we must earn well"—a maxim sufficiently observed in practice that AT&T was a blue chip stock. But the industry's quasi-governmental role gave it a distinctive

65. Minutes of AT&T Executive Policy Committee meeting, August 23, 1973. These minutes, marked "private," and some of the other AT&T internal documents used in the following pages became available to the public because they were introduced in evidence in MCI's antitrust suit against Bell. Both MCI and AT&T provided assistance in our use of the documents.

66. See Gormley, *Politics of Public Utility Regulation,* chap. 1, which shows that similar conditions prevailed generally in public utilities regulation until the late 1960s and early 1970s. By now, however, "the consensual years have come to an end."

ethos and an esprit de corps. As retired AT&T executive Alvin von Auw has written, the company traditionally claimed to be principally motivated by "the spirit of service," rather than "the lesser incentives of other callings."[67] As a result, when the FCC began to adopt procompetitive policies in the late 1960s and early 1970s, it represented an attack on the industry's special status and a rejection of its values. The chairman of the board of AT&T, John de Butts, was troubled, he said, by the changes FCC policy would require of the company in pricing, service responsibility, and priorities for research and development. But even more troubling to him was the "potential impact of that policy on the fundamental character of our business." The service motivation—"bred in the bones of telephone people over the course of a hundred years"—would be supplanted by a market motivation. "I for one cannot help but feel we would be the poorer for it and so would the public we serve."[68]

AT&T'S POLITICAL DECISIONMAKING. The industry's profound feelings against competition might have been turned to effective political use. To do so would have required political skill and sensitivity and the use of restraint. Because of its dominance, AT&T would have had to provide the needed control; but neither its leadership nor its organization for political decisionmaking prepared it for the task.

Restraint was, in particular, no part of the style of de Butts, who had become the company's chairman and hence principal political strategist in 1972. Having headed the government relations office in Washington for several years, de Butts was by no means a political novice. By his personal manner and disposition, however, he was poorly matched to a political role—at least in circumstances, such as Bell faced, that demanded the ability to compromise. De Butts was considered by many to be arrogant and aloof; AT&T had been less effective at the FCC than it might have been, a former official of the agency judged, because de Butts had not "condescended to visit the commissioners." He was the sort, said another FCC official, whose mere presence polarized debate. According to von Auw, who served as his personal aide, "He was not given to brooding over even the most complex questions. When he had come to a decision, be it at mid-meeting or at meeting's end, he made no secret of what he had decided." In a speech de Butts described himself as "the perennial

67. Von Auw, *Heritage and Destiny,* p. 373.
68. *Telecommunications Reports,* November 8, 1976. p. 23.

optimist, the true believer," who always says that "whatever the Bell System sets its mind on doing it does."[69] This disposition was reinforced, undoubtedly, by the magnitude of the company's political resources and its reputation for power—which would have created temptations for any leader of AT&T to act boldly.

AT&T was organized for political decisionmaking just as for any other companywide decisionmaking. During the late 1960s, oddly, Bell had no well-developed apparatus for central decisionmaking on any matters. It was felt that the company's early response to procompetitive policies lacked clarity partly for that reason. So in 1970 AT&T set up an Executive Policy Committee (EPC) as the primary forum for considering issues, political and otherwise, that affected the company as a whole.[70]

Despite the concern for political efficacy, the EPC did not incorporate a particularly prominent role for specialists in politics. The committee consisted mainly of the company's operating leadership—that is, the chairman, his personal assistant (who served as secretary), the president, vice-chairman, general counsel, and several functional vice-presidents. On issues of special importance, it consulted with the heads of the local operating companies in an EPC–Presidents' Conference before reaching a decision. Other AT&T officials gave presentations or attended EPC meetings by invitation when they were needed. The head of public affairs, based in Washington, was thus not a full-fledged member of the company's principal decisionmaking body, though he sometimes participated in its deliberations. The position, in any case, was merely one rung on a general career ladder and not occupied by a political professional. However constituted, the EPC was necessarily an instrument of the chairman as chief executive, to be consulted, dominated, or ignored as he saw fit. De Butts, who saw fit to dominate it, used the EPC to bring about a hardline defense of the traditional monopoly.

Initially, the question of how AT&T should deal with the trend toward competition evoked internal disagreement between strict traditionalists and those who advocated a more flexible posture, recognizing advantages

69. Interview, Walter Hinchman, former chief of the Common Carrier Bureau, FCC, May 21, 1981; interview, anonymous FCC staff member, December 12, 1980; von Auw, *Heritage and Destiny*, p. 331; and John de Butts, speech delivered to the Pioneer General Assembly, Houston, Texas, October 22, 1974.

70. Interview, Alvin von Auw, former vice-president and assistant to the chairman of the board, AT&T, August 10, 1982; and von Auw, *Heritage and Destiny*, pp. 312–21.

to competition in some areas or seeing a need for political realism. In a crucial EPC–Presidents' Conference in May 1972, the disagreement came to a head. "What is our philosophy vis-à-vis competition?" asked one participant, complaining that the company's response had not been vigorous. Observed another, referring to the headquarters' address on Broadway in New York: "We have no direction from 195."[71]

The most fundamental differences concerned terminal equipment. Some doubted that AT&T should even continue to serve that diverse and innovative market and suggested withdrawing from at least parts of it. Deeply rooted practices, such as never refusing a customer's business, would hamper the company's competitive performance, and by trying to compete against the whole array of specialists entering the market, warned one of the presidents, "we're going to get run out of business." In regard to political strategy, the main question was whether Bell should agree to the FCC's development of a certification program for competing manufacturers' terminal equipment. Leading to direct interconnection of the equipment to the Bell System network, such a concession would be to acquiesce in competition where it was most established. Thus far, Bell had obscured its position by opposing certification but nevertheless offering to cooperate with regulatory bodies in studying it. "We are arguing with ourselves," a vice-president said. Some AT&T officials, such as Illinois Bell President William Ellinghaus (later president of AT&T), considered certification inevitable. "Let's work like hell to get certification on our terms," he therefore advised.[72]

"The question of do we want to compete has been answered," said an impatient de Butts. "We do." Rejecting the suggestion to accept certification, he attacked the very notion of compromise, which he considered irresponsible. "We must ask ourselves," he insisted, "is it really in the public interest to be anything other than a monopolist?" Claiming to see some signs of support for the company's position, he refused to concede that certification was inevitable and added: "My experience has been I'm going to lose every fight I don't set out to win." Having heard de Butts's speech, the meeting treated the issues as closed. Later, in remarks closing the conference, de Butts emphasized that the public interest was "the *only*

71. Notes of Bell System Presidents' Conference, Key Largo, Florida, May 10, 1972.
72. Ibid.

supportable criterion" for determining the company's position, and in light of this reiterated a pledge that the company "wouldn't hear John de Butts saying 'We welcome competition.' "[73]

As its political strategy gradually emerged, AT&T seems to have barely considered the feasibility of its objectives, though by 1973 there was clear warning of impending trouble. Even though the public, as a poll showed, was generally satisfied with telephone service under the monopoly, to stop the trend toward competition or secure new anticompetitive policies would not be easy.[74] Another poll, as summarized by the public relations staff, had given "a discomforting confirmation of the immensity and complexity of the task" of convincing the public of the need for monopoly. Standing in the way were "deeply held beliefs about the American way of life"—especially the belief in the "inherent benefits of competition." An additional problem was the public's ambivalence toward big business—which, the analyst explained, "we are seen to be."[75]

Undeterred, the EPC agreed in August to take the company's case to Congress and the public. Opening the campaign before a convention of state regulatory officials, de Butts delivered a speech that, as he later described it, put "the world on notice that the Bell System is ready to fight for what it believes." "Having taken our stand, there is no turning back," de Butts told AT&T executives after the speech. Acknowledging that their viewpoints initially had been "quite diverse," he now trusted that they shared a common conviction "without reservation" and urged their "common responsibility" to see it prevail. In furtherance of this conviction AT&T developed policy positions that conceded virtually no role for competition in the industry. It first called upon the FCC to institute a lengthy pause in the expansion of telecommunications competition,

73. Ibid.; and de Butts, "Closing Remarks," Presidents' Conference, Key Largo, Florida, May 12, 1972.

74. According to an AT&T-sponsored survey in 1973, 82 percent of the public rated telephone service good or excellent, and 76 percent believed that prices were reasonable or very reasonable. *The Industrial Reorganization Act,* Hearings before the Subcommittee on Antitrust and Monopoly of the Senate Committee on the Judiciary, 93 Cong. 2 sess., pt. 6: *The Communications Industry* (GPO, 1974), p. 4648.

75. "Prices and Services—Subscriber Reactions to Copy Statements (Illinois): An Overview," an undated, unsigned memo reporting results of an Illinois Bell test of anticompetitive promotional literature, reprinted in *The Industrial Reorganization Act,* Hearings, pt. 5: *The Communications Industry,* p. 3456.

describing this as "a moratorium on further experiments in economics." When the commission refused, Bell took the next step and began to work for reversal by Congress.[76]

THE BELL BILL. For the drafting of legislation, AT&T enlisted the participation of a broader industry group, including representatives of USITA, several of the major independent telephone companies, and a rural telephone association, which met in USITA's offices in Washington. The expanded group was no less ambitious and parochial collectively than Bell was alone. The independents were just as opposed to competition, and USITA's representative supported extreme proposals, he later felt, partly because he was new to the job and lacked experience. Within AT&T, decisionmaking in the legislative phase was handled more narrowly than before, largely by de Butts and Edward Crosland, recently promoted from head of the Washington office to executive vice-president at headquarters in New York. In the judgment of a union official, "two more willful men could not be found." In a long series of predominantly harmonious meetings, spanning several months, the group produced numerous drafts of a proposed bill, but it made no effort to determine what kind of restrictive legislation, if any, the Ford administration or congressional leaders would support.[77]

The Consumer Communications Reform Act (CCRA), the name given the resulting bill, was designed overtly to suppress competition. In transmission services it simply prohibited "duplication" (and hence competition) in services that the established carriers provided or that they might provide. In terminal equipment the bill did not prohibit competition but, in an apparent attempt to approximate the result, it transferred regulatory jurisdiction from the FCC to the states. (As de Butts explained in a meeting with company executives, some states might use this authority to prohibit competition within their borders.[78] At a minimum, it would

76. John de Butts, speech delivered to the National Association of Regulatory Utility Commissioners, Seattle, Washington, September 20, 1973; speech to Pioneer General Assembly; "Opening Remarks," EPC–Presidents' Conference, Portland, Oregon, October 2, 1973; and interview, John de Butts, May 29, 1981.

77. Interview, Jack Harrington, governmental affairs, United States Independent Telephone Company, August 29, 1981; the nature of AT&T's decisionmaking was described in similar terms by two close observers who did not speak for attribution.

78. De Butts, "Opening Remarks," EPC–Presidents' Conference, Portland, Oregon, October 2, 1973.

mean that competitors would have to obtain state-by-state approval to offer their products in what was otherwise a national market.) Finally, in perhaps the *coup de grace,* the bill provided antitrust immunity so that AT&T's competitors, driven from the market as independent firms, could be absorbed by merger into the Bell System.

In promoting the bill, introduced in Congress early in 1976, AT&T used methods as blunt and uncompromising as the proposed provisions. Pressure from AT&T was threatening in Congress if only because of the company's size and the resources it committed to the effort. In the second quarter of 1976, AT&T reported spending $1 million on lobbying and public relations on behalf of the campaign—a sum extracted from the ratepayers, which did not include expenses for the Washington office. AT&T was represented on Capitol Hill, if anything, excessively well. In an incident that became notorious, Representative Timothy Wirth, Democrat of Colorado, asked all the Bell employees in a large, crowded hearing room to stand up and identify themselves—revealing that they accounted for most of the audience. Bell took care that such overstaffing was not repeated, but even the local operating presidents alone were a large and imposing force of lobbyists. In using the presidents routinely, von Auw later believed, Bell had failed to show the political sensitivity appropriate for a major corporation.[79]

Yet a forceful, even coercive approach also was obviously intended. If Congress did not soon put a stop to the FCC's expansion of competition, "we would feel obliged to move promptly toward a drastic realignment of our rates," de Butts threatened. "In every jurisdiction we would have to file sharply increased rates for basic exchange service." Such threats, frightening in the extreme for members of Congress, were not justified by the data and projections produced by the FCC in an elaborate inquiry. Challenging Bell's basic contention, the commission even doubted that the services then becoming competitive had ever been used as a source of cross-subsidies. In any event, it concluded, the incursions of the competitors under current or contemplated policies (which were much more restrictive than those the courts imposed later) would be far too modest to force an appreciable change in the company's rates. Bell was using "totally unsubstantiated scare tactics," said John Eger, who was then depart-

79. Von Auw interview.

ing as director of the Office of Telecommunications Policy in the Ford White House.[80]

When most of the committee leaders withheld support from the proposed bill, the industry, rather than compromise, tried to bypass or overpower them. Lobbying intensely among the rank and file, Bell and its allies by late 1976 had enlisted 175 cosponsors in the House, a figure approaching a majority, and 17 in the Senate—many of whom called for early consideration of the bill. Particularly in the House, the subcommittee leaders and staff felt resentful and anxious: "We were afraid the bill would be taken out of our hands," the staff counsel later explained.[81]

The campaign for the CCRA, derided by opponents as the "Bell bill," proved to be an ignominious failure and counterproductive as an attempt to stop the expansion of competition. Telecommunications policymakers and analysts were appalled by its provisions. Alfred Kahn, who was then chairman of the New York State Public Service Commission—and who was expert mainly in telecommunications and had served AT&T as a consultant—was prominent among the critics. Even though Kahn had doubts about the advisability of competition in some parts of the industry, he told Congress that the Bell bill was so extreme it was "an abomination." Congressional leaders on telecommunications largely agreed. Except for Senator Vance Hartke, Democrat of Indiana, who was in line to become Communications Subcommittee chairman and cosponsored the bill "by request," none of the leaders in either house supported it, and several worked hard to stop other members from joining in sponsorship. Even presumptive allies were inclined to defect. The Communications Workers of America (CWA), whose members were losing jobs to Bell's competitors, nevertheless found the bill extreme and refrained from giving a specific endorsement. USITA, which had helped in drafting it, soon recognized that the bill was a mistake and stopped asking for hearings to

80. *Telecommunications Reports,* November 8, 1976. The FCC had been making its own inquiry into the economic effects of competition. See the testimony of chairman Richard Wiley and supporting documents, *Competition in the Telecommunications Industry,* Hearings, pp. 733–39, 763–950. For Eger's statement, see *Washington Star,* June 3, 1976. Bell's warning would have been more convincing if it had been addressed to the potential long-run effect of competition in public long distance service (as opposed to specialized service and private lines). This would have virtually endorsed the then-current FCC policy, which did not contemplate establishing competition in that market.

81. Interview, Harry M. Shooshan III, former chief counsel, House Communications Subcommittee, September 11, 1981.

consider it. Despite all the pressure on its behalf, the CCRA did not get far in Congress. The subcommittees in both houses held hearings on the telecommunications industry, but the tone of the hearings was mostly favorable toward competition, and both chairmen made it clear that the CCRA was not on the agenda.[82]

After the fact, industry officials consoled themselves (and turned aside criticism) by claiming the bill had at least focused Congress's attention on the issue of competition. This was a patent rationalization that ignored the damage done to the industry's cause. The episode created a hostile political climate for the industry. AT&T in particular lost credibility and good will in Congress, as senior subcommittee members took stances that were in varying degrees adversarial toward the company; two key Democratic leaders, Senator Hollings and Representative Wirth, became sharp critics. Four years later, in 1981, a Bell official based in Washington still was uncertain whether the political fallout had entirely dissipated.[83] Another result of the episode was the mobilization of Bell's competitors. To fight for survival, they formed one new organization, the Ad Hoc Committee for Competitive Telecommunications (representing common carriers), and intensified lobbying activity at the federal level in such existing organizations as the North American Telephone Association (for manufacturers of terminal equipment) and the Computer and Business Equipment Manufacturers' Association. These groups remained active after the bill's defeat, giving procompetitive forces vigorous, organized advocacy that was lacking earlier. The changes in Bell's political environment had tangible effects on its subsequent strategy: the company still had the power to veto a bill, a House staff member observed, but after the CCRA it could no longer initiate one.[84]

Finally, the campaign for the CCRA squandered what may have been a genuine chance to obtain moderate statutory limits on competition. The industry might have succeeded, for example, with a proposal to restrict

82. *Competition in the Telecommunications Industry,* Hearings, pp. 1–5, 973; *Telecommunications Reports,* April 5, 1976; Harrington interview; and *Domestic Telecommunications Common Carrier Policies,* Hearings before the Subcommittee on Communications of the Senate Committee on Commerce, Science, and Transportation, 95 Cong. 1 sess. (GPO, 1977), pt. 1, pp. 1–2.

83. Interview, Pickard Wagner, AT&T's principal public relations spokesman in Washington, August 29, 1981.

84. Interview, Herbert Jasper, executive director, Ad Hoc Committee for Competitive Telecommunications, June 12, 1981; and Shooshan interview.

competition in public long distance service, the source of roughly half of AT&T's revenues. Perhaps resembling a measure advocated earlier by the state regulatory commissioners, such a bill would have been plausible because in the mid-1970s there were few advocates of competition in that market. By no means did considerations of economic efficiency clearly support it; and long distance service was the main source of the cross-subsidies for rural and residential users. More generally, a plausible bill might have required, for any expansion of competition, an administrative finding that it would not tend to increase rural or residential rates. Some such restrictions might have had broad support. The FCC then still opposed public long distance competition, and in rejecting AT&T's demands for a reversal of policy, congressional leaders spoke only in defense of "limited competition." It is, of course, impossible to judge whether any restrictive legislation could actually have passed. But the enactment of a moderate restrictive bill—one that constrained competition in certain respects but also ratified and facilitated it where it was already becoming established—was by no means inconceivable.[85]

Instead, the CCRA guaranteed a prolonged delay in congressional action, allowing the trend toward competition in the industry to proceed further. Congress needed a lengthy period for educating the members, negotiation, and cooling off before new legislation could be seriously contemplated. In 1978 House Communications Subcommittee Chairman Lionel Van Deerlin introduced a proposed procompetitive revision of the entire communications act (including the broadcasting sections), but the bill, nicknamed "the rewrite," was intended mainly for preliminary discussion and it was late in 1979 before any bill advanced to subcommittee markup in either house. During the delay, predictably, organized political opposition to AT&T only grew. Through such organizations as the International Communications Association and the National Retail Merchants' Association, business users of communications equipment and services became more active, most often supporting Bell's competitors.

---

85. The Home Telephone Act, proposed in the early 1970s by the National Association of Regulatory Utility Commissioners, would have discouraged long distance competition by instructing the FCC, in its regulation of long distance service, to stress the maintenance of low rates for residential customers. Challenging competition indirectly, it would have required the commission to reevaluate policies "whose continuation may have a significant impact on increasing the rates for telephone exchange service in the future." *Congressional Record* (June 4, 1974), p. 17429. That some such moderate bill might have been feasible, with support from AT&T, seemed likely in retrospect to some of the participants in the debate, including a union official and a legislative assistant to Wirth. Aylward interview.

Even within the established industry, divisions developed as General Telephone and other major independents increasingly entered competitive markets. Most important, the FCC and the courts continued to adopt policy changes, some of them decisively adverse for AT&T.

The Conversion of AT&T

The first important telecommunications bill after the CCRA—Van Deerlin's proposed "rewrite" of the communications act—declared in its statement of purpose that "the Commission shall . . . place maximum feasible reliance on marketplace forces . . . [and] rely on competition to provide efficiency, innovation, and low rates."[86] Introduced in June 1978, the rewrite demonstrated that the congressional agenda on telecommunications was controlled by the committee leaders, not AT&T, and that the agenda consisted of measures to ratify or extend competition, not restrict it. With the independents generally following, Bell soon began to act in ways more closely parallel to the airline and trucking industries. Driven ultimately by administrative and judicial action, it gradually consented to procompetitive policies that Congress otherwise could not have approved. For this to occur, however, required a basic conversion of AT&T—not only a revision of its political objectives, but a change of leadership and at least the beginnings of a new corporate ethos.

After AT&T had tried and failed to stop the rise of competition by legislation, the only available course was to come to terms with it—a difficult task with both managerial and political elements. As early as 1972, when he became chairman, de Butts had recognized that if the company could not prevent competition by political action, it would have to transform itself in order to compete.[87] Overall, observers said, AT&T's competitive response was hampered by a "public utility mentality." AT&T's research and development subsidiary, Bell Laboratories, was insulated from the marketplace; it exercised broad discretion in setting its priorities and responded sluggishly to competitive challenges and customer demands. AT&T's marketing people were not aggressive, competitive salespersons and managers, it was often said, but passive order

86. *The Communications Act of 1978,* Hearings before the Subcommittee on Communications of the House Committee on Interstate and Foreign Commerce, 95 Cong. 2 sess. (GPO, 1978), p. 48.

87. De Butts, "Closing Remarks," Presidents' Conference, Key Largo, Florida, May 12, 1972.

takers. And prices for AT&T's services corresponded only very roughly to their separate costs, which its accounting system, designed for other purposes, was largely unable to identify. Because historically there had been no compelling need to control them, the costs in any case were generally high.[88]

Besides needing to change its internal management and marketing practices in order to compete, AT&T needed to negotiate favorable governmental policies for competitive activities because policies intended to foster competition often constrained the former monopolist. The FCC in the mid-1970s was trying, although without much effect, to control AT&T's economic response to competition. In order to stop AT&T from setting predatorily low prices for competitive services, the commission was developing a new methodology for determining rates; by requiring the company's competitive services to cover a larger share of overall costs, the new approach threatened to make them less attractive. The FCC also showed an increased disposition to restrict AT&T's role under the terms of the 1956 consent decree. Because it limited Bell to providing regulated communications services, the decree barred the company from providing products or services that involved data processing—the most dynamic segment of the telecommunications market—except insofar as the FCC defined them as communications services subject to regulation. As of 1978 the FCC had not blocked any AT&T offerings. But one important product, a terminal device called the Dataspeed 40/4, had been approved narrowly and only because a commission majority overruled the staff. Commission approval for Bell's Advanced Communications System, a project in which the company had made a huge investment, was considered uncertain. Bell denounced these constraints as unfair and incoherent, as mere protection for its competitors from competition by Bell.[89]

Another threat, ultimately more fundamental, had been created by the Justice Department and was slowly developing in federal court. In the massive antitrust case, *United States* v. *American Telephone and Telegraph Co.,* which was filed in 1974 and finally went to trial in 1980, Justice accused Bell of having used a variety of illicit methods to undermine competition. The complaints, similar to those made in several private antitrust suits, included AT&T's refusal to interconnect with competitors,

88. For a discussion, see "Behind AT&T's Change at the Top," *Business Week,* November 6, 1978, pp. 114–39.

89. *Telecommunications Reports,* February 5, 1978.

predatory pricing, and use of dilatory tactics and arguing in bad faith before regulatory bodies.[90] Justice asked the court to order AT&T split into two or more separate companies for the sake of protecting future competition. Bell's leadership had a profound aversion to divestiture, which they argued would harm service and undermine the competitive prowess of the resulting companies. Bell spent vast sums defending the suit, over $100 million in 1979, which it then condemned as a waste of resources.

To have a chance of overcoming these hazards, AT&T would have to come to terms with competition and reach an accommodation with pro-competitive policymakers in the FCC, the Justice Department, and especially Congress. De Butts once again took decisive action. In order to compete more formidably, he ordered a massive reorganization of the company, designed to enhance the marketing function. Affecting about 250,000 employees, it was described as the largest reorganization in business history. The company stepped up its efforts to recruit new executives with entrepreneurial attitudes and skills and to create a more competitive corporate climate, bringing changes that compromised service ideals and elicited resentment from the company's traditionalists.[91]

In addition, de Butts took a step that, under the circumstances, substantially enhanced AT&T's potential effectiveness in the political process: he chose to retire. Having been the industry's doctrinaire leader in the campaign against competition, he could not credibly be its leader in accepting it. Some of the hostility toward the company in Washington focused on him. Although de Butts gave only personal reasons to explain his decision,[92] he may also have recognized that he had become an encumbrance in the company's pursuit of political goals.

His successor as chairman, Charles L. Brown, whom de Butts helped select, was better suited. A son of two Bell employees, Brown had started his career in the company with summer jobs as a linesman, joined after college as an engineer, and worked his way up through the management ranks. Although steeped in the monopoly culture, he was also flexible,

90. Justice Department, Plaintiff's Memorandum in Opposition to Defendant's Motion for Involuntary Dismissal under Rule 41b, *United States* v. *American Telephone and Telegraph Co.,* filed August 20, 1981.

91. "Behind AT&T's Change at the Top," p. 117; and von Auw, *Heritage and Destiny,* pp. 158–79. Von Auw calls this conflict a "clash of cultures," and his extremely interesting book is a testament to the traditionalists' depth of conviction.

92. De Butts interview.

intelligent, and tactful. Unlike the traditionalists in the industry, he viewed competition not only as a threat but also as an opportunity and challenge. In contrast with de Butts, whom even some high officials found imperious, Brown dealt directly and respectfully with congressional staff.

"I intend to be guided by what I have called a new realism," Brown told the Senate Commerce Committee in April 1979. "This new realism recognizes that competition is a fact of life in our business and that, thus far at any rate, its effects haven't been all bad." This did not mean that AT&T was abandoning hope of restraining the expansion of competition. But the main corporate political objective would be to secure Bell's own freedom from governmental interference.[93]

Brown also changed AT&T's manner and methods as a political organization, as the result of which its centralized structure and vast resources finally were put to effective use. Like de Butts, Brown personally controlled the company's political operation and made most of the significant political decisions; but unlike de Butts, he constantly consulted the Washington office and he paid due attention to the political realities. In the poisoned atmosphere created by the CCRA, Bell found it expedient to use milder, less direct political tactics. In the six years after de Butts's departure, Bell neither overtly sponsored nor gave unqualified support to any bill, though Congress considered telecommunications legislation throughout the period. Assuming almost a passive role, the company revealed its positions mainly by reacting to proposals by committee leaders. In reaching these positions, Brown negotiated personally with congressional leaders and even their staff. He used a low-key, cooperative manner, and instead of bringing a retinue of other executives, he generally came unaccompanied.[94]

AT&T's conversion, encompassing changes of leadership, strategy, and political methods, prepared it far better than it had been prepared in the early 1970s to reach the necessary accommodation with the forces of reform. As before, Bell could deploy an extraordinary lobbying network, bringing to bear the political resources of the local operating companies,

93. *Amendments to the Communications Act of 1934,* Hearings before the Subcommittee on Communications of the Senate Committee on Commerce, Science, and Transportation, 96 Cong. 1 sess. (GPO, 1979), pt. 1, p. 215. See also Brown's speeches, *Telecommunications Reports,* November 27, 1978; February 5, 1979; and March 5, 1979.

94. Brown's methods were described to us by a close observer in the company: interview, John Fox, vice-president for public affairs, AT&T, August 31, 1982. Observers outside the company had similar perceptions: Shooshan interview.

and yet still have the coordination and discipline of a single hierarchy. Now it also could conduct political affairs with sensitivity and skill on behalf of realistic objectives. The CCRA had taken a toll in political good will, but Bell still could negotiate from a position of strength. At least until the divestiture agreement of January 1982, which sharply diminished its political stature, AT&T was presumed able to block any significant telecommunications bill that it strongly opposed. Thus combining discipline, political sensitivity, and lobbying power, AT&T enjoyed a strategic luxury not available to the trucking industry or especially the airlines. According to circumstances, it could make orderly, precisely calibrated concessions, setting limits that were certain to stick.

The concessions needed, nevertheless, were drastic and more fundamental than might have been needed, given comparable political restraint, in 1976. AT&T conceded more quickly on some issues, more slowly on others. The differences reflected the substance and politics of the issues as well as further developments in the FCC and the courts.

The Consensus on Competition

The most fundamental policy question in telecommunications—the scope of competition in the industry—was also the question most easily settled. So quietly and gradually it was hardly noticed, the question by early 1980 had been definitively resolved entirely in favor of competition. This did not occur because Congress was determined to impose such a clear-cut result. Even the reformist committee leaders tended to be more cautious; and against AT&T they were in no position to impose anything. The resolution occurred, rather, because further developments in the FCC and the courts made radically procompetitive policies seem politically balanced and compelled concessions by AT&T.

The industry's legislative initiative having come to nothing, administrative and judicial action was free to continue. On terminal equipment, where the FCC was most confident of the benefits of competition, the commission took decisive steps. As some AT&T officials had long expected, in 1977 the FCC decided to establish a registration program that would certify competitors' equipment for direct connection to the Bell network. AT&T, in a last-ditch effort to retain a vestige of monopoly control, proposed what it called the "primary instrument concept," requiring that every customer use at least one instrument provided by the Bell system. Although the subcommittee chairmen in both houses, Hollings and Van Deerlin, pronounced the proposal worth considering, the FCC saw no need for the restriction and dismissed Bell's proposal out of hand.[95]

In long distance transmission, however, the FCC refused to grant MCI authorization for its "Execunet" service—a switched, or public, service intended for business. Unrestricted competition in the long distance market was authorized through intervention by the courts. In a ruling that had enormous consequences for public policy and the development of the industry, although it was based entirely on a procedural issue, the Court of Appeals for the D.C. Circuit held that the commission had erred in the Execunet case (since it had not adequately examined the need for monopoly in long distance service) and reversed its decision.[96] In January 1979 the Supreme Court denied the government's petition for certiorari, and MCI, Southern Pacific, and other competing carriers were free to offer any kind of long distance service they wished.

The FCC quickly began a new proceeding, the MTS-WATS market structure inquiry, in which in theory it could have corrected the alleged error and returned long distance service to monopoly control. But the prospects of actually accomplishing this were remote. It would take many months to complete the inquiry; and, as one commissioner worried in an early meeting, to try to restore monopoly after a lengthy period of competition would be "like trying to unscramble eggs."[97] By early 1979, therefore, decisions by the FCC and the courts had made Bell's chances of hanging on to any monopoly protection, either in terminal equipment or in long distance service, exceedingly dim.

These developments transformed the politics of procompetitive policy in telecommunications. It became politically possible—indeed, it was no longer particularly daring—to advocate further expansion of competition in the industry. AT&T, which unlike its competitors was still legally barred from important markets, would have the most to gain from the expansion. By adjusting the provisions on a number of specific issues,

95. According to the chief of the Common Carrier Bureau at the time, Walter Hinchman, the FCC considered the proposal a nuisance—an attempt to reopen an issue, terminal equipment competition, that had already been thoroughly examined and completely resolved.

96. *MCI Telecommunications Corporation* v. *Federal Communications Commission,* 580 F. 2d 590 (D.C. Cir., 1978); and 561 F. 2d 365 (D.C. Cir., 1977).

97. *Telecommunications Reports,* April 23, 1979.

proposals for a wide-open procompetitive policy could be designed to strike a cautious political balance or could even be tilted toward AT&T.

The change in politics was reflected by a change in the position taken by the Carter administration. Like Ford before him, Carter had been less willing than congressional leaders to become embroiled in the issue of competition in telecommunications and had kept a low profile in the controversy over the CCRA. The domestic policy staff disapproved of the bill. But CWA president Glenn Watts, who had been the first leader of a major labor union to endorse Carter for president and could not easily be ignored, pressed him to support the bill's major goals. On the advice of his staff, with the CCRA already dying in Congress, Carter was noncommittal with Watts and kept personally out of the debate on the bill.[98]

But later, as administrative and judicial decisions abolished protections for AT&T, the administration became more involved, permitting statements of policy to emanate from the Department of Commerce. Henry Geller, the director of the National Telecommunications and Information Administration, an agency established there in 1978 to replace the White House Office of Telecommunications Policy, began to argue publicly for wide-open entry. A former general counsel of the FCC and a widely respected expert on the industry, Geller offered a loosely defined set of proposals that assumed free entry in all aspects of telecommunications—not only for fledgling competitors but also, in a greater departure from existing policy, for AT&T.[99] However radical these proposals would have seemed a year or two earlier, under the new circumstances the committees in both houses adopted Geller's suggestions without difficulty as a new starting point for deliberations, and in his 1980 State of the Union message Carter emphasized his personal support of the congressional effort.[100]

98. White House memorandum: Rick Neustadt to Barry Jagoda, Si Lazarus, and Elizabeth Cook, "Visit with Communications Workers of America," February 4, 1977; draft memorandum: Stu Eizenstat and Rick Neustadt to the president, "Letter from Communications Workers," undated; and Rick Neustadt to Stu Eizenstat, "Competition in the Telephone Industry," October 20, 1977, and "The Bell Bill," March 7, 1977.

99. Interview, Ellen Deutsch, program manager, Domestic Common Carrier Program, National Telecommunications and Information Administration, December 9, 1980; and *Telecommunications Reports,* November 12, 1979.

100. "The State of the Union, January 23, 1980," *Public Papers: Carter, 1980–81,* bk. 1 (GPO, 1981), pp. 194–200. Carter also had given a general endorsement of legislative efforts on telecommunications in the fall, shortly before the release of Geller's proposals. "Regulatory Reform of the Telecommunications Industry, September 21, 1979," *Public Papers: Carter, 1979,* bk. 2 (GPO, 1980), p. 1699.

In its response to these administrative and judicial actions and legislative proposals, AT&T's political realism under Brown clearly emerged. By one analysis, an aggressive second effort to overturn competition was possible. After the courts' Execunet ruling, the chief of the FCC's Common Carrier Bureau, Walter Hinchman, feared that AT&T might retaliate by rapidly deaveraging rates on long distance service, using the loss of regulatory protection as justification. This would send rural and small-town rates sharply upward and Congress, predictably, into an uproar; perhaps, Hinchman implied, something like the CCRA might be resurrected.[101] AT&T, even though outraged by the decision, instead used marked restraint in forming a response. It neither deaveraged rates suddenly nor, in contrast with its behavior in 1976, threatened to deaverage in the near future. Bell supported the MTS-WATS market structure inquiry, urging that the long distance monopoly be restored. At the same time it pressed forward with FCC-sponsored negotiations to set access charges for the competitors' use of the local network. AT&T thus indicated its presumption that long distance service competition was probably permanent.

As AT&T sought mainly to remove restraints on its own conduct, it began abandoning efforts to preserve monopoly. Testifying before the Senate in 1979, Brown capitulated on terminal equipment competition, even granting that it might be possible to deregulate that market.[102] By early 1980, the company had thrown in the towel on competition. It suggested to the FCC that it drop the MTS-WATS inquiry and the pretense, as the company now saw it, that monopoly might be reestablished in the long distance market. Finally, three years after promoting a bill to virtually end competition, Bell agreed to support a House bill that allowed no restriction on the scope of competition; in exchange, AT&T was to gain access to important markets in data processing. Reported by the Commerce Committee in the waning days of the Ninety-sixth Congress, the bill was the first telecommunications measure approved in committee during five years of continuous effort.[103]

101. Remarks by Walter R. Hinchman, chief, Common Carrier Bureau, before the International Communications Association, Las Vegas, Nevada, May 15, 1978; and Hinchman interview.

102. *Amendments to the Communications Act of 1934,* Hearings, pt. 1, p. 215.

103. Because the bill, H.R. 6121, had implications for antitrust policy, it was then referred sequentially to the Judiciary Committee, which reported it adversely. With no counterpart nearing passage in the Senate, it was allowed to die without being debated on the House floor.

After AT&T had given up the cause of monopoly, the issue of the scope of competition in telecommunications ceased to exist. Neither the independents nor the CWA defended ground that had been abandoned by AT&T. In Congress and the executive branch, a set of principles for telecommunications policy far more procompetitive than anyone advocated a few years earlier were taken as given. The Bell system would face competition in every part of its business that competitors chose to enter—that is, all of its business with the possible exception of local telephone services—and the competitors, lacking any significant market power, would be deregulated. AT&T, in turn, would receive clear title to offer services involving data processing, and almost any other services; and where it faced adequate competition, Bell too would be deregulated except for some constraints designed to ensure that it competed fairly. The consensus contemplated exceptions to the policy of free entry only in certain peripheral lines of business, such as burglar alarm systems and classified advertising, where incumbents claimed special vulnerability if AT&T was allowed to enter. The new principles were not enacted into law immediately, or even soon. But they shaped all subsequent legislative proposals and guided administrative policy and the behavior of the industry. The consensus on these principles represented a policy change of the first importance.

The Issue of AT&T's Structure

The end of conflict on the scope of competition was not the end of conflict on telecommunications, because other questions remained in dispute. Several issues were sharply contested, among them charges to competing common carriers for access to AT&T's network; measures to moderate the increases in rural and residential rates that were expected now that long distance service would be fully competitive; and the extent of deregulation for AT&T, which dominated many markets where it was no longer a monopoly. The most difficult issue, though, and the one most responsible for frustrating legislative efforts from 1979 to 1982, concerned the methods for preventing anticompetitive behavior by AT&T—in particular, whether and how this was to be accomplished by structural means.

A brief sketch of this lengthy, complicated dispute will suffice to show why it proved so difficult to resolve, and yet why here also AT&T eventually surrendered. The issue of AT&T's structure contrasted substantively, and hence politically, with other issues of procompetitive reform; in the long run, however, developments outside Congress produced a similar outcome.

The structure of AT&T was controversial not primarily because of its size, but because it operated in both competitive and monopoly markets and because it owned most of the local telephone networks, which were needed by AT&T's competitors to provide their services. So constituted, many believed, AT&T was an intrinsic threat to competition. To create an advantage for its own services, Bell could interfere with competitors' use of the local networks—withholding technical information, for example, or providing inferior service. To gain a price advantage, Bell could cross-subsidize its competitive services by allocating costs in a biased manner.[104] By 1981, in a number of private antitrust suits, plaintiffs such as MCI, Litton, and others had accused AT&T of using these and other anticompetitive tactics, and courts had agreed.

DEADLOCK IN CONGRESS. As Congress began considering procompetitive legislation in 1978, there was no important disagreement about whether to try to prevent anticompetitive actions by AT&T, but much disagreement about how to do so. AT&T's competitors, for the most part, demanded that the company be forced to divest its operations that served competitive markets, removing the financial incentive to discriminate in their favor. Denying that it had ever competed unfairly, AT&T claimed sufficient protection was possible without structural change through accounting improvements and regulatory controls. Rejecting the two extremes, congressional leaders were inclined to compromise with a limited reform in which AT&T would create a special subsidiary for competitive operations—to be kept separate, financially and in other ways, from the monopoly business. This "fully separated subsidiary," proposed in numerous versions, was intended to bring the relationship between AT&T's competitive and monopoly activities into the open and thus make it easier to control. But the compromise was immediately satisfactory to neither AT&T nor the competitors.

The issue peculiarly resisted resolution largely because the debate was

104. For statements of this concern, see *Telecommunications Act of 1980,* Hearings before the Subcommittee on Monopolies and Commercial Law of the House Committee on the Judiciary, 96 Cong. 2 sess. (GPO, 1980), especially pp. 379–427, 554–87. See also Donald E. Ward, "The Case for Structural Reform of the Bell System as a Means of Eliminating Anti-Competitive Incentives," prepared for the Ad Hoc Committee for Competitive Telecommunications, September 1977.

peculiarly ambiguous. The question of AT&T's appropriate structure, unlike many other issues of procompetitive reform, had no clear answer in economic analysis: economists could predict neither the degree to which proposed measures (short of divestiture) actually would prevent anticompetitive behavior, nor the degree to which (as Bell warned) structural reforms would undermine the company's efficiency. The NTIA requested proposals, but could find no consultant with expertise to help design a separate subsidiary for the purpose at hand.[105]

Even the prescription to promote competition failed to provide definite guidance. To some, the danger was that AT&T would destroy competition by exploiting its position, while to others it was that AT&T's competitors were seeking to hamper a major rival. Experts who were independent of the interested parties exhibited a confusing array of opinions on the issue. According to subcommittee chairman Van Deerlin, who was annoyed by the resulting lack of help, the experts were "all over the lot" on the structural issue.[106]

These ambiguities gave rise to partisan and ideological conflict in Congress and divided the committee leaders. Democrats, who tended to dislike big business but not necessarily big government, generally supported more ambitious structural reforms; Republicans, with the opposite attitudes, argued against them. In the Senate Commerce Committee, two senior Democrats, Cannon and Hollings, advocated strong structural reforms, and three Republicans, Barry Goldwater, Harrison Schmitt, and Bob Packwood, put forth weaker ones. In the House, the partisan alignments were roughly similar, although the committee leaders often managed to agree on compromise measures. Added to the powerful resistance to strong measures by AT&T, these conflicts produced a deadlock in Congress on the structural issue lasting from 1978 until 1982, by which time the issue was moot.

COMPROMISE IN THE FCC. Administrative decisions, in this instance, did not help to resolve the issue. Having essentially the same conflicts, the FCC was able to act on AT&T's structure before Congress did so only by acting in a highly compromised, tentative manner. The commission addressed AT&T's structure as part of its May 1980 ruling in *Second*

105. Note the radically conflicting opinions of academic experts testifying in *U.S.* v. *AT&T* in *Telecommunications Reports,* November 9, 1981. See also Brock, *The Telecommunications Industry,* chap. 10, which views divestiture as excessively radical; and Deutsch interview.

106. Interview, Lionel Van Deerlin, November 27, 1980.

Computer Inquiry (Computer II), the historic decision deregulating "enhanced" services (those involving data processing) and terminal equipment. Following the advice of the commission staff, Chairman Charles Ferris wanted to order a sharp separation between AT&T's competitive and monopoly activities to reduce the risks of deregulation; but, resisted by other commissioners more responsive to Bell's objections, he could not assemble a majority to do so. In order to act, Ferris settled for what he could get. The commission ordered a version of the separate-subsidiary requirement that was weaker than those being considered in Congress—indeed, being negotiated there with AT&T. Even so, in both dissenting and concurring opinions, several commissioners criticized the requirement as too severe, and the chairman, holding together a fragile majority, promised to reopen the issue if it proved unduly burdensome for AT&T to set up the subsidiary as ordered.[107]

The FCC's structural ruling in the Computer II case neither was taken as definitive nor eased the way for action by Congress, which was just as deadlocked after the decision as it had been before.[108] As the Ninety-sixth Congress neared an end, Cannon and Hollings refused to begin committee action because AT&T would not agree to a bill that required a separate subsidiary and preserved FCC authority to order further structural reforms. In the House, the Commerce Committee approved a milder bill, supported by AT&T and attacked by its competitors, but the more liberal and antitrust-oriented Judiciary Committee obtained sequential referral of the bill and managed to kill it. Under Republican control in the next Congress, the Senate passed an essentially similar bill, sponsored by Bob Packwood, that was again acceptable to AT&T, but this time the House was more demanding. Timothy Wirth, who had assumed the chairmanship of the House subcommittee, criticized the Packwood bill as lax and, with the Senate, AT&T, and President Reagan arrayed against him, chose to undertake an elaborate staff study and hold more hearings before proceeding. Thus early in 1982 the structural issue in Congress stood quite favorably for AT&T. It was nevertheless then that AT&T, ending years of fervent resistance, agreed to divest.

THE ANTITRUST SETTLEMENT. Rather than legislative or administrative action, AT&T was driven to retreat on the structural issue by the Justice

107. 77 FCC 2d 384–522 (1980). Interview, Charles Ferris, July 28, 1981; and interview, anonymous FCC staff official, December 12, 1980.

108. Interview, Bernard Wunder, House Communications Subcommittee, majority staff, December 10, 1980.

Department's antitrust suit, *U.S.* v. *AT&T,* and the manner in which it was developing in federal court. A massive and controversial venture for Justice, the AT&T case often seemed destined to end in failure. Although plaintiffs had made similar allegations successfully in private suits, there was doubt that the staff of the Antitrust Division, weakened by turnover and outnumbered by AT&T's army of lawyers, could effectively prosecute the case. Granting that it could, there was even more doubt that a district court judge would take it upon himself, as the department asked, to dismember an enormously complicated and vital enterprise like AT&T.[109] The Carter administration was uncertain and internally divided on the case's importance. In 1980 it supported the House bill, with its relatively weak structural provisions, and overruled Justice's objection that the case would be hurt by the bill's enactment. After Carter's defeat in the election, the department offered to settle with AT&T on easy terms, requiring only a token divestiture, which a confident Bell declined to accept. The Reagan administration, hardly disposed by ideology to break up large corporations, was even less committed to the suit and debated a recommendation by the Commerce Department that it be dropped.

The case's fortunes rose sharply in late 1981, however, and with them the danger it posed for AT&T. In cabinet-level meetings Reagan's assistant attorney general for antitrust, William Baxter, a conservative professor of antitrust law also trained in economics, argued against dropping the case and won at least a temporary reprieve. In the trial itself, a clear trend emerged favoring the government. When Justice rested its case, AT&T petitioned for dismissal. In denying the petition, Judge Harold Greene issued an opinion so detailed and emphatic that, before Bell's defense was even presented, it strongly suggested a final verdict: "The testimony and the documentary evidence adduced by the government demonstrated that the Bell System has violated the antitrust laws in a number of ways over a lengthy period of time."[110] In questioning witnesses about the proposed structural remedy, Greene showed open skepticism toward Bell's objections and no apparent reluctance to order divestiture.

Addressing his board of directors in December 1981, AT&T's Brown was able to give several reasons for accepting a settlement he had negoti-

---

109. Wunder interview; Deutsch interview; interview, Rick Neustadt, January 11, 1981.
110. *United States* v. *American Telephone and Telegraph Co.,* 524 F. Supp. 1336, 1381 (D.D.C. 1981).

ated with Baxter.[111] Although Bell probably could defeat drastic structural reform in Congress, it had become obvious that without such reform any feasible bill would impose other burdensome constraints. Perhaps, as Baxter had urged in offering the settlement, divestiture would be the simpler, more workable solution for the company. Moreover, Justice had agreed to drop the restrictive provisions of the 1956 consent decree; though Congress also was preparing to drop them, the settlement would bypass the uncertainties of the legislative process. Finally, in the privacy of the boardroom, Brown may have predicted that, if it did not settle, AT&T probably would lose the case, with results that could be significantly worse. Above all, Bell worried that Judge Greene might order a vertical divestiture—splitting off the research, development, and manufacturing arms (Bell Laboratories and Western Electric)—which the company felt would leave it incapable of competing against vertically integrated companies like Xerox and IBM.[112]

In January 1982, with the board's approval, AT&T and the government jointly announced they had reached a settlement in the eight-year-old case and that, as part of it, Bell would divest the twenty-two local operating companies, representing about half its total assets. One of the largest corporate divestitures in history, this would sever the local monopolies from the competitive parts of the business. It was what most of Bell's competitors and their strongest supporters in Congress had wanted from the beginning, but few expected ever to occur.

While resolving one difficult issue, the settlement also raised others and thus opened a new phase of congressional debate.[113] But it was a debate in which the fundamental questions had already been answered, largely through concessions by Bell: competition, much of it deregulated, would extend throughout the industry and would be protected by the most decisive structural reforms from unfair competition by AT&T. Nevertheless, by conducting political affairs in a rational, disciplined manner with Brown as chairman, AT&T by no means had suffered unqualified defeat. It gained access to the key markets involving data processing; kept its research, development, and manufacturing subsidiaries; and to a considerable degree was deregulated itself.

Also concluded with the settlement was the era, almost a century long,

111. On the board meeting, see *New York Times,* January 11, 1982.

112. Von Auw interview; and "Behind AT&T's Change at the Top."

113. Michael Wines, "Divorce, American Style—Breaking Up AT&T Could Trigger a Battle Royal," *National Journal,* vol. 14 (January 30, 1982), pp. 189–93.

in which a single firm was the dominant political force in the telecommunications industry. As late as the end of 1981, it still had been taken for granted that Congress could pass no significant telecommunications bill without Bell's imprimatur. The announcement of the settlement cast doubt on AT&T's ability to speak for the local companies, the principal source of its political power; and its diminished political stature was soon apparent. The Wirth subcommittee drafted a new bill intended to strengthen the local companies after the breakup and, despite Bell's violent opposition, unanimously approved it. No longer able to command sufficient votes to prevent passage, Bell relied instead on delaying tactics by a few supporters in the full committee. As the session drew to a close Wirth abandoned the bill, but Judge Greene, threatening to resume the antitrust trial, got AT&T to agree to incorporating some of its provisions in the settlement with the Department of Justice.[114]

Conclusion

In airlines, trucking, and telecommunications, Congress thus gave approval to strong and even radical procompetitive policies. In part, as discussed in chapter 4, this approval reflected the ability of the reform forces in Congress to defeat intense opposition by the regulated industries. But, as shown in this chapter, it also reflected the narrowing or ending of that opposition—the reformers' ability, in the end, to obtain the industries' consent.

The behavior of the industries was at variance in some respects with prevailing notions of how major economic groups participate in policymaking. As a rule, such groups are presumed to act with coordination, skill, and firm resolve on behalf of their interests—failing to do so only when, as occasionally occurs, fundamental conflicts of interest divide them.[115] The industries in our cases, with a few exceptions (most notably United Airlines), did not change their minds about the merits of reform, and differences within them were marginal compared with the interests

114. *Congressional Quarterly Almanac,* vol. 38 (1982), pp. 331–32.

115. Under such circumstances, of course, organizational difficulties are to be expected. See Raymond H. Bauer, Ithiel de Sola Pool, and Lewis Anthony Dexter, *American Business and Public Policy* (Atherton Press, 1963), which also shows that business firms can fail to notice an issue affecting their interests—a phenomenon wholly absent from our cases.

they had in common. Nevertheless, their resistance was ineffective and tended to deteriorate. Considered broadly, the sources of this weakness suggest reasons—although certainly not the only ones—why organized groups may at times be less able to obstruct policy change than the magnitude of their political resources would lead one to expect.

In the first place, political institutions that were fragmented and decentralized proved a mixed blessing, at best, to opponents of change. This was so, despite their presumed advantages for such groups, because parts of these institutions could act independently. Before new legislation was enacted, procompetitive decisions by the commissions and sometimes the courts made unyielding opposition not just ineffective, but impossible. These decisions tended to vitiate the regulatory regimes as bulwarks of protection from competition, even while regulatory forms and procedures remained in effect. The existing statutory provisions, drained of much of their value to the industries, were less urgent for them to defend. The industries' distress was exacerbated by the administrative and judicial mode of policy change. As adopted by commissions and courts, policy change came in fits and starts, with no predictable schedule or end point. It thus caused uncertainty that was hard to bear for executives of regulated firms; perhaps as much as they wanted opportunity for profit in the long run, they wanted to know how to run their firms in the short run. As the uncoordinated result of separate cases in separate forums, such policy change also contained no careful balancing of interests or equities, but rather imposed burdens on particular firms and industry segments almost randomly. Most important, policy change by the commissions and the courts, instead of subsiding, accelerated. This implied that the industries could win reliable limitations on the scope or pace of reform, if at all, only by consenting to legislation.

Although the importance of these considerations varied among the industries and over time, their combined effect was powerful in each, and sooner or later substantially vitiated each industry's ability to resist. In the circumstances, passage of a reform bill became desirable for them even if its terms were to be only mildly favorable—if the bill corrected inequities of piecemeal change, had some moderating effect on the reform process, or at least brought policy change to a conclusion. Because of the political strength of the reform forces in Congress, it was in fact only such mildly favorable terms that could be obtained. In the end, all three industries made drastic concessions to procompetitive reform, and as a result a large amount of such reform became noncontroversial in Congress.

Besides this pronounced strategic disadvantage, the industries encountered difficulties of political organization and decisionmaking and in two cases they failed to devise and implement appropriate action.[116] In part because they were on the defensive and under stress, the industries faced three internal obstacles to the conduct of a coherent and well-adapted political effort.

Even as they were threatened with the loss of cherished prerogatives of long standing, the industries had to set themselves feasible goals and refrain from overly ambitious or aggressive action. Ironically, this was difficult for them partly because their arguments in defense of anticompetitive regulation were mainly sincere, based on genuine, even if self-serving, beliefs about the public interest. Because they were convinced themselves, industry executives expected others also to be convinced of the need for regulation once the reasons were explained, and they often overestimated the prospects for building support. Each industry had an important, sometimes dominant group that demanded an unyielding stand against reform. Each industry also had advice from political specialists who worked in trade associations, in Washington law firms kept on retainer, or in corporate governmental affairs offices located there. These political specialists generally had a realistic view of the situation. What they did not have, at times, was a powerful role in making the industries' political decisions.

Another problem was that an industry easily could lack unity and coordination in political effort. This was a danger because even with realistic assessments, decisions on political strategy were sufficiently ambiguous that conflict over them could rise from even marginal differences of interest or priority. One could not say with certainty, for example, whether the passage of a reform bill had become inevitable or whether endorsing a moderate proposal would limit the severity of the resulting bill. Those firms or segments that felt they had relatively more to gain or less to lose by reform concluded more readily that compromise was needed, while others, more fearful of reform, disagreed with that judgment and sometimes distrusted the motives behind it. Separate firms or segments of industries were inclined to insist on their own views of political strategy—even if doing so imperiled the effectiveness of the whole industry.

116. On the difficulties of organizations as they are preoccupied with maintaining themselves, see Wilson, *Political Organizations,* chap. 15.

Finally, as some airlines demonstrated, there was a danger that parts of an industry—contemplating the time-consuming and expensive task of lobbying and the costs of alienating political leaders—would opt out of the industry's effort. The executives might stay home and run their businesses, which, though one response to a discouraging situation in Congress, was not likely to improve it.

In dealing with the internal hazards, two very different forms of political organization exhibited weaknesses. The most vulnerable condition was that of the airlines—an industry consisting of several large and medium-sized firms, each with a capacity of its own for political action. In an industry so structured, firms are likely to become victims of their own independence. The airlines supported a well-staffed, politically active trade association, but because each firm had its own views and the ability to express them, the association was permitted to take positions and serve as spokesman for the industry only in cases of unanimous agreement. It is just when such an industry confronts a serious political threat, with differences emerging over strategy, that the trade association is likely to be paralyzed and the separate firms, lacking a mechanism to resolve differences, are unable to concert efforts.

Also prone to failure, for very different reasons, was the centralized political organization of the traditional telephone industry, consisting of an overwhelmingly dominant AT&T and the independent telephone companies. The political performance of such an industry depends on the capacities and behavior of the dominant firm—a condition not in itself disabling, but very clearly unreliable.

In such an industry, the hierarchical organization of the dominant firm guarantees a high degree of coordination, even if the firm is, like AT&T, exceedingly large. But neither that firm's leadership nor its principal structures for decisionmaking will generally have been selected for political tasks, to which they may be poorly adapted; and the firm's political specialists, as persons of lower corporate rank located in Washington, may have limited influence in political decisions. Much depends in such a case on the kind of leadership the company happens to have, especially its chief executive, and the political methods he adopts. Under one chairman in the mid-1970s, AT&T demonstrated the risks of insulated, politically unsophisticated leadership, adopting such an extreme anticompetitive program and using such aggressive methods that it created a backlash and lost any remaining chance to establish lasting boundaries to competition. Later, with a new chairman, and after learning a lesson from political defeat, AT&T adopted a sensitive and realistic approach that for the first time made a genuine political advantage of centralization. Bell used this improved political capacity with substantial success to secure its own freedom to compete.

The only consistently effective mode of political organization was based, paradoxically, on the most fragmented economic organization. One might have expected the trucking industry—with over 16,000 regulated firms, differing widely in size, economic characteristics, and type of service—to be incapable of coherent political action.[117] In fact, this fragmentation did not prevent the development of a large, well-financed national organization, the American Trucking Association, but only enhanced that organization's political effectiveness. Unlike the airline association, the ATA could act with far less than the unanimous agreement of its members or executive committee, and its actions were virtually immune to challenge within the industry. Unlike AT&T, the ATA was an organization with a largely political mission, led by political specialists, and located in Washington. The trucking industry alone, among the three industries, acted with unity in a firm yet calculating manner to oppose reform; and it alone secured legislative provisions that in any significant way limited deregulation and competition.

117. Compare Olson, *The Logic of Collective Action,* which argues that unconcentrated industries are at a disadvantage in political organization.

CHAPTER SIX

The Limits of Deregulation

IN THE preceding chapters we sought to lay a basis for generalizing about deregulation by examining in depth three cases that promised to be especially revealing because, as we argue, they are "hard" and "clear." In this chapter, we seek to lay the basis for refining and elaborating generalizations, and judging their scope of application, by briefly examining some cases that are plainly contrasting. In these cases, presidents sought to reduce regulation but achieved much less than in our three cases; or they conspicuously failed even to endorse reduction, despite the pleas of economic advisers.

For simplicity's sake and because they are not at all comparable with our cases, we do not discuss regulations that are addressed to other governments in the federal system, although they have been encompassed in recent attempts at reducing regulation. For example, the Reagan administration sought to reduce the regulations governing transportation of the handicapped by municipal transit systems and those imposed on school districts to govern education of handicapped children. Concerned only with regulations imposed on private activity, we have chosen five cases that are like ours in that analytic advocates of regulatory reform concentrated on them and managed to achieve some degree of concentration by presidential staffs and one or more presidents as well, even if the presidents did not always become advocates of reform. The five are natural gas pricing, air pollution control, wages paid on federally supported construction projects, milk marketing, and ocean shipping. Our aim is to account for the lesser success of the reform movement in them compared with our three.

We approach this exploration of the limits of deregulation with an expectation that they will vary with the party composition of the government. Given the intense commitment to deregulation associated with the conservative Republican administration of Ronald Reagan, the inclusive sweep of its deregulatory goals, which encompassed the new regimes of health, safety, and environmental regulation, and the election results of 1980, which produced a Republican Senate, one would have predicted extensive gains for deregulation beginning in 1981. There turns out to be some validity to this, yet the difference in deregulatory outcomes before and after the 1980 election is not as plain as one might suppose. To discern where the limits of deregulation have lain and why, it is best to look at particular cases. For the most part we will defer drawing conclusions from them until, in chapter 7, we can juxtapose the additional data they supply with data from the three cases that have been central to our analysis.

Natural Gas Pricing

The Natural Gas Act of 1938 charged the Federal Power Commission with securing "just and reasonable" prices of natural gas. Under this law and a crucial interpretation of it rendered by the Supreme Court in 1954, the commission has regulated firms that produce natural gas for sale in interstate commerce and those that transport it for resale in interstate commerce. Economists attacked this example of price regulation much as they had attacked others, but with particular volume and vehemence as the energy crisis of the mid-1970s deepened, for the critics believed that regulation was to blame for a shortage of natural gas.[1]

In response to presidential proposals, deregulation of the price of natural gas was debated in the mid- and late 1970s, roughly coinciding with the debate over airline deregulation, but with a far more equivocal outcome. Results were embodied in the Natural Gas Policy Act of 1978, passed on October 15, the same day as the Airline Deregulation Act, after an exceptionally prolonged and tortuous path through Congress that was marked by a filibuster in the Senate and conference deadlock of many

1. Stephen G. Breyer and Paul W. MacAvoy, *Energy Regulation by the Federal Power Commission* (Brookings, 1974); Robert B. Helms, *Natural Gas Regulation: An Evaluation of FPC Price Controls* (American Enterprise Institute for Public Policy Research, 1974); Patricia E. Starratt, *The Natural Gas Shortage and the Congress* (American Enterprise Institute for Public Policy Research, 1974); and Paul W. MacAvoy and Robert S. Pindyck, *Price Controls and the Natural Gas Shortage* (American Enterprise Institute for Public Policy Research, 1975).

months. Given this history, it is no surprise that what came out was a byzantine compromise, an almost incomprehensible mix of regulatory and deregulatory measures. Prices were indeed to be deregulated, but with several years' delay and so many qualifications that it was impossible to say what side had won. The new law brought the intrastate markets in natural gas under federal controls for the first time; created no fewer than seventeen categories of gas, each with its own pricing and regulatory specifications; and stipulated a complex pricing plan that was designed to protect residential consumers from the brunt of higher prices by shifting a disproportionate share of the costs onto industrial users.

One major reason that officeholders found it hard to agree on deregulation was that expert analysts could not agree on what the consequences would be. The central problem was defined as a shortage of natural gas, part of a more general shortage of domestic energy supplies, and the central aim of policy measures was to increase supply. Some analysts argued that to remove price controls would give producers the necessary incentive to develop new sources of supply and increase production, whereas others, pointing out that repeated price increases granted by the Federal Power Commission between 1967 and 1976 had not had the desired effect on production, doubted that further measures would be any more effective. Over the years, the results of econometric simulations of natural gas production under alternative pricing scenarios had often proven unreliable, with the result that congressmen "began to lose appetite for this sort of rational analysis."[2]

Related to the uncertainty among experts over the probable results were sharply differing perceptions among the contestants about the underlying structure of the industry. Those who believed the industry to be basically competitive also believed that increases in supply would follow from higher prices. Others believed that a free market in energy was unattainable, that shortages were contrived by the industry, that prices for years had been higher than they needed to have been, and that the only result of decontrol would be bigger profits.[3] Even assuming perfect competition among domestic gas producers, such persons argued, market

2. Pietro S. Nivola, "Energy Policy and the Congress: The Politics of the Natural Gas Policy Act of 1978," *Public Policy,* vol. 28 (Fall 1980), pp. 531–32. Our account of natural gas pricing policy relies heavily on this source.

3. Neil de Marchi, "The Ford Administration: Energy as a Political Good," in Craufurd D. Goodwin, ed., *Energy Policy in Perspective: Today's Problems, Yesterday's Solutions* (Brookings, 1981), p. 477.

forces were not freely determining the price of energy supplies because an international cartel, the Organization of Petroleum Exporting Countries (OPEC), was seeking to control the price of world crude oil.

Deeply at odds over the likely effects of decontrol on supply and profits, the contestants nonetheless agreed that, at least in the short run, decontrol would mean higher prices. The principal effect of regulation of the natural gas industry had been to restrain maximum prices; government had never overtly restricted competition by controlling or sanctioning control of the minimum price, as in the transportation industries. Appraisals of the magnitude of the prospective price increase were extremely divergent. Partisans of decontrol adduced reasons why the price increases would not be sudden, severe, and unsupportable, and added that higher energy prices were inevitable anyway. Opponents anticipated both a sharp rise in retail prices and unequal distribution of the burden among social classes. Consumer groups were implacably opposed to decontrol.

Within Congress, natural gas deregulation produced an unusually sharp partisan cleavage, closely correlated with liberal-conservative ideologies. The limited credibility of academic analysis contributed to this result, but so did the public credence given to the notion that energy shortages were contrived by the industry. The corporate giants of the petroleum and gas industry elicited the suspicion of bigness latent in the general public and were natural targets of the neopopulist hostility to business that characterized the consumer movement. Under these circumstances, liberal Democrats in Congress fought deregulation as hard as they could.

The partisan cleavage was evident in congressional votes on natural gas throughout the 1970s.[4] The Republican presidents of the 1970s, Nixon and Ford, favored decontrol, as did their party in Congress almost to the point of unanimity, but the opposition of Democrats in Congress thwarted it.[5] Although Jimmy Carter as a presidential candidate endorsed deregulation (for example, in a letter to the governors of Oklahoma, Texas, and Louisiana several weeks before the election), as the head of a Democratic administration he backed away from it and submitted to

4. Nivola shows that whereas party affiliation was a powerful predictor of votes on natural gas deregulation after 1970, it was a poor one in the 1950s, but he offers no explanation for the change. Nivola, "Energy Policy and the Congress," pp. 541–43.

5. See A. James Reichley, *Conservatives in an Age of Change: The Nixon and Ford Administrations* (Brookings, 1981), chap. 17, especially pp. 371–73.

Congress a plan that, though it allowed natural gas prices to rise, called for a firm statutory ceiling on them and extended federal controls to intrastate markets. It was the Carter proposal that Congress debated with such difficulty in 1977–78. Except for sharp divisions among Democrats in the Senate, the administration's plan would have prevailed; it did so in the House, where the Democratic majority held firm in support of it.[6]

Not party, but ideology (as measured by "liberal quotients" compiled by the Americans for Democratic Action), was the most powerful predictor of votes on deregulation. Congressmen with liberal voting records consistently rejected decontrol; those with more conservative records consistently backed it. One scholar argues that it was this deep division on principle that made the 1978 bill so difficult for Congress to act on.[7]

Because natural gas politics were much affected by the special complexities introduced by the energy crisis of the mid-1970s, which exposed domestic policymaking to international influences and made supply and national self-sufficiency the central problems for policy resolution, one hesitates to assert general propositions about "the politics of deregulation" on the basis of this case or to offer any simple explanation for the relative failure of natural gas deregulation. Yet this much seems clear: when the result of deregulation was expected to be an increase in consumer prices, a large part of the Democratic party declined to support it. For liberal Democrats to support deregulation of maximum prices, it was crucial both that the structure of the affected industry be judged competitive and that such competition be judged likely, in the event of deregulation, to moderate prices. Having a relatively weak preference for free markets and having much greater skepticism about the likelihood of their actually being attained in the real world, liberals in Congress, most of whom were Democrats, were unwilling to expose consumers to the risks of the attempt in this case. They preferred shortages, if necessary, to a sharp increase in prices as a rationing device. Thus the bipartisan coalition of conservatives and liberals that formed to support deregulation of the transportation industries (and the deregulation of telecommunica-

6. In addition to Nivola, "Energy Policy and the Congress," see David Howard Davis, "Pluralism and Energy: Carter's National Energy Plan," in Robert Lawrence, ed., *New Dimensions to Energy Policy* (Lexington Books, 1979), pp. 194–95; and Jimmy Carter, *Keeping Faith: Memoirs of a President* (Bantam Books, 1982), pp. 91–103. M. Elizabeth Sanders offers an interpretation of natural gas politics that contrasts with Nivola's, emphasizing a regional clash of economic interests (producers versus consumers) rather than party or ideology. See *The Regulation of Natural Gas* (Temple University Press, 1981).

7. Nivola, "Energy Policy and the Congress," p. 543.

tions, insofar as the telecommunications industry was seen to be competitive) did not form in support of natural gas deregulation. Liberals remained emphatically on the opposite side.

Air Pollution

In the wave of health and safety regulation newly authorized by Congress in the 1960s and 1970s—often loosely called "social" regulation to distinguish it from the "economic" regulation that accumulated earlier— by far the most costly both to governments and businesses was that designed to control air and water pollution. A survey of forty-eight companies released by the Business Roundtable in March 1979 found that 77 percent of the costs of the six regulatory programs selected for study stemmed from environmental rules.[8] "If anything can be predicted in the new administration," the *National Journal* reported as Reagan took office, "it is an effort to trim the powers of the Environmental Protection Agency (EPA) and other environmental regulators."[9]

The need to cut back on environmental regulation had been one of the president's campaign themes. He had called for returning the primary responsibility for environmental regulation to the states. "They've got rules that would practically shut down the economy if they were put into effect," David Stockman remarked of the EPA soon after the election. As director-designate of the Office of Management and Budget, Stockman wrote an apocalyptic memorandum warning that the recent buildup of industrial regulation would "sweep through the industrial economy with near gale force, pre-empting multi-billions in investment capital, driving up operating costs and siphoning off management and technical personnel in an incredible morass of new controls and compliance procedures." But incoming officials believed that with sufficient resolve and the backing of a Republican Senate, the new administration could achieve impor-

8. Timothy B. Clark, "New Approaches to Regulatory Reform—Letting the Market Do the Job," *National Journal*, vol. 11 (August 11, 1979), p. 1317. The six agencies whose regulations were selected for study were the Environmental Protection Agency, Occupational Safety and Health Administration, Equal Employment Opportunity Commission, Department of Energy, Federal Trade Commission, and the administrators of the Employee Retirement Income Security Act, for which the Department of Labor and Internal Revenue Service share responsibility.

9. Lawrence Mosher, "Reagan and Environmental Protection—None of the Laws Will Be Untouchable," *National Journal*, vol. 13 (January 3, 1981), p. 17.

tant legislative reforms.[10] The Clean Air Act was the leading target, not just because it was very costly in the aggregate and very burdensome to particular major industries that were in serious trouble (steel and autos), but also because it was due to be renewed in 1981 and because it prohibited the EPA from considering costs in setting national ambient air quality standards. This law epitomized for the economically oriented the irrationality and extremism of much of the new social regulation.

No important legislative reforms occurred, however, and none were proposed by the administration. Rather than submit legislation, in the summer of 1981 the president sent Congress a set of eleven broadly worded principles to guide legislation. Their tone was much more moderate than what had been anticipated from the administration and had in fact been leaked in an early draft. Perceiving that there was not enough support for a major reduction of air pollution regulation, the administration chose not to risk a public defeat on the issue—a "shrewd political move," according to Robert T. Stafford, Republican of Vermont, chairman of the Senate Committee on Environment and Public Works.[11] The lack of support was in fact remarkably pervasive, embracing different strata of the population and both political parties.

Critical though many were of air pollution regulation, expert analysts nonetheless had not mounted against it the kind of fundamental assault that they had brought to bear on controls of price, entry, and exit in multifirm markets. One after another, analyses of these regulatory regimes yielded findings that were unusually stark and sweeping: there was no justification for regulation, and no public benefits were realized from it. The policy recommendation was correspondingly extreme and unambiguous: regulation should be eliminated. By contrast, expert critiques of air pollution regulation accepted the underlying rationale for it—to take account of externalities—but argued that costs were not sufficiently being taken into account or that benefits had not been shown to justify the costs. Arguments revolved around the rationale and procedures for standard setting, the quality of scientific evidence used, the logic with which it was applied, and marginal differences in allowable amounts of particular pollutants. The issue was not whether to deregulate; it was how, and how extensively, to regulate. Prescriptions for reform resulted in a stream of presidential contrivances for achieving better analysis and review.

10. "1-Year Moratorium Recommended on New Regulations," *Washington Post*, November 9, 1980; and "The New OMB Director's Gloomy Memo on the Economy," *National Journal*, vol. 12 (December 20, 1980), p. 2188.

11. *Congressional Quarterly Almanac*, vol. 37 (1981), p. 507.

If expert analysts failed to support deregulation, so did the public, with even greater visibility. The passage of air pollution control legislation in 1970 owed a great deal to a surge of public opinion in support of clean air, and a decade later pollsters reported that the country had not changed its collective mind on this question. The CBS News–*New York Times* poll in the fall of 1981 found that nearly two-thirds of adult Americans wanted to keep clean air laws "as tough as they are now" even if "some factories might have to close."[12] A Harris poll at about the same time found that 51 percent of respondents wanted to leave the Clean Air Act unchanged, 29 percent wanted it to be stricter, and only 17 percent wanted to relax it. No important subgroup favored relaxation, not even conservatives or voters for Reagan. Questions on environmental issues elicited no important differences among age, income, occupation, or partisan and ideological groups, except that people of low socioeconomic status were more likely than others to profess unfamiliarity with the issues.[13] Poll results, besides being exceptionally consistent among polls and among population subgroups, were exceptionally well publicized. Harris presented his findings to a House subcommittee in the fall of 1981 in terms that any layman could understand and any newspaper reporter would wish to quote: "Mess around with the Clean Air and Clean Water acts, and you are going to get into the deepest kind of trouble. The Republican Party is at a crossroads on this. . . . I am saying to you just as clear as can be, that clean air happens to be one of the sacred cows of the American people. . . . "[14]

Active, organized interests were arrayed on both sides of the issue, as one would expect, with environmentalists pitted against industry; yet "in-

12. Ibid., p. 512.

13. Everett Carll Ladd, "Clearing the Air: Public Opinion and Public Policy on the Environment," *Public Opinion,* vol. 5 (February–March 1982), pp. 16–20. For later data from a Harris poll, see "A Call for Tougher—Not Weaker—Antipollution Laws," *Business Week,* January 24, 1983, pp. 87–88.

14. *Congressional Quarterly Almanac,* vol. 37 (1981), p. 512. Nevertheless, poll data on public attitudes toward pollution were not without ambiguity. In a list of thirteen "concerns" surveyed in Roper polls, pollution of air and water consistently ranked at or near the bottom between 1974 and 1982. As of January 1982, it was tied with alcoholism for last place. *Public Opinion,* vol. 5 (February–March 1982), p. 33. This suggests that the public was not really very passionate about pollution control, but the evidence that it was quite united in support of control, to the extent that it held an opinion, is persuasive. Politicians apparently were impressed by the poll results. Senator Stafford called the Harris poll of the fall of 1981 "the most extraordinary poll I've ever read." *Congressional Quarterly Almanac,* vol. 37 (1981), p. 512.

dustry" was not cohesive. An industry to supply pollution control equipment had sprung up with over $2 billion a year in sales, including associated costs in construction and instrumentation. Some firms had been quicker than others to comply with regulations and therefore had a stake in making sure that everyone else would be forced to comply too. While some business organizations were extremely critical of the regulatory regime, others sought to enter into a coalition for the purpose of securing moderate, pragmatic changes.[15] No one sought repeal—least of all the consumer movement, despite the costs to consumers from regulation-induced price increases, especially of automobiles, which were now freighted with pollution control devices. An ideological close cousin of the environmental movement, sharing with it sponsorship, leadership, goals, and adversaries in industry, the consumer movement was most strongly moved to protest the costs of regulation to consumers when government collaborated with business in imposing those costs. It was this collaboration in support of industry-serving ends, and not the higher prices per se, that made anticompetitive regulation outrageous to the neo-populists in the consumer movement.

Observing this array of forces—disinterested critics whose criticism focused on technical and procedural issues, a public overwhelmingly favorable to pollution control, an environmental movement not yet spent, and a business community in less than unanimous opposition—Republicans in Congress did not rush to support the Reagan administration in an attempt at relaxing controls. Nor had Republicans in Congress stood for weak controls in the past. In sharp contrast with natural gas pricing, pollution control measures had not elicited a clear and consistent pattern of party differences. President Nixon had sponsored clean air legislation in 1970, and the two houses of Congress had passed it with only one dissenting vote between them. In 1977, when the act was renewed after prolonged and arduous deliberation, partisan differences appeared on some issues, but at least in the Senate Committee on Environment and Public Works pollution control remained very much a bipartisan cause.[16]

15. Lawrence Mosher, "Clean Air Act an Inviting Target for Industry Critics Next Year," *National Journal*, vol. 12 (November 15, 1980), pp. 1927–30; and "EPA's Drive to Loosen Some Rules Angers Firms That Have Complied," *Wall Street Journal*, September 23, 1982.

16. R. Shep Melnick, *Regulation and the Courts: The Case of the Clean Air Act* (Brookings, 1983), chap. 2; and Norman J. Ornstein and Shirley Elder, *Interest Groups, Lobbying and Policymaking* (CQ Press, 1978), chap. 6.

Had incoming administration officials acknowledged this fact after the election of 1980, they would have expected no particular help on this issue from the newly Republican Senate, where in fact they got none. The sixteen-member Senate committee, acting in bipartisan fashion with only one, two, or three Republicans dissenting, approved only minor changes in the Clean Air Act. There was more support for relaxing regulation in the House, though it was still under Democratic control. A bipartisan majority of the forty-two-member Energy and Commerce Committee prepared a bill that both the Reagan administration and the major industrial interests endorsed, though a large faction within the committee remained opposed. Led by the committee chairman, John D. Dingell of Michigan, the Democrats who favored major modifications of the act were mostly from the decaying industrial heartland of the Midwest, often from districts in which important elements of the automobile industry or its suppliers were located. The contending congressional factions were unable to agree on a bill.[17]

Unable to win regulatory relief from Congress and unwilling, as things turned out, even to invest political resources in the attempt, the Reagan administration was forced to pursue its goals through executive action. In so doing, it had the advantage, by comparison with its predecessor, of internal cohesion. The Carter administration's attempts to have professional inflation fighters in the president's office supervise regulation touched off a round of fights in 1978–79 between the White House and the executive agencies as well as oversight hearings by agency protectors in Congress and court suits brought by agency allies in organized labor and the environmental movement, all challenging the right of the president to intervene or the economic logic on which intervention was based.[18] James C. Miller III, the OMB official who initially headed the Reagan administration's attempts at economic oversight of rule making,

17. Lawrence Mosher, "Clean Air Supporters Are Outflanked by Sponsors of a 'Bipartisan' Bill," *National Journal,* vol. 14 (February 6, 1982), pp. 237–40; Robert M. Cohen, "Congress Likely to Ignore Reagan's Request for Clean Air Act Passage," *National Journal,* vol. 14 (November 27, 1982), pp. 2027–28; "Committee Completes Work on Clean Air Act Rewrite," *Congressional Quarterly Weekly Report,* vol. 41 (August 21, 1982), pp. 2066–67; "Reagan Goal of Easing Environmental Laws Is Largely Unattained," *Wall Street Journal,* February 18, 1983; and *Congressional Quarterly Almanac,* vol. 39 (1983), p. 339, and vol. 40 (1984), p. 339.

18. For example, see "Battle Intensifies over Authority of President to Control Agencies," *New York Times,* January 17, 1979; and Timothy B. Clark, "When the President Tries to Regulate," *National Journal,* vol. 10 (December 16, 1978), p. 2029.

told Congress that his task would be "hopelessly impossible" if he had to deal with Carter's regulatory appointees instead of Reagan's.[19]

Even with the advantages of internal cohesion, the Reagan administration, relying on executive powers alone, made limited and halting headway against the established body of environmental regulation. It refrained from promulgating some regulations that the Carter administration had prepared, and the rate at which new regulations were issued slowed down, but other branches delayed or thwarted substantive changes of major importance. When the EPA under Reagan sought to extend application of the "bubble" concept—an EPA scheme, instituted under Carter, that gave firms increased flexibility in managing factory emissions—the U.S. Court of Appeals of the District of Columbia found the change impermissible, although the Supreme Court subsequently overturned its decision.[20] The Senate Environment and Public Works Committee, proceeding with its markup of amendments to the Clean Air Act, not only failed to endorse changes the administration wanted, but approved by wide margins two amendments that were specifically designed to block pending EPA proposals to relax emission controls for trucks.[21]

To the extent that deregulation of pollution control occurred under Reagan, it resulted from the one kind of action that the executive could take unilaterally. Reductions in personnel and in levels of enforcement occurred in the EPA and other regulatory agencies throughout the federal executive branch.[22] For this, the administration did receive indirect con-

19. *Role of OMB in Regulation,* Hearings before the Subcommittee on Oversight and Investigations of the House Energy and Commerce Committee, 97 Cong. 1 sess. (Government Printing Office, 1981), p. 67. However, the EPA of the Carter years, under Douglas Costle, did not conspicuously resist the effort of Executive Office economists to enhance the rationality of regulation, but on the contrary developed a reputation for conceptual innovation and sophisticated analysis.

20. *Natural Resources Defense Council* v. *Gorsuch,* 685 F. 2d 718 (D.C. Cir., 1982); and *Chevron, U.S.A.* v. *Natural Resources Defense Council,* 44 *Supreme Court Bulletin* (Commerce Clearing House, 1984), p. B3841–43. Under the "bubble" concept, EPA applied emission limits to an entire plant rather than to each pollution source, such as a smokestack or vent, within it. Application of this concept meant that a reduction in pollution from one source within the plant could offset an increase from another source.

21. *Congressional Quarterly Almanac,* vol. 37 (1981), p. 509.

22. Lawrence Mosher, "Will EPA's Budget Cuts Make It More Efficient or Less Effective?" *National Journal,* vol. 13 (August 15, 1981), pp. 1466–69; Lawrence Mosher, "Move Over, Jim Watt, Anne Gorsuch Is the Latest Target of Environmentalists," *National Journal,* vol. 13 (October 24, 1981), pp. 1899–1902; and Lawrence Mosher, "Reagan's Environmental

gressional endorsement in the form of cuts in appropriations. Budget reductions, which the administration sought for their own sake, constituted a crude, backdoor approach to deregulation even when it could not be achieved directly.

The politics of deregulation with respect to health, safety, and the environment—the subjects of the post-1967 wave of new regulation— were entirely different from the politics of procompetitive deregulation. Even Reagan in his earliest statements drew a distinction. "We have no intention of dismantling the regulatory agencies," he told the nation within three weeks of taking office, "especially those necessary to protect [the] environment and to ensure the public health and safety."[23] No one advocated deregulation, if by that one means literally the abolition of regulatory regimes. Industry opponents asked for less exacting standards or delays in enforcement; disinterested critics asked for more rationality in regulatory decisions. But with respect to pollution control, even piecemeal relaxations and procedural reforms were resisted by the environmental movement and were subject to delay or defeat by the courts and a bipartisan majority in the Senate.

The cases of natural gas pricing and air pollution control, when juxtaposed with those that we have already analyzed in depth, suggest the following formulation: deregulation succeeded best with respect to regulatory regimes in which government agencies were allied with producers in such a way as to foster anticompetitive pricing and hence to inflate consumers' costs. It was only this pattern of regulation that plainly elicited deregulation as a policy prescription from disinterested analysts and brought liberals (attentive to consumerism) and conservatives (attentive to free enterprise) together in a bipartisan coalition for reform. But did this pattern invariably yield to regulatory reform, and if not, why not? In search of answers, we will turn next to an examination of the Davis-Bacon Act and milk price supports, two additional cases of anticompetitive regulation that have drawn much analytical fire.

Federalism—Are the States Up to the Challenge?" *National Journal,* vol. 14 (January 30, 1982), pp. 184–88. More generally, see, for example, the *Washington Post,* November 22, 1982, for a table showing the decline in employment between 1980 and 1983 at the independent regulatory agencies.

23. *Congressional Quarterly Almanac,* vol. 37 (1981), p. 18E.

Davis-Bacon Act

Passed in 1931 and importantly amended four years later, the Davis-Bacon Act provides that the federal government shall pay the locally prevailing wage to workers under contract for the construction and maintenance of buildings and other public works, and more than seventy other statutes extend this practice comprehensively to construction aided with federal funds. About a fourth of the annual volume of construction in the United States is directly affected by these statutory requirements.

Although the volume of scholarly, analytic literature on the subject is not large, numerous economists and Congress's own overseer of federal spending, the General Accounting Office, argued during the 1970s that the act is wrong in principle—that no valid public purpose is currently served by protecting the wages of construction workers—and that biased or ineffectual administration by the Department of Labor has compounded the intrinsic flaw by yielding wage determinations that were too high. "Davis-Bacon determinations have tended to raise wages in the construction industry, and have spread high wages to various geographic localities irrespective of the wage rates actually prevailing in those localities," one study found.[24] The alleged result was to raise the costs of federal construction by an estimated several hundred million dollars per year. A series of nine critical reports from the GAO over more than a decade culminated in a flat recommendation for repeal of the act.[25]

The inflationary effects of the Davis-Bacon Act began to receive presidential attention during the Nixon administration, at a time when prices generally were rising very fast and the price of construction was rising even faster. Nixon's leading economic advisers—Arthur Burns and Paul McCracken—repeatedly told the president that he ought to suspend the Davis-Bacon Act or push for its repeal, and in fact he did suspend it, though for a mere six weeks, at the outset of his campaign to control wages and prices. Repeal, however, was not a cause in which Nixon

24. John P. Gould and George Bittlingmayer, *The Economics of the Davis-Bacon Act: An Analysis of Prevailing-Wage Laws* (American Enterprise Institute for Public Policy Research, 1980), p. 39. This study, a first version of which was published by AEI as Special Analysis No. 15 in 1971, synthesizes the analytic literature on the Davis-Bacon Act.

25. *The Davis-Bacon Act Should Be Repealed,* Report to the Congress by the Comptroller General of the United States (GAO, 1979). Appendix 1 lists previous reports and briefly summarizes their contents.

showed any interest. According to one White House staff member, William Safire, he seems to have actually welcomed the existence of the Davis-Bacon Act as a weapon that the government could wield against construction workers by threatening to suspend it. According to another staff member, John D. Ehrlichman, he was so unwilling to pay the political price of an effort at repeal that he gave instructions to dissuade a conservative Republican senator, John Tower of Texas, from pushing for it: he said to tell Tower that "the unions would put Nixon on the spot if Tower kept beating the drum. The President would be forced to be for the unions if Tower didn't lay off."[26]

Under Ford, anticompetitive regulation came under fairly comprehensive and systematic review as a result of the work of the Domestic Council Review Group on Regulatory Reform, and the Davis-Bacon Act was briefly singled out, along with occupational safety and health regulations, as a likely target of reform within the Department of Labor. A Domestic Council staff member speculated that other Department of Labor programs, such as those under the Equal Pay Act and the Fair Labor Standards Act, were "too sacrosanct and too well defended to take on immediately," whereas at least administrative alterations of Davis-Bacon regulations might be possible. However, when the DCRG approached the Department of Labor, it found that the Davis-Bacon Act was also sacrosanct. Secretary John T. Dunlop preferred "to approach problems in the construction field through long range planning and mutual agreement . . . [rather] than by the confrontation that would result from an assault on the Davis-Bacon Act."[27] The Ford administration's efforts thereafter were confined to a study by the Council on Wage and Price Stability. During the 1976 presidential campaign Ford conspicuously ducked a question on the Davis-Bacon Act at a meeting of the Houston Builders Association, in Senator Tower's presence. Asked if he favored repeal and would support a one-year suspension to demonstrate the possibility of savings, Ford said it would be "premature" to make any decision until the GAO issued its next report on the subject, which was known to be forthcoming.[28]

26. William Safire, *Before the Fall* (Ballantine Books, 1977), pp. 762–63; and John D. Ehrlichman, *Witness to Power: The Nixon Years* (Simon and Schuster, 1982), p. 329.

27. Memo, Lynn May to Rod Hills, August 13, 1975, and memo, May to Rod Hills, Cal Collier, and Paul MacAvoy, August 22, 1975, in Box 32, Edward C. Schmults papers, Gerald R. Ford Library.

28. "Remarks and a Question-and-Answer Session at a Forum in Houston, April 28, 1976," *Public Papers of the President: Gerald R. Ford, 1976–77*, bk. 2 (GPO, 1979), pp. 1273–77.

During the Carter administration, an interagency task force considered the case for reform and spelled out the options, but that administration took no action except to propose minor changes in regulations, such as making it easier for wage determinations to be appealed.[29] Running for reelection in 1980, Carter courted the construction unions with repeated promises to veto any attempt at repeal, even though nothing in congressional behavior suggested that repeal was imminent. Throughout the 1970s, conservative Republicans in the Senate and the House routinely introduced bills for repeal, but until the very end of the decade they attracted few cosponsors and received no hearings. In the Ninety-sixth Congress, which sat in 1979–80, repeal acquired new backers and momentum, but still not enough to approach success. In the presidential campaign of 1980, Reagan, like Carter, pledged not to support repeal. Nonetheless, under Reagan there was an effort at administrative reform.

Until the arrival of the Reagan administration, efforts at change were confined to a coalition of government procurement officials, businessmen (both peak associations, such as the Chamber of Commerce and National Association of Manufacturers, and builders' organizations), and conservatives in Congress, who repeatedly sought waivers to exempt particular segments of construction, such as subsidized housing or military facilities. Within the executive branch, the issue pitted contracting agencies, such as the Department of Housing and Urban Development and the Department of Defense, and a central procurement office, the OMB's Office of Federal Procurement Policy, against the Department of Labor. In parallel fashion, in Congress it pitted committees with an interest in construction, such as Armed Services or Banking and Currency (with jurisdiction over housing legislation), against the Labor committees.

In the late 1970s it was common for conservative members of the Armed Services or Banking and Currency committees to sponsor a waiver of Davis-Bacon Act provisions in military construction or housing authorization bills and to be defeated on the floor, sometimes after an adverse report from the Labor Committee. Democrats voted overwhelmingly against Davis-Bacon waivers, while Republicans were divided.[30] Though

29. See *Oversight on the Davis-Bacon Act,* Hearings before the Subcommittee on Labor of the Senate Committee on Labor and Human Resources, 97 Cong. 1 sess. (GPO, 1981), pp. 2–21 for the task force memorandum and p. 34 for speculation that the failure to act was politically motivated. The Carter rules changes were about to take effect when the Reagan administration entered office and withdrew them. They appear in 44 Fed. Reg. 77026–33 (1979).

30. In votes in 1976 and 1977 Republicans were divided evenly. In 1979 they began voting for waivers roughly in the proportion of two to one.

liberal Republicans were not in the forefront of the reform effort, they were sometimes aligned with conservative members of their party on this issue. Thus, Senator Stafford, a liberal Republican who was at odds with the Reagan administration over pollution control, was sharply critical of the Labor Department's administration of the Davis-Bacon Act and called on the Reagan administration to correct the department's "costly and damaging application of the law."[31] The Democratic party's traditional commitment to protecting organized labor was not crosscut by pressures from the consumer movement, which took no interest in the Davis-Bacon Act. Senator Edward M. Kennedy, the Democrat who had led a consumer-oriented campaign in Congress for procompetitive deregulation of the airline and trucking industries, was a leading defender of the Davis-Bacon Act.[32] The proximate "consumers" in this instance were government procurement officials. It was they and their agencies who bore the brunt of higher prices, though of course the general taxpayer paid ultimately.

The arrival of the Reagan administration, in view of the president's campaign pledge, added nothing to the efforts at repeal or other legislative modification. Republican backers of a military construction waiver in 1981 were badly disappointed when Reagan did nothing to help them.[33] On the other hand, the Reagan administration made a serious effort at administrative modification, in which Secretary of Labor Raymond J. Donovan wholeheartedly participated. When he took office, Davis-Bacon regulations were inescapably on his agenda as a result of strong recommendations from a Reagan transition task force and very mild proposals for revision that had been formally promulgated by the Carter administration. Donovan, who was a building contractor and had been active in contractors' associations, promptly endorsed strong action and withstood the vigorous protest of building trade union leaders.[34]

31. *Oversight on the Davis-Bacon Act,* Hearings, p. 27.
32. See ibid., pp. 24–25, for a statement by Kennedy.
33. William J. Lanouette, "Golden Silence," *National Journal,* vol. 13 (November 14, 1981), p. 2039.
34. Officials who worked closely with Donovan did not regard his background as a contractor to be a sufficient explanation of his position. He had been a union contractor, one of them pointed out, and union contractors, like the unions, were protected from competition by the Davis-Bacon Act. Several different sources said Donovan judged the old regulations to be unfair in principle. One thought that his willingness to defy the construction unions might have been heightened by the fact that they were at that time engaged in an attack on him, alleging corruption in his private business conduct before entering

The new regulations that the Department of Labor issued in 1982 were designed to reduce the added construction costs imposed by the Davis-Bacon Act in several ways. Among other things, they based determinations of prevailing wages solely on private construction, omitting work done under government contracts; prohibited the use of data from metropolitan counties for wage determinations in neighboring rural counties; permitted the increased use of semiskilled "helpers" in lieu of skilled laborers; and defined a "prevailing wage" as that paid to the majority of a class of laborers or mechanics, whereas in the past a wage had been defined as prevailing if at least 30 percent of workers were receiving it. (If no wage so "prevailed," both the old and new regulations provided for use of an average.)[35] These changes were intended to remove the principal sources of upward bias that critical analysts had identified in the Department of Labor's practices for determining prevailing wages. More specifically, they were meant to reduce the probability that the union-negotiated wage would automatically be defined as the prevailing wage.

In the courts, the Department of Labor's new regulations were at first largely struck down and then, on appeal, largely upheld. The differences between the rulings of U.S. District Judge Harold H. Greene, who overturned most of what the department sought to do, and that of the U.S. Court of Appeals for the D.C. Circuit, which overturned most of Judge Greene's ruling, derived from the respective courts' conflicting interpretations of the scope of discretion permitted the secretary of labor by the Davis-Bacon Act.

Greene's opinion conceded that the legislative history of the Davis-Bacon Act was ambiguous and could be interpreted to support the new regulations. Nonetheless, the court resolved doubts in favor of the plaintiffs "because each of the regulations . . . is wholly inconsistent with administrative interpretation contemporaneous with the enactment of the statutes about 1935 and consistent administrative practices since then." In short, the Department of Labor must adhere to its original, long-standing regulations because they were original and long-standing. Greene found that the reasons the government gave for wishing to make the change were insufficient: "When an agency abruptly changes a long-

---

office. Interviews, Christopher DeMuth, former administrator, Office of Information and Regulatory Affairs, OMB, August 30, 1984; John Cogan, associate director of OMB, September 6, 1984; and Sue Messenger, deputy undersecretary of labor and head of the Employment Standards Administration, September 18, 1984.

35. 49 Fed. Reg. 23644–79 (1982).

standing administrative position . . . it may be expected at a minimum to show that the earlier understanding of the statute was wrong or that experience has proved it to be defective. . . . The Secretary has done neither; his primary reliance throughout has been on cost and cost savings—matters neither of novel experience nor of special expertise, but well known to and considered by the Congress as early as 1931." The basic purpose of the Davis-Bacon Act, Greene wrote, is "to protect the wages of construction workers even if the effect is to increase the costs of construction to the federal government." Moreover, he argued, the secretary's right to make changes in light of expertise and experience, though "unexceptionable in the abstract," is "also more directly applicable to the exercise of broad public-interest type discretion than it is to actions which are essentially exercises in statutory construction."[36]

The circuit court of appeals, in overruling Greene, said: "Our disagreement with the District Court's heavy reliance on administrative practice stems from our view that . . . the Secretary was acting in an area as to which he had some discretion to reach a number of different results rather than an area of pure statutory interpretation as to which there is in theory only a single answer. As the District Court recognized . . . prior administrative practice carries much less weight when reviewing an action taken in the area of discretion . . . than when reviewing an action in the field of interpretation, where it is thought that the agency's contemporaneous and consistent interpretation of one of its enabling statutes is reliable evidence of what Congress intended."[37]

Contractors' associations hailed the circuit court opinion as a victory for competition and for the regulatory reform effort of the Reagan administration. But it was a victory heavily dependent on the fortunes of judicial scrutiny. Had the district judge's ruling stood, deregulation would have been defeated.

Milk Marketing

For decades, several forms of federal government policy have prevented a free market in the production and sale of milk, the most impor-

---

36. *Building and Construction Trades Department, AFL-CIO* v. *Raymond J. Donovan*, No. 82–1631, slip opinion at 13, 14 (D.D.C. July 22, 1982).

37. "Decision of U.S. Court of Appeals for District of Columbia Circuit in AFL-CIO Building and Construction Trades Department v. Donovan," *Daily Labor Report* (Bureau of National Affairs, July 6, 1983). The case was decided on July 5, 1983.

tant of which are a qualified antitrust immunity for dairy cooperatives; marketing orders, through which prices for grade A milk (fit for consumption in fluid form) are set by the Department of Agriculture; and price supports, under which the price of grade B milk (fit for manufacturing purposes) has been guaranteed by the government through promises to purchase excess supplies.[38]

Of these forms of intervention, marketing orders most clearly fit a conventional definition of regulation. A federal milk order is a restraint on private conduct prescribed by the secretary of agriculture; it is published with other federal regulations in the Federal Register and is codified in the Code of Federal Regulations. It sets the minimum prices that milk dealers may pay dairy farmers for raw grade A milk. Rather than one nationwide order, there are different orders for different regions, areas with similar production characteristics, of which there were fifty-six as of the late 1970s. All are administered by the Dairy Division of the Agricultural Marketing Service within the Department of Agriculture. Each order has a local marketing administrator, a Department of Agriculture employee, who is responsible for operating the order, making audits, collecting and disbursing funds, and making statistical reports. However, efforts to reduce anticompetitive government intervention have focused less on these marketing orders than on statutory price supports, with which they are closely interrelated. In practice, the price of grade B milk, which has been determined through the statutory price support program, has been used by the Department of Agriculture as the base for calculating the grade A prices that have been prescribed in marketing orders.[39] "The current dairy situation is more a product of the price support program than of other dairy programs," two professors of agricultural economics wrote in 1981. "The price support program has been largely responsible for excessive milk supplies in many federal orders."[40] Thus

38. The antitrust immunity was provided by the Capper-Volstead Act of 1922; the marketing orders were authorized by the Agricultural Adjustment Act of 1933 as amended in 1935 and 1937; and the price supports were introduced in the 1930s, expanded in World War II, and made permanent in 1949. Other interventions have included import quotas and prohibitions on the sale of reconstituted milk.

39. Paul W. MacAvoy, ed., *Federal Milk Marketing Orders and Price Supports* (American Enterprise Institute for Public Policy Research, 1977), pp. 2–7, 107. This is a condensation of a report prepared by staff members of the Antitrust Division of the Justice Department.

40. Emerson M. Babb and Robert D. Boynton, "U.S. Dairy Programs—The Track Record," *Dairy Field* (February 1981), pp. 71–76. Note that the term "order" is often used to refer to the area encompassed by the order.

the politics of deregulation have revolved less around the direct regulatory scheme—the marketing orders—than around the statutory price support program on which the precise effects of the regulatory scheme have depended.[41]

Through the 1970s, when presidents were struggling to control inflation and were willing to take politically risky initiatives on behalf of procompetitive deregulation to that end, they were constantly on the defensive concerning milk price supports. From their perspective, the issue was not whether to put an end to government intervention. It was whether to resist (and, if so, how hard) the efforts of an aggressive Congress, urged on by a rich and very active dairy lobby, to drive price supports up.

Nixon, Ford, and Carter all were presented with farm bills that did more for the dairy industry than the presidents said they wanted. In 1973 a bill that moved in the direction of greater reliance on the free market for basic crops singled out dairy farmers for special treatment by fixing dairy price supports at 80 percent of parity for the next two years, over the objection of the Nixon administration.[42] During the Ford administration, the president used his veto three times to prevent Congress from making dairy price supports even more generous to farmers by raising them to 85 percent of parity or calling for quarterly or semiannual adjustments of support prices in order to keep up with the effects of inflation. During the Carter administration, Congress finally did enact more frequent adjustments as part of a general farm bill that was far more expensive than what Carter said he would accept. The president threatened a veto but in the end failed to use one.[43]

41. Marketing orders apply to many agricultural commodities besides milk. Roughly half of the $12 billion worth of fresh fruits, vegetables, and nuts marketed annually in the United States is regulated by marketing orders that, for example, assign quotas to packers and set standards for quality and packaging. These orders affect prices by affecting supplies, but only the orders for milk actually set prices. As of 1982, the Reagan administration's deregulators in the OMB were trying to restrict the use of agricultural marketing orders, against the opposition of the Department of Agriculture. See "Fruit Growers' Control of Market Assailed," *New York Times,* March 23, 1981; "U.S. Agricultural Marketing Orders," *Regulation,* vol. 6 (March–April 1982), p. 30; and "Farm, Budget Officials Clash on Supply Curbs by Marketing Boards," *Wall Street Journal,* December 7, 1982.

42. Parity, a central concept in the agricultural price support programs enacted in the 1930s, was designed to stabilize the purchasing power of farmers, using the pre–World War I period, which was a prosperous time for farmers, as a base.

43. *Congressional Quarterly Almanac,* vol. 29 (1973), pp. 285–307; *Congress and the Nation,* vol. 4 (Congressional Quarterly, 1977), pp. 729–39; and *Congressional Quarterly Almanac,* vol. 33 (1977), pp. 415–20.

The dairy industry has had many partisans in Congress and no consistent critics. As one would expect, members from milk-producing states—Wisconsin and Minnesota, for example—and members of the Agriculture committees and their dairy subcommittees have been particularly outspoken advocates of the industry's interests, but, less predictably, so have members whose support cannot be explained by region or committee position, such as Speaker Carl Albert and Ways and Means Committee Chairman Wilbur Mills in the 1970s. (In Mills's case, the dairy lobby financed his abortive campaign for the Democratic presidential nomination in 1972.) Proponents of reform looked to Senator Kennedy for help, and while he gave a hard-hitting keynote speech at a consumer-oriented conference late in 1975, he never pursued the reform of milk marketing as he pursued the airlines and trucking. The senator, a staff aide said, was "more in sympathy" with dairy farmers than with airline executives. Congress not only failed to provide a platform for analytic criticism of government protection of the dairy industry (such as the Kennedy hearings on the CAB), it even went so far as to prohibit one of the government's in-house critics of protective legislation, the Federal Trade Commission, from studying or prosecuting any agricultural cooperative.[44]

The combined (and presumably related) aggressiveness of the Congress and the dairy lobby made it difficult for the executive branch to decide where to set price supports each year. The Agriculture Act of 1949, which contained a permanent authorization of dairy price supports, permitted the secretary of agriculture to set them at 75 to 90 percent of parity. Because the stakes were large for dairy farmers and consumers and because all administrations in the 1970s professed to be fighting inflation, setting supports became one of the most delicate and heated of domestic questions. Nixon's decision in 1971 to override his secretary of agriculture, Clifford M. Hardin, in order to fix a support price higher than the one Hardin had announced was one of several scandals that in combination became the Watergate scandal; evidence was adduced to show that

44. Michael McMenamin and Walter McNamara, *Milking the Public: Political Scandals of the Dairy Lobby from L.B.J. to Jimmy Carter* (Nelson-Hall, 1980), pp. 226–29, 235. The prohibition was contained in the Federal Trade Commission Improvements Act of 1979. It was sponsored by Mark Andrews, Republican of North Dakota, who had received frequent contributions from the dairy industry's political action committees, but the dairy industry was not the only beneficiary. The FTC had an investigation pending against the Ocean Spray cranberry cooperative as well as Dairymen, Inc., and it was preparing to prosecute Sunkist Growers, Inc., a large California-based cooperative, for illegally monopolizing the western citrus fruit industry.

Nixon was influenced by the promise of a contribution of $2 million from the dairy lobby to his reelection campaign in 1972. Other evidence shows that Nixon expected Congress to raise the support price by law if the administration did not do so, and if that happened, he remarked in a private meeting with members of his administration, "I could not veto it. Not because [the dairy farmers are] militants, but because they're farmers. And it would be just turning down the whole middle America, where . . . we . . . need support. And under the circumstances, I think the best thing to do is just . . . relax and enjoy it."[45] Although Ford vetoed statutory price support increases in 1975 and 1976, his secretary of agriculture in both years allowed lesser price rises through administrative action. One of the first acts of the Carter administration, in the spring of 1977, was to allow a sizable increase in the support price. When a skeptical reporter asked Carter how he reconciled this action with his anti-inflation program, the president replied that "milk is a special case."[46]

Neither the Department of Justice nor most economists nor advocates of consumer interests thought that milk was "a special case." Late in 1975 the Community Nutrition Institute, a consumer-oriented organization specializing in food and nutrition, sponsored a well-publicized conference at which the typical array of economist-critics gave the typical array of critical papers—one each from COWPS, the Department of Justice, the FTC, and the Public Interest Economics Center. The Antitrust Division had brought three major suits in the early 1970s against milk producer cooperatives, the most important of which—against Associated Milk Producers, Inc. (AMPI)—ended with a consent decree in the spring of 1975 in which AMPI agreed to refrain from the price-fixing and predatory practices specified in the suit. Under Ford, the Justice Department prepared a major study criticizing the operation of milk marketing orders

45. Cited in ibid., p. 106. Just as this was not the only scandal in which Nixon was implicated, it was also not the only scandal in which the dairy lobby was implicated. The manager of Hubert Humphrey's 1968 presidential campaign was convicted of soliciting illegal corporate political contributions from the Associated Milk Producers. Nixon's secretary of the treasury, John B. Connally, was indicted but found not guilty in connection with charges that he had been bribed by a lobbyist for the dairy industry. The lobbyist who sought to bribe him pleaded guilty and received a suspended sentence. Ibid., pp. 54–62, 124–70.

46. *Public Papers of the President of the United States: Jimmy Carter, 1977* (GPO, 1977), bk. 1, p. 635. (Hereafter *Public Papers: Carter.*) Carter went on to explain that the profit margin of dairy farmers was "precariously imbalanced," and that what his administration had granted was much less than the dairy interests had sought.

and price supports that subsequently was published by the American Enterprise Institute for Public Policy Research.[47]

Though a critical analysis of milk price supports was developing in the late 1970s, it was considerably less voluminous and concerted than that which had been successfully applied to reform of the transportation industries.[48] Very likely, the lag in criticism reflected a lag in the development of monopoly practices. While protective legislation for the dairy industry dated from the 1920s and 1930s, its extreme effects were much more recent. As of 1940 milk marketing orders covered only 20 percent of all raw milk produced; not until the late 1960s were the proportions reversed, such that only 20 percent of total production was not covered. The large and very powerful cooperatives also dated from the late 1960s, when they were formed in a wave of mergers. Thus the representatives of Ford's Domestic Council Review Group who approached the Agriculture Department with requests to consider regulatory reform were relatively ill prepared to challenge this new behemoth of American politics. They also discovered that they could anticipate no help from Secretary of Agriculture Earl Butz, who told them that he favored milk marketing orders. The Agriculture Department's plan for regulatory reform, prepared at the DCRG's request, was quite diffuse, comprehensive, and unproductive. It covered many of the department's activities and had a measurable effect on none.

The presidential-level effort at reform of milk marketing orders, barely begun under Ford, did not continue under Carter, who was less willing

47. MacAvoy, *Federal Milk Marketing Orders.*
48. For the analytic case, see, in addition to ibid., Tanya Roberts, "An Evaluation of Federal Milk Price Regulation: History, Impact, and Options for Reform," in *Study on Federal Regulation,* prepared for the Senate Committee on Governmental Affairs, S. Doc. 96-14, 96 Cong. 1 sess. (GPO, 1978), pp. 485-585. One sign of the lack of an elite consensus comparable with that pertaining to the transportation industries was the inability of a Carter-appointed commission on antitrust laws and procedures to make "a definitive recommendation concerning the current exemption for milk marketing orders." *Report to the President and the Attorney General of the National Commission for the Review of Antitrust Laws and Procedures* (GPO, 1979), p. xii. The commission did recommend that sec. 2 of the Capper-Volstead Act, which authorizes the secretary of agriculture to take action against an agricultural cooperative that unduly enhances prices, be amended to define undue price enhancement more clearly and that responsibility for enforcement of this provision be separated from the promotional responsibilities of the Department of Agriculture. The secretary of agriculture has never used that provision of the law. McMenamin and McNamara, *Milking the Public,* pp. 253, 260. See also Ralph H. Folsom, "Antitrust Enforcement under the Secretaries of Agriculture and Commerce," *Columbia Law Review,* vol. 80 (December 1980), pp. 1623-43.

than his predecessor to oppose dairy interests and also less willing to encourage critics in COWPS and the Department of Justice to persist in their criticism. When his secretary of agriculture, Robert Bergland, attacked the Justice Department's study of milk marketing orders for "factual, legal and interpretive errors," Carter's Justice Department did not reply.[49] In a campaign speech late in his administration, Carter boasted of having increased milk price supports, supported farm cooperatives, and defended the Capper-Volstead Act.[50] Nor was the effort resumed under Reagan, whose task force on regulatory relief elected to tackle only a select few of the many agricultural marketing orders, among which dairy orders were not included.

At the beginning of the 1980s, government policies extremely favorable to the dairy industry began to produce extreme effects. Government outlays for purchase of surplus dairy products rose from $0.3 billion in fiscal year 1979 to $1.9 billion in 1981. Government purchases in 1980 accounted for 7 percent of the nation's milk production. Billions of pounds of cheese, butter, and powdered milk were accumulating in government warehouses.[51] A broadening array of consumer interests began to complain of the rising price of dairy products—not just the Community Nutrition Institute, but also Common Cause, a public interest lobby with a broadly inclusive agenda, and the industrial purchasers of milk products, such as pizza and chocolate manufacturers and restaurants. The *Wall Street Journal* reported that a 6 percent increase in government price supports for dairy products in the fall of 1980 would cost Pizza Hut an additional $3.6 million a year for cheese. The new OMB director in 1981, David Stockman, said dairy price support levels were "a scandal." The new secretary of agriculture, John R. Block, pointed out that the cost of the dairy program amounted to one-half of the whole farm bill and that it was "entirely unfair" for a single industry to receive so much. Even members of the dairy industry were on the defensive. An executive of Land O' Lakes, Inc., was quoted by a trade publication as saying that the price support program "must not be abused to such an extent that it becomes a continuing political embarrassment. . . . The dairy industry cannot

49. McMenamin and McNamara say that the attorney general did not allow critics of milk marketing orders in Justice to reply. *Milking the Public*, p. 231.

50. *Public Papers: Carter, 1980–81* (GPO, 1982), bk. 3, p. 2468.

51. For example, see Robert J. Samuelson, "The Land of Milk and Money," *National Journal*, vol. 13 (May 16, 1981); and Congressional Budget Office, *Food and Agriculture Policy in the 1980s: Major Crops and Milk* (GPO, 1981), pp. xiv–xvii, chap. 4.

continue to produce eight billion pounds of milk more than consumers will purchase."[52]

In this situation, agricultural politics underwent major change. Whereas throughout the 1970s Congress had produced agriculture bills that especially pleased dairy interests, its actions in 1981 especially displeased them. First it denied dairy farmers a scheduled price increase in April at the request of Reagan—one of his first legislative victories. Then, at the end of the year, it enacted a farm bill that sharply lowered price supports for milk and partially severed their link to parity.[53] Dairy interests lobbied hard against the bill, and the chairman of the Livestock, Dairy and Poultry Subcommittee of the House Agriculture Committee urged the House to vote against any farm bill rather than accept the one that came to them from the House-Senate conference. The bill passed the House by only two votes, 205–203.[54]

The result depended critically on use of the congressional budget process, with its hitherto unexploited provision for "reconciliation," to put a ceiling on agricultural expenditures. Under reconciliation in 1981, the Agriculture committees, like other authorizing committees in Congress, had to adjust their programs to dollar ceilings specified by the budget resolution.[55] This pitted agricultural commodity groups against one another, to the disadvantage of the hitherto much-privileged and protected dairy industry. In addition, the administration, with support from party leaders in the Senate, used threats of a veto.

The new law, however, did not halt the rise in the government's purchases of milk, nor did it represent more than a fleeting departure from the well-established congressional pattern of favoring dairy farmers with protective legislation. Dairy farmers responded to the drop in price sup-

52. "Big Cost Churns Up Opposition to Dairy Supports," *Wall Street Journal,* October 16, 1980; "Dairymen Yielding Little on Subsidies," *New York Times,* February 2, 1981; and "Dairy Price Support Program Enters New Era of Visibility," *Dairy Field* (September 1981), pp. 17, 118–19.

53. The precise provisions were complicated. The law specified price supports in dollars per hundredweight for the coming three years in terms roughly equivalent to 70 percent of parity, but provided for a return to parity in certain contingencies—if government purchases of dairy products were less than $1 billion a year, or if annual purchases fell below stipulated volumes of weight.

54. *Congressional Quarterly Almanac,* vol. 37 (1981), pp. 535–52.

55. For a description and analysis of the procedure, see Allen Schick, *Reconciliation and the Congressional Budget Process* (American Enterprise Institute for Public Policy Research, 1981).

ports, and to a coincidental drop in the price of cattle feed prices in the early 1980s, by increasing production; as a result, the government's outlays for surplus dairy products rose to $2.2 billion in fiscal year 1982 and $2.7 billion in 1983, equivalent to 10 to 12 percent of the nation's milk production. Congress in turn promptly passed the Dairy Production Stabilization Act of 1983, which both continued the price support program at a slightly lower level and required the Department of Agriculture to make sizable "diversion payments" to dairy farmers who reduced production. Far from being a move toward a free market in milk, this was a precedent-setting new departure from it. The Reagan administration opposed the bill, but despite the pleas of his economic advisers, the president declined to veto it.[56]

The Davis-Bacon Act and myriad government policies on milk marketing have fostered anticompetitive pricing and inflated costs to consumers and the taxpaying public, and for those reasons have been sharply attacked by economic analysts, but reform has been limited by comparison with what occurred in our three central cases of success. Davis-Bacon reforms have been confined to those procompetitive changes in departmental regulations that reviewing courts would permit, and milk-marketing reform has been confined to what Congress would enact contrary to the interests of the dairy industry. We will leave to the next and final chapter the question of more precisely what these cases show and why they yielded different outcomes than our central cases. But before proceeding to the conclusions, we wish to introduce yet one more illustration of the limits of reform—the maritime industry.

On their face, our three cases of success share an obvious difference from the Davis-Bacon Act and milk marketing. They entailed regulation by independent multimember commissions having very broad grants of authority from Congress, whereas the two contrasting cases entailed more circumscribed grants of regulatory discretion to line agencies of the executive branch. This leads us to wonder whether there is something about the form or powers of independent regulatory commissions that made them especially susceptible to attempts at reform or especially prone to respond with effective measures of deregulation. If we are to weigh such a possibility, we must consider the anomalous case of the maritime industry and the Federal Maritime Commission (FMC), its regulatory patron. In

56. Michael Wines, "Less Milk Could Mean More Money for Dairy Farmers, Higher Federal Costs," *National Journal,* vol. 15 (December 31, 1983), pp. 2667–69.

fact, among the anticompetitive regimes administered by the independent regulatory commissions, only that governing the maritime industry proved altogether impervious to procompetitive change. Presidents who endorsed strong measures of procompetitive deregulation in other regulatory commissions and other transportation industries either did nothing to reform maritime regulation or endorsed new anticompetitive measures.

The Maritime Industry

The Shipping Act of 1916 authorizes the Federal Maritime Commission to regulate organizations of shipping companies, called "conferences," whose members ship goods to and from American ports. Consisting of both American flag and foreign flag companies, these conferences set shipping rates and terms of service and are supposed to file their agreements with the FMC when they involve trade at American ports. Conference agreements approved by the FMC have been exempt from antitrust laws.[57]

In the Ford administration, a task force of the Domestic Council Review Group on Regulatory Reform considered the subject of shipping conferences, but with a notable lack of urgency. The task force organizer, a staff member of the Council of Economic Advisers, suggested in a memo to the DCRG that "conferences and the FMC are not much of a problem." Weakened by free entry and by a competitive fringe of tramp and independent lines, the conferences were periodically subject to price wars and outright disintegration, while the FMC had few regulatory powers compared with the Interstate Commerce Commission, and was "not very aggressive about exercising those that it has." He concluded that the real problems in ocean shipping appeared to be in the area of subsidies and cargo preferences rather than regulation, and recommended limiting the task force effort to the gathering of more data.[58]

---

57. For analysis of the FMC's use of its powers, see Edward Mansfield, "Federal Maritime Commission," in James Q. Wilson, ed., *The Politics of Regulation* (Basic Books, 1980), pp. 42–74.

58. Memo, Fred Peterson to Domestic Council Review Group, December 17, 1975, in Box 24, Paul C. Leach Papers, Ford Library. Unofficial critiques of maritime policy had likewise concentrated on subsidies and cargo preferences rather than regulation. See Allen R. Ferguson and others, *The Economic Value of the United States Merchant Marine* (Northwestern University, Transportation Center, 1961); and Gerald R. Jantscher, *Bread upon the Waters: Federal Aids to the Maritime Industries* (Brookings, 1975).

Domestic policymakers in Carter's Executive Office were more committed to maritime reform. They reasoned that because protective regulation was being challenged in other transportation industries, it might be challenged for the maritime industry as well. An interagency task force was assembled in the spring of 1978 and before long split into two opposing groups, those that favored strengthening the conferences and the FMC's regulatory powers (the Departments of Commerce, Labor, and Defense, and the FMC) and those that favored weakening the conferences and the FMC so as to achieve greater competition (Treasury, Justice, the OMB, COWPS, and the CEA). The Departments of Transportation and State were allied with neither camp. The first group sought to allow conference members to pool revenues, permit agreements among conferences so as to limit competition between rival trade routes, permit exclusion of new firms from conferences, and prevent nonconference lines from competing on some routes. The procompetitive group argued that rebating should be legalized and that additional limitations should be imposed on the conferences' powers of collective action, possibly even ending their exemption from antitrust laws. The procompetitive reformers suffered a major defeat within the task force when the chairman, who was a member of the domestic policy staff, decided that their preferred positions, such as ending the antitrust exemption for conferences and abolishing the FMC, were so extreme and politically unrealistic that they could not even be included in the options paper that went to the president. What did go to him put forth a middle-ground option, an ambiguous mixture of new pro- and anticompetitive measures, which the procompetitive side felt was not a middle ground at all but a step backward, at least in the context of the time. Carter chose what had been presented to him as a "middle ground."[59]

"The political pressures from industry and the unions were clearly pointing in the direction chosen," an economist on the president's staff wrote of this decision, but then he added, quite correctly, that the same could have been said about the airline and trucking industries before their deregulation. What appears to distinguish the maritime industry from these others is its poor financial condition, indicated by stagnant tonnage, a declining share of the U.S. trade, and bankruptcies, along with its exposure to competition from foreign companies whose governments own,

59. Lawrence J. White, *Reforming Regulation: Processes and Problems* (Prentice-Hall, 1981), pp. 166–75.

protect, or subsidize them with no compunctions about restraints on competition. Using the argument that the U.S. maritime industry must be protected from foreign competitors, the House Merchant Marine and Fisheries Committee and its counterpart, the Merchant Marine Subcommittee of the Senate Commerce, Science, and Transportation Committee, have constantly promoted fresh legislation to that end. Finally, there are the defense and diplomatic implications of these issues, to which presidents are necessarily sensitive. The Department of Defense as well as overt partisans of the industry argue that a healthy U.S. maritime industry is needed to assure the availability of cargo capacity in case of war. That the Soviet Union has a large and modern merchant marine fleet and has increasingly penetrated the U.S. trade tends to reinforce this argument, whatever the merits of it may be. And there is concern that strict imposition of procompetitive U.S. laws against foreign flag carriers will raise troublesome diplomatic issues.[60]

Presidents have signed some of the maritime protection bills that Congress has sent them and have vetoed others, objecting to the adverse effects on diplomatic relations, although Ford also stressed the effects on domestic inflation in his veto of a bill that would have guaranteed American flag tankers 30 percent of the oil cargo imported to this country.[61] No president has endorsed procompetitive deregulatory measures. Carter took what his economic advisers believed were backward steps, not only in choosing a "wrong" option from a wrongly conceived options paper, but by signing bills that tightened the FMC's control over predatory price setting by foreign flag carriers (a measure aimed primarily at Soviet penetration of the U.S. trade) and that sought to increase the FMC's power to curtail rebating by foreign flag firms.[62] The Reagan administration, though willing to endorse a reduction in the FMC's powers of regulatory review as well as to reduce the subsidies with which the government has helped the maritime industry, did not wish to end the antitrust immunities that the industry has enjoyed. On the contrary, it proposed to enlarge

60. Ibid.; *Congressional Quarterly Almanac,* vol. 34 (1978), pp. 517–19; and Michael Wines, "Reagan's Cure for Maritime Industry—Fewer Subsidies and More Protection," *National Journal,* vol. 14 (April 24, 1982), pp. 725–30.

61. "Memorandum of Disapproval of United States Tanker Preference Legislation," *Public Papers of the Presidents: Gerald R. Ford, 1974* (GPO, 1975), p. 782; and "Veto of Bill Concerning Shipping Rebating Laws," *Public Papers: Carter, 1978,* bk. 2 (GPO, 1979), pp. 1962–63.

62. White, *Reforming Regulation; Congressional Quarterly Almanac,* vol. 34 (1978), pp. 517–19; and *Congressional Quarterly Almanac,* vol. 35 (1979), p. 349.

them. It elected to accept shipping cartels on the theory that the U.S. shipping industry should be allowed to join, if it could not beat, the rest of the world. Encouraged by backing from the Reagan administration as well as the maritime industry and unions, Congress passed a bill in 1984 that broadened and clarified antitrust exemptions for shipping conferences. Though agreements that set rates and terms of service still have to be filed with the FMC, after forty-five days they become effective automatically unless the FMC rejects them, and the grounds for rejection are practically nonexistent.[63]

In sum, the maritime case represents an inversion of procompetitive deregulation, not an unsuccessful attempt at it. Most regulatory regimes run by independent regulatory commissions may indeed have been more susceptible to reform than those run by line agencies (the Ford administration tentatively found that to be the case), but the recent history of maritime regulation establishes that the organizational form did not by itself necessarily make them more vulnerable.

63. *Congressional Quarterly Weekly Report,* vol. 42 (March 10, 1984), pp. 567–68.

CHAPTER SEVEN

The Politics of Ideas

POLICYMAKING, reduced to its simplest, requires agreeing on what to do and having the means to effectuate the agreement—to embody it in an authoritative form, typically law, and then put it into practice. As a general rule, reaching agreement is hard in the United States because it is a free and diverse society with many conflicting interests and opinions and no important restraints on organizing to promote them, and because its policymaking institutions are quite accessible and are designed to work slowly, responding only when a high level of agreement has been achieved. Implementing agreements is also typically difficult, among other reasons, because of the extreme organizational fragmentation associated with federalism and a confused mingling of the public and private sectors.

On top of these "normal" or built-in obstacles to action, our three cases posed additional obstacles. For procompetitive deregulation to occur, a diffuse, ill-organized, broadly encompassing interest had to be favored over particularistic, well-organized, putatively very powerful interests, and long-established government policies had to be reversed, agencies' routines profoundly altered, and their powers reduced.

Our first task in this chapter is to summarize why it was possible for presumptively sluggish institutions to agree on and implement procompetitive deregulation, even under the especially difficult circumstances posed by the cases. Then we will discuss the implications of our study for two subjects of broader concern: the role in policy change played by economic analysis; and the capacities of the American political system in its current state, called by some the "new American political system."

237

The Explanation of Success

We conclude that deregulation of the airline, trucking, and telecommunications industries occurred for the following principal reasons, which with some significant qualifications for telecommunications are applicable in common to our three leading cases.

1. *Elite opinion converged in support of reform.* Within the academic world the convergence was interdisciplinary, and within the political-governmental world it cut across political parties, ideological groupings, and branches of the government. Perhaps most important was the convergence of the two worlds when analytic prescriptions, instead of depending upon technical and abstruse arguments, proved adaptable to political rhetoric and position taking.

Drawing upon both theory and empirical research, economists were convinced that much economic regulation in fundamentally competitive markets had large costs yet yielded no benefits, and their analysis reinforced the work of other disciplines that had criticized regulatory agencies as captives of the regulated industries. Policy research organizations and a cadre of officials in executive agencies of the government advocated reform. And political leaders, primarily presidents seeking cures for inflation and responses to the public's restiveness with government intervention, embraced the advocates' prescriptions. Procompetitive reform then proved to have a broad political appeal, engaging liberals (led by Senator Edward M. Kennedy), who stressed the benefits of lower prices for consumers and an end to government protection of business, and conservatives (led by President Gerald R. Ford), who stressed the benefits of reducing the burden of government regulation in private markets. Conversely, anticompetitive regulation found scant support in any of the widely held perspectives on public policy—ideological or analytic—and thus industry opponents of reform had an unusually distinct appearance of special interests.

Where regulation was not anticompetitive—that is, where it did not restrict the minimum price of goods and services—elite opinion did not similarly converge. This was the case in natural gas pricing, where sharp partisan differences persisted, and air pollution control, where a Republican president was at odds with Republican senators and both parties were internally divided in Congress. Nor did all procompetitive deregulation elicit the firm, broadly inclusive agreement that marked our two transportation cases. Though economists had produced critiques of the Davis-Bacon Act, milk marketing orders, and maritime regulation without provoking any important professional dissents, their analyses in all three cases were thinner, more recently developed, and less widely noticed and invoked than those the analytic community had produced about the airline and trucking industries. Among officeholders, only Republicans were critical of the Davis-Bacon Act, and they were divided. Democrats, apparently detecting no general appeal to consumers in Davis-Bacon reform, did not in this instance abandon their traditional prolabor position. There was no support among officeholders in either party for maritime or milk-marketing reform. And on some of the issues in telecommunications, there was no convergence even among economists. In the absence of consensus regarding long distance service and the structure of AT&T, policymaking was tortuous, conflicted, and ultimately left by default to the judicial process, which does not depend on consensus.

2. *Officeholders in positions of leadership took initiatives.* There is an unmistakable pattern in our leading cases: presidents, commission chairmen, and congressional committee and subcommittee leaders generally advocated reform. We infer that such leaders are especially induced or constrained to serve broad, encompassing, diffuse interests. Any officeholder faces conflicting pressures of personal conviction, desire for reputation, and political interest; some of these pressures will encourage service to broader, diffuse interests while others certainly will not. For leaders, the pressures that encourage such service are markedly enhanced by the very fact of leadership, which makes their actions visible to a wider public, exposes them to observation and comment among the political and governmental elite, and tends to elicit a more compelling sense of responsibility. If any officeholders have adequate incentives to prefer diffuse over special interests, leaders do.

We do not suppose that leaders always act in that way, or that all classes of leaders are subject to the same constraints in the same degree. It is worth noting, for example, that departmental secretaries generally do not appear in our account as advocates of reform except as it applied to regimes other than those over which they presided. (However, our data that bear on this point, besides being thin, are inconsistent, given the support of Ronald Reagan's secretary of labor, Raymond J. Donovan, for procompetitive administrative reform of the Davis-Bacon Act.) Although three successive presidents appear in our analysis as leaders of procompetitive deregulation, their leadership was quite selective. None risked a personal commitment to repeal of the Davis-Bacon Act. None risked a frontal assault on the dairy industry's price supports until Reagan did so briefly at the outset of his presidency. None advocated procompetitive reform of the maritime industry. They took no stand or only a very vague one on telecommunications reform. Even in our clearest cases of success, airlines and trucking, leadership was sometimes ambivalent or inconsistent; Reagan appointed an ICC chairman who did not believe in procompetitive reform.

In selecting actions to emphasize, leaders make matches between the prescriptions that advocates thrust upon them and the public problems and political opportunities or necessities that are cast up and unpredictably restructured by the stream of events.[1] They appear to be influenced by several properties of the prescriptions and their fit to a perceived problem. One is ripeness. The legislative prescriptions that Ford embraced had been in preparation for some time, and the Kennedy hearings were a positive spur to action from Congress. Leaders are sensitive to timing—that is, to the general readiness for what it is they propose to do—and though they cannot insist on guarantees of success, they are unlikely to risk advocacy unless they detect some possibility of it. A second consideration is room on the agenda. When we asked Ford why he had pursued, for example, deregulation of trucking but not milk marketing, he replied quite simply that "Congress can do only so much at once." It follows from that, of course, that a prudent president, husbanding his own influence, will ask it to do only so much at once. As presidents gave their endorsement to successive reform bills, it became less likely that they would endorse additional bills unless passage of preceding ones created room on the agenda and gave promise of further successes. To some extent, the choices of issues by leaders have no more fundamental explanation than the need to choose. A third factor that influences choice is the merits of the issue, which is to say the magnitude of the anticipated benefits. Before they undertake risks in order to serve the general good, leaders need to be convinced that it will be served significantly if they succeed. Finally, leaders' choices are influenced by prior commitments, which very often are shaped in election campaigns. It is perhaps no accident that the first president to lead the drive for procompetitive deregulation held the office not through election, but because of the resignation of his predecessor.

1. For an extended analysis of agenda formation, showing how problems, policies, and politics come together to lay the basis for action, see John W. Kingdon, *Agendas, Alternatives, and Public Policies* (Little, Brown, 1984).

As an issue develops, demonstration, imitation, and competition among leaders become extremely important influences. Kennedy prodded Ford. Jimmy Carter seized on deregulation very early in his administration largely because Ford had prepared the issue for action. Other commission chairmen followed the well-publicized example of Alfred E. Kahn. In Congress, Kennedy influenced Howard Cannon. At least in telecommunications, the commission chairman competed with a subcommittee chairman. When numerous leaders in different parts of the government became involved and began competing with one another, policy change occurred very fast.

In our limiting cases, some or all of the conditions that encourage leaders to select issues were absent, and the competitive, dynamic process that carried our leading cases so far down the path of procompetitive policy change was never set in motion.

The case for maritime deregulation was relatively weak on the merits; in the Ford administration not even economic analysts were prepared to press it aggressively, and in the Carter administration several executive agencies argued against it. Congress was not merely unreceptive to reform, but quite aggressive on the industry's behalf, while presidents were inhibited by a variety of international influences unique to the case. It is one thing to dismantle a domestic cartel and another to pay the price, including possible complications in diplomatic relations, of defying an international one.

Without cooperation from the secretary of labor, Ford's presidential staff was unable to make Davis-Bacon reform ready for action, and Reagan's campaign promise precluded any attempt at repeal in his administration; nonetheless, the issue by then was ripe for administrative action, which Reagan's secretary of labor proved willing to take, making this a case of qualified success.

Political leaders' estimates of the merits of milk-marketing reform appear to have been much affected by the perception that dairy farmers were more deserving of protection by the government than other industrial interests. Senator Kennedy was "more in sympathy" with them than with airline executives, while Richard Nixon was unwilling to use his veto against them "because they're farmers." Much as Kennedy and Ford were joined in a willingness to attack airline regulation, Kennedy and Nixon were joined in an unwillingness to attack dairy farmers. For any president to risk a major initiative on milk-marketing reform was unthinkable in light of the fact that there was no sign of congressional receptivity to such reform, but there were many signs of Congress's wholehearted support of the dairy industry. (This was especially true, of course, among regional partisans of milk producers, for whom there was no congressional counterpart in the airline, trucking, or telecommunications industries.) Such an initiative was not possible even for Ford, who, unlike Nixon, was willing to use his veto against price support increases. Among political leaders, someone has to take the first step for an issue to ripen through advocacy and reach the policy agenda. In regard to milk marketing orders, no political leader showed any disposition to take that step unless one counts Reagan's brief, anomalous use of the budget process to force a cut in milk price supports in 1981, after government policies had created surpluses so extreme that even the industry was embarrassed.

It might be supposed that leaders were inhibited from acting by the tangible political power—measured by campaign contributions, votes, and lobbying efforts—of the dairy industry, or the construction trade unions in the Davis-Bacon case, or the maritime industry and unions in the maritime case. We do not doubt that leaders were so inhibited, yet the power of the interests that escaped concerted, vigorous attempts at reducing government protection was not demonstrably greater than that of the interests that were subjected to such attempts. Differences in such power cannot have been crucial. The dairy industry's very large campaign contributions in the 1970s may have given it some special measure of political protection, yet they could easily have backfired and made it an especial target of reform. Here again, we believe that the politicians' perception of that industry as especially deserving tended to spare it. When AT&T was aggressive, overbearing, and profligate in politics, officeholders reacted with hostility and sarcasm. Dairy cooperatives, still approved of as farmers rather than despised or feared for their lately attained corporate size, were freer to use their financial power with impunity.

Whatever issues they pick, leaders are often thwarted by officeholders having narrower constituencies, less visibility, or a less urgent sense of responsibility, and hence less concern for general, encompassing interests. Typically, it is through Congress—a large, representative, elected body—that particularistic interests assert themselves, yet Congress posed no serious obstacles to reform in our cases.

3. *Congress did not have to act for deregulation to occur.* It is hard to overstate the importance of this fact for our cases. It is crucial. An instrument was available—the independent regulatory commission—that had broad powers to act and was driven to do so by a combination of external sanctions and criticism and entrepreneurial leadership committed to re-

form. Action by the commissions promptly elicited the desired economic responses from industry, since removing anticompetitive restraints compelled firms to compete whether they wanted to or not. And action by the commissions precipitated legislation (in the transportation cases) or adequately substituted for it (for terminal equipment in telecommunications). Moreover, insofar as the commissions failed to institute reforms, courts were available as an alternative instrument; it was a court, not the legislature or a commission, that in effect dictated that long distance telephone service should become competitive.

Had Congress alone been able to take effective, authoritative action, far-reaching reform would have been much less likely to occur. In the absence of action by the commissions, Congress would not have felt that its prerogatives were being challenged; it would not have come under pressure from the regulated industries to take action as a way of restoring stability; and, insofar as it might have preferred to preserve the old regimes, it would not have borne the considerable political burden of reversing reform measures already instituted.

Had the independent regulatory commissions not been both very vulnerable to external influence and exceptionally endowed by statute with authority to act, they would have been less capable of forcing Congress's hand. Although the commissions were no more independent of congressional oversight and judicial review than more conventional agencies, their "independent" status set them apart from the rest of the executive branch, and, ironically, rendered them more than ordinarily vulnerable to presidential efforts at reform. Presidential staffs, which were inhibited by law and tradition from intervening in commission decisions or disciplining their members, for that very reason felt no obligation on their behalf and freely joined in criticizing their basic functions, using the rival expertise of the line agencies of the executive branch. Although the Civil Aeronautics Board and Interstate Commerce Commission moved toward reform through rule making and adjudication of individual cases, it was primarily the Department of Transportation, actively supported by the president's staff, that planned the legislation through which transportation regulation was largely dismantled. Ford's staff found it harder to devise effective tactics and useful sources of expertise when it sought to curb the regulatory activities of the conventional (not "independent") agencies.

The broad, flexible grants of statutory authority enjoyed by the commissions emboldened reform-oriented chairmen to fundamentally reverse long-standing practices and presumably would have helped the commissions to withstand court tests if congressional action had not made most of those tests moot. It is significant that when the Reagan administration tried to achieve reform of the Davis-Bacon Act by changing the regulations of the Department of Labor, judicial review almost prevented it. Drawing an implied distinction between the authority granted to independent regulatory commissions to exercise "broad public-interest type discretion" and the much more limited power of the department to construe specific statutory provisions, a district court struck down most of the new regulations. Reversal by an appeals court made the outcome favorable to deregulation, but if it had decided the other way, the administration would have had to abandon regulatory reform or depend on Congress to achieve it. And, if it had had to depend on Congress, there would have been no reform.

4. *Yet Congress did act.* In the airline and trucking cases, Congress passed strongly or radically procompetitive bills. Even in the face of intense interest group opposition, majorities in committee and on the respective floors proved willing to endorse reform. They were persuaded, of course, partly by the positions and efforts of the committee leaders, the administration, and the commissions. In addition, certain features of reform advocacy helped to achieve broader congressional support by overcoming the ordinary members' lesser attention to substantive debate. Reform advocates managed to provide simple and vivid cues on the merits of the issues; to answer questions about the effects on supposedly vulnerable geographic constituencies (primarily small towns and rural areas) with research and special provisions of legislation; and to make a rhetorical connection between deregulation and larger concerns of the general public. Eventually, when the opposition of the industries waned as the result of commission action, Congress endorsed deregulation very strongly.

In the telecommunications case, committee leaders made patient, devoted efforts on behalf of reform, but the advocacy never achieved comparable clarity or persuasiveness if only because some major issues were impossible for disinterested analysts to decide or for leaders to agree on. Congressional support for reform in this field was correspondingly less robust. This support was manifested not in finished legislation, but in refusal to consider the anticompetitive "Bell bill" in the mid-1970s, then establishment of a procompetitive agenda for legislative action, and, once AT&T had retreated, a radically procompetitive consensus sufficient to guide administrative policy and economic behavior even though ancillary issues still precluded final action.

In offering this account, we rejected the fashionable academic view that members of Congress concern themselves exclusively with reelection as opposed to programmatic or ideological goals, and that narrow, well-organized, particularistic interests necessarily dominate their electoral concerns. Very often, of course, Congress acts in just the ways that this suggests. But, as we argued at some length, this view not only overlooks the looseness and ambiguity of the members' electoral constraints; it also ignores the reasons for even wanting to be a member of Congress as well as the subtle and indirect ways (hardly observable in opinion polls) in which widely shared interests and values can have electoral effects.

5. *Affected industries had only a limited ability to protect their interests through political action.* They were put at a strategic disadvantage and forced to retreat as deregulation by the commissions and courts proved economically unsettling, diminished the reality of regulatory protection, established new baselines for legislative action, and threatened rapidly to go even further—all of which suggested the need for compromise in order to pass legislation and restore stability. Moreover, the industries' political responses often were not well suited to limit the damage, but suffered in varying degrees from unrealistic estimates of their political capabilities, lack of coordination and unity, or the failure of firms to sustain an energetic political effort. The nature and extent of these weaknesses depended above all on how the industries were organized for political action. The airline industry, with a number of firms each capable of representing itself, underwent a political collapse, while the telecommunications industry, dominated by a politically insulated, overbearing AT&T, in a fit of aggressiveness missed its best chance to limit the expansion of competition. Only the trucking industry, represented by a dominant, politically sophisticated trade association, managed its political resources reasonably well, yet even so succeeded only in limiting the magnitude of its defeat.

To sum up the analysis in the broadest terms, the explanation for success in our cases has three principal elements: the fit between a well-developed analytic prescription and the need of politicians for positions that were responsive to current public concerns (inflation and intrusive government), appealing on ideological grounds, and easy to comprehend and explain; the presence of leadership roles and institutions, especially the commissions and courts, that facilitated action; and the difficulty encountered by the affected interests, though mobilized in opposition, in converting economic resources effectively to political use.

The Role of Analysis

As vividly and impressively as possible, our cases demonstrate the role that disinterested economic analysis can play in the formation of public policy. If economists had not made the case for procompetitive deregulation, it would not have occurred—at least not on the scale the nation has witnessed. Yet economists' advice is not always so well heeded. Why was economic analysis so influential in these cases, and what general lessons can be drawn about the conditions for its influence?

Our account suggests that advice tends to be efficacious insofar as it has two general attributes, which are by no means necessarily related: substantive soundness—the quality and persuasiveness of analysis as judged by the criteria of analysts themselves; and political adaptiveness—the ability of analysis to meet further criteria inherent in the political process and to underlie rhetoric that meets those criteria. With important exceptions on some issues in telecommunications, the analysis supporting procompetitive deregulation had both attributes in unusual degree.

Reform analysis was substantively sound because it was grounded in both microeconomic theory—which is generally held to be the most powerful body of theory in the social sciences—and empirical research. The analysis was persuasive in that, to a remarkable extent, economists agreed; and its findings were clear, giving generally unqualified support to procompetitive deregulation. Moreover, apparent proofs of the validity of the analysis were promptly forthcoming. When deregulation began to be instituted in the airline industry, the promised reductions in fares rapidly ensued, and there were also immediate, if less dramatic, benefits from new competition in trucking and telecommunications.

In addition to strong evidence of validity, reform analysis offered relatively complete guidance for the actions of officeholders. Procompetitive deregulation did not depend on complex strategies of implementation. Instead of creating new institutions—something done only in telecommunications and then very late, with the restructuring of AT&T—deregulation called mainly for removing constraints on existing institutions and restoring markets in classic form. It stands in contrast, for example, to the federal government's promotion of health maintenance organizations, a case in which an effort to strengthen markets encountered unforeseen difficulties in building a novel form of organization.[2]

2. Lawrence D. Brown, *Politics and Health Care Organization: HMOs as Federal Policy* (Brookings, 1983), chap. 9.

Politically adaptive at the same time, reform analysis was in several ways well suited to the needs of political actors. Conforming to common sense and traditional values, it could be rendered in simple, symbolic, intuitively appealing terms. Procompetitive deregulation differed in this respect, for example, from the use of effluent taxes to control pollution, a measure roughly as convincing to economists but difficult for laymen to comprehend. Both liberals and conservatives found in the proposals the opportunity to assert their principles. At least in the transportation cases, deregulation posed no deeply divisive issues of equity among social groups or geographic areas or of the relative worth of competing goals. Finally, and crucial to overriding interest group opposition, these intrinsically rather obscure proposals could be linked rhetorically to larger public concerns—inflation and big government—which gave them potential to be widely noticed.

Rather than products of effort and strategy, the strengths of reform analysis were mainly advantages presented, more or less fortuitously, by the cases—because of the clarity of economic findings on anticompetitive regulation, for example, and the inflation of the mid-1970s, which gave those findings a new pertinence. Still, the efficacy of analysis is not entirely a matter of luck. To some degree, whether analysis is likely to meet both substantive and political requirements for effectiveness depends on how it is conducted and on the organizational arrangements under which it is produced.

Before it can produce policy change, policy analysis must undergo three stages of development, each based in different organizational settings and concerned with a somewhat different set of analytic problems. In the first stage, analysts evaluate existing policies and, in broad outlines, propose alternatives. Judgment is based on general conceptions of the public interest, such as an economic definition of social welfare, and as much as possible on scientific theory and empirical evidence.[3] Much of this analysis is performed in universities and policy research organizations that have a partly academic orientation, such as Brookings and the American Enterprise Institute.

One advantage of such settings is that analysis can be carried on with little concern for the near-term political feasibility of recommendations. Pessimism about political feasibility did not prevent the development of

3. Much of policy judgment, however, must be based on "ordinary knowledge." See Charles E. Lindblom and David K. Cohen, *Usable Knowledge: Social Science and Social Problem Solving* (Yale University Press, 1979).

reform analysis because academic practitioners of analysis face no compelling need for political success: for them a study is successful enough if it persuades (and favorably impresses) other analysts. The indifference of academic analysts to short-term feasibility helps to expand the range of possible policy changes in the long term.

The weakness of analysis in academic settings, from the standpoint of policymaking, is that the selection of topics and analytic approaches, shaped by academic purposes and resource limits, may diverge quite significantly from that which any test of political importance, short term or long term, would suggest. Because the CAB provided conveniently usable data on airlines, economists analyzed that industry early and extensively; the trucking industry, which was far more important to the economy but harder to analyze, had been neglected for many years. Little work had been done other than by AT&T's own economists on the daunting subject of that company's appropriate structure. In all cases academic research had focused mainly on the consequences of regulation for allocative efficiency and general price levels, matters central to the theoretical interests of economists, and had largely ignored questions, central to policy design and political judgment, of its distributive effects.

In the second stage, analysis must be introduced into the political process in the form of advice to policymakers who are capable of initiating action—especially, but not only, the president. Such advice is concerned in large part with choosing among issues—which ones to adopt and how hard to push them—and takes into account how they bear on the larger national problems and political goals with which policymakers are occupied. In a speculative, preliminary way, it also considers feasibility.

Organizational arrangements for economic advice, once lacking, were well established by the mid-1970s. In recent decades, policy analysis and initiation of proposals have been developing as distinct functions of the Executive Office of the President and of secretarial-level staffs in the executive departments. The principal motive behind this development is to liberate executive policy planning from the parochialism of career program specialists in the operating bureaucracy and thereby to foster innovation, rationalization, and coordination. Economists have come to dominate these various central planning agencies, especially the offices of planning and evaluation that are now often found in cabinet departments under the direction of an assistant secretary. Additionally, economists command a respected, well-established place in the Executive Office of the President—the Council of Economic Advisers, which was created by law in 1946 to give the president advice on how to maintain full employment and has since given him whatever advice about economic policies he has asked for or its members have thought he ought to have.

Their high organizational place under these arrangements was a great asset to economists in our cases. Their presence in the CEA, the Council on Wage and Price Stability, the Department of Transportation, and elsewhere in the government gave them access to the president and made possible the development of an informal, professionally based network of deregulation advocates, which in turn facilitated the creation of a more formal advisory group in the Ford administration. And even in the regulatory commissions, formerly ridiculed as bastions of economic ignorance, economic analysis units rose in sophistication and power after reform-oriented chairmen took charge.

If these organizational developments have a serious liability, it would be that economists and their view of the world are too dominant in policy analysis within government. Because economic analysis is ill equipped to deal with some important dimensions of public policy, such as moral issues and psychological effects, economists generally omit them from policy discourse. They also try to extend the logic of economic analysis to the functioning of institutions other than markets, often with results that noneconomists find implausible.[4] The dominance of the economic perspective posed no difficulties in our cases, however, because the matters that economic analysis neglects were not much involved, while the proper functioning of markets was precisely the issue. Compared, for example, with proposals to alter health, safety, or environmental regulation, the issues in our cases were far more susceptible and appropriate to prescription derived exclusively from economics. Under the circumstances, economists brought to policy prescription the freedom from organizational inhibition and indifference to tradition, legal precedent, and vested interests that are the raison d'être of central staff members, while at the same time they were able to command a large measure of the credence and respect that tend to be reserved for specialists.

Finally, a third stage of analysis is concerned with adjusting proposals, devising selling points, and answering objections to enlist the support of

---

4. For a penetrating discussion of the limitations of the economist's world view, see Steven E. Rhoads, *The Economist's View of the World: Government, Markets, and Public Policy* (Cambridge University Press, 1985).

a larger group of decisionmakers—most often the members of Congress. In many cases the congressional rank and file use criteria of choice that are different from, or additional to, those used by presidents or congressional leaders. It was very evident in these cases that they set stronger constraints on distributive effects of policy change, protecting favored social groups or geographic areas against loss even if at a cost to the nation as a whole. They require complicated arguments on behalf of proposals to be translated into simpler and more vivid terms.

The analytic task of seeing that these requirements are met falls largely to staff units that are directly engaged in policy promotion—in our cases regulatory analysis groups in the Departments of Transportation and Commerce, parallel units in the commissions themselves, even the staffs of congressional committees. All of these assisted in constructing reform advocacy and initiated, sponsored, or conducted studies aimed at overcoming congressional resistance. Solving the problems of this stage requires close collaboration between analysts and lobbyists and perhaps ideally involves versatile individuals who are both, so that research can be performed to address politically decisive issues as directly as possible.[5] It also requires analysts who, unlike most academics, are willing to do research under short deadlines with laymen as the intended audience.

Intrinsically difficult to plan, analysis for policy promotion was the least effectively performed of the three stages in our cases. Although the studies of the small-community service issue proved sufficient to the task of winning the support of most senators from rural states, it was far from ideal that almost all of the research had to be carried out in a great rush, with congressional debate already under way. One of the major barriers to legislation in the telecommunications case was that no one could gauge with reasonable precision the amount of cross-subsidy in the system or the likely effects of market-based pricing on the structure of rates.

It is worth considering whether the conduct of policy analysis by economists and others could be more closely linked to the policy process so that analysis would respond in more timely fashion to the political agenda and apply more politically relevant criteria of choice. A dramatically strengthened linkage does not seem likely or even advisable, but

5. This point is emphasized in Dorothy L. Robyn's account of "the strategic use of analysis," "Braking the Special Interests: The Political Battle for Trucking Deregulation" (Ph.D. dissertation, University of California–Berkeley, 1983), chap. 4. See also John Mendeloff, *Regulating Safety: An Economic and Political Analysis of Occupational Safety and Health Policy* (MIT Press, 1979).

limited improvement may be possible. One policy-oriented economist, former CEA member George Eads, has urged that to be more relevant to policymaking economists should devote less attention to policies' consequences for allocative efficiency and more to their distributive effects that bear on equity.[6] Such a change seems unlikely. The concern with efficiency is part of the basic structure of economic theory, and, by the resulting professional bias, central to the normative outlook of most economists. In short, economists are no more likely to stop asking whether policies are efficient than are political scientists to stop asking whether political processes are democratic.[7]

What is perhaps more feasible is a modest increase in governmental capacity to anticipate policy debate and to conduct, or at least plan, pertinent research before it is needed. After Congress had begun debating proposals for a substantial divestiture by AT&T, and several years after the Justice Department first sued for such a measure, the Commerce Department's National Telecommunications and Information Administration tried to let a contract for a study of the issue, only to conclude that no consulting firm knew how to do one.[8] Even though Ford submitted a bill in 1975 to deregulate the trucking industry and Carter showed an interest in it from the beginning of his term, the crucial research on how it would affect small-community service was not done until 1979. Such tardiness is more than merely inconvenient. The later that significant information is introduced in policy debate, the more decisions and commitments will have been made before it arrives. In addition, one can doubt the advisability of basing policy decisions on research that is done by consulting firms or professors under the pressure of tight deadlines.

The most appropriate organizational setting for an expanded governmental effort to anticipate debate is probably not in the executive branch, where research cannot easily be separated from the policy commitments of the current administration. A more suitable location would be provided by one or more of the congressional staff agencies—the Con-

6. George Eads, "Economists versus Regulators," in James C. Miller III, ed., *Perspectives on Federal Transportation Policy* (American Enterprise Institute for Public Policy Research, 1975), pp. 104–06.

7. On the relation between disciplinary concerns and normative outlooks in the behavioral sciences, see Duncan MacRae, *The Social Function of Social Science* (Yale University Press, 1976).

8. Interview with Ellen Deutsch, program manager, Domestic Common Carrier Program, National Telecommunications and Information Administration, December 9, 1980.

gressional Budget Office, Office of Technology Assessment, and Congressional Research Service. The norms in such agencies, requiring political neutrality and responsiveness to individual committees and members of Congress, would permit research on proposals that have attracted some interest but are not yet on the immediate agenda. Because these agencies need to maintain bipartisan support in Congress, they have credibility. And, as parts of the legislative branch, they are well situated to address the special concerns of members of Congress.[9] Of course, no amount of effort will succeed in anticipating all of the particular issues that may arise in the legislative process, or even which proposals among the many that at any given time are attracting interest will "catch on" sufficiently to be acted upon. As John Kingdon has shown, proposals long under discussion often rise to preeminence quite suddenly and unpredictably.[10] Under such circumstances, to be ready with pertinent analysis at a propitious time is extremely difficult, and there may be no escape from the need to do "on demand" the highly applied analysis of stage three. Still, the history of most major proposals is sufficiently long to allow some analytic basis for legislative debate to be prepared by the time they are ready for disposition.

The success of procompetitive deregulation demonstrates not only the influence of economic analysis but also certain capabilities of the political system. In the closing section, we expand on our explanation of that success by inquiring into the system's general properties.

The U.S. Political System

The democracy of the United States, like any democracy, is prey to a tendency for policymaking to be dominated by narrow perspectives and interests or to reflect ill-considered, superficial opinions or the impulses of the mass public. These dangers were avoided in our cases as expert, well-considered analysis was successfully linked with broader fashions and sentiments, and political institutions proved responsive to the resulting definition of what public policy ought to be. Thus the cases are of use in

9. The contribution of nonpartisan analytic staffs to the quality of policy debate is stressed in William K. Muir, *Legislature: California's School of Politics* (University of Chicago Press, 1982).

10. Kingdon, *Agendas, Alternatives, and Public Policies*, p. 85.

assessing such threats to the performance of American democracy and in recognizing some of its strengths.

That a union of expert analysis and mass attitudes occurred was partly the result of unusual properties of the cases. In particular, the cases were characterized by an unusually inclusive agreement among analysts and political actors oriented toward broad constituencies and an unusually sharp, clear cleavage between them and the particularistic, apparently self-serving interests that opposed them. Ordinarily there is much more ambiguity and dispute about what the general good requires. If consensus always attained such a high level and if the only dissent from it could always be discounted for self-interestedness, policy choice would be much easier than it generally is, and the performance of U.S. political institutions would be rated more highly. Beyond that, built-in obstacles to action were unusually easy to overcome because the independent regulatory commissions, which through monumental irony had become the instruments of reform, were able to use their exceptionally broad statutory powers. Exposed to oversight from all three main branches of the government, yet vested with extraordinary power to act independently, the commissions could respond effectively to concerted pressure for action and thus compensate for the dispersion of authority that so often paralyzes U.S. government.

Yet on the whole the commissions neither initiated the reforms we have analyzed nor took the actions that, in the end, were definitive. To draw broader inferences from what happened, it is necessary to look at the whole set of governing institutions and not just one rather anomalous part of them. We argue that the outcome of our cases was attributable to properties of the political system—some of them new, or at least newly more pronounced—that endow it with a greater capacity than is usually acknowledged to transcend particularism and incorporate responsible analysis in decisions.

The decisive features of the political system were, above all, leadership that is attentive to broad audiences; widespread competition for leadership, both within Congress and between Congress and other institutions; and extreme receptivity by leaders and other officials, including rank-and-file members of Congress, to the materials of policy advocacy, that is, argument, symbols, and ideas. These features are in part enduring attributes of American politics, but they also reflect widely remarked changes in political institutions and their context—including the rise of the mass media, the decline of political parties as organizations capable of electing or controlling officeholders, the growth of analytical staffs in both legislative and executive branches, and the decentralization and democratization of power in Congress. These changes have altered the conditions, opportunities, and definitions of success in political careers: they encourage officeholders to rely on themselves, rather than political parties, for security and advancement; to appeal for support to larger segments of the public rather than interest groups; to prefer, as a general rule, policies that can be defended with impressive supporting analysis; and, where opportunities are presented, to seek a prominent role and distinctive achievement in the politics of issues. These inducements apply not only to elected officials, but also in large part to appointive ones, and they enhanced the capacity of political institutions to respond favorably to procompetitive deregulation.

Other analysts, observing roughly the same features of the contemporary American political system, have commented on them unfavorably, finding in them the source of several pathologies. Extreme fragmentation, it is said, makes it difficult to concert action and subjects the government to policy immobilism. According to another argument, not necessarily incompatible, when action does occur it is likely to be impulsive and ill considered, because it is driven by ideas that derive much of their persuasive force from symbolism and mass appeal. And, while the power of the classic iron triangles has declined, the issue networks that have arisen more recently weaken democracy. Drawing power from shared bodies of policy knowledge, these networks intimidate politicians, alienate the public from policy discourse, and resist effective control by elected leaders, including the president.[11]

In our cases of procompetitive deregulation, these pathologies arose only in mild form or not at all, and insofar as they did arise the political

11. Anthony King explains why action has become very difficult, stressing "atomization," by which he means, above all, the disintegration of distinct, stable political formations out of which coalitions can be formed. James Q. Wilson, agreeing with King about atomization—as manifested, for example, in dispersion of power within Congress and the declining power of leaders and vested interests—argues that action nevertheless remains possible because of the enhanced importance of ideas and ideology. King, "The American Polity in the Late 1970s: Building Coalitions in the Sand," in Anthony King, ed., *The New American Political System* (American Enterprise Institute for Public Policy Research, 1978), pp. 371–95; and Wilson, "American Politics, Then and Now," *Commentary*, vol. 67 (February 1979), pp. 39–46. Wilson's analysis invites inquiry into the processes whereby certain ideas become dominant. Our findings are generally consistent with his analysis, and we believe that our own analysis illustrates the processes by which ideas can precipitate coherent and even profound policy change.

system demonstrated compensating capacities. Fragmentation and competitive leadership did not prevent action, but rather prodded sometimes reluctant leaders to act more boldly. For example, Senator Kennedy, using a subcommittee that lacked jurisdiction to fashion a bill, prompted support for airline deregulation from the Ford administration, previously inarticulate on the subject, and from a decidedly skeptical Commerce Committee. Under more orderly, centralized arrangements, Kennedy would have lacked authority to become involved, and the leaders who had authority might have chosen to avoid a difficult issue. The current political system encourages rival credit claiming and competition for proprietary sponsorship of promising issues, and this means that few issues with potential for successful action are likely to be ignored.

With a partial exception in telecommunications, ultimate decision was reached through a process of orderly deliberation in which symbolism played some, but not a dominant, role. On airline and trucking deregulation, Congress was induced to act by the commissions, which had thrown the existing regulatory regimes into turmoil. In each case Congress took about two years, from the first hearings before legislative committees to passage of a bill, to consider the issues. In deciding what action to take, Congress caused a substantial body of information to be gathered, ranging from analysis based on economic theory to surveys of small shippers' opinions. Either it called for such information, or analysts anticipated a call. Congress then apparently was influenced by the major findings. Potential side effects were debated at length. Although sweeping rhetoric was used concerning inflation and big government, and although the very term "deregulation" acquired a symbolism of moderate potency that supplied some of the momentum for reform proposals, the proposals and the rhetoric were also guided by the best dispassionate analysis available. Symbolism, rather than dictating the content of policy, gave some salience to otherwise obscure subjects. No one can contend that policymaking must be free of any nonrational elements, nor has it ever been: party loyalty, lately exalted for the coordinating power it once brought to American politics, also depended heavily on symbolism.

The network of specialized policy experts, ardently committed to reform, was very much at the service of elected officials. During the Ford administration, reform-minded economists and others developed into an issue network, or part of one, and by creating the Domestic Council Review Group on Regulatory Reform, Ford made it a presidential instrument. Giving it leadership and using its support, he was able to propose coherent, carefully considered initiatives for policy change that clearly suited his own preferences. The trucking industry would eventually complain that the Senate Commerce Committee had been captured by a staff composed of doctrinaire reformers, but this staff had been hired by the chairman, Howard Cannon, who felt satisfied to give it generally worded instructions for the drafting of a bill and was manifestly pleased with what it helped him accomplish. In fact, rather than being doctrinaire, the staff aimed at some degree of moderation, in keeping with the chairman's wishes.

Criticisms of American political institutions find some support, on the other hand, in the process of policy change in telecommunications. An issue network came into play with the potential for monopolizing power because of its understanding of enormously complicated issues and its use, inescapably, of an esoteric language to conduct debate. It was subjected to little scrutiny by nonspecialists; even serious, energetic legislators on the communications subcommittees complained of having unusual difficulty comprehending the subject. The main defect of policymaking in this instance, however, was not that the issue network monopolized power; it resulted, if anything, from the profound inability of the issue network to find consensus.

Confronting issues so complex and ambiguous that they failed to elicit agreement even among disinterested policy experts, and confronting as well the political power of AT&T, Congress failed to produce a new telecommunications statute in six years of effort. Policy decisions of vast significance—the opening up of all telecommunications markets to competition and the breaking up of AT&T—were disposed of under vague statutes by the Federal Communications Commission and the federal courts. These were not necessarily the policies that a hesitant, divided, compromise-seeking Congress would have been likely to choose, if it had been capable of choosing. The new policies became for all practical purposes final when AT&T, seeing the futility, stopped challenging them. This, we presume, is not the way democratic policymaking should be conducted. Interests of such magnitude and variety were involved, on issues with implications so manifold and widespread, that one is inclined to think a representative legislature should have resolved them.

Yet, even here, the political system manifested certain strengths. The outcomes yielded by nonlegislative forums lend no support to the proposition that the political system is severely biased in favor of powerful, well-organized interests: AT&T, a truly monumental organization, was a truly monumental loser. Furthermore, they demonstrate that even when Congress is stalemated, the political system as a whole may not be. Democratic procedures, though certainly altered and perhaps compromised by administrative and judicial initiatives, were not thereby nullified.[12] In principle, Congress could have changed the decisions of the FCC and the courts if it had strongly disagreed with them. In fact, telecommunications policy leaders in Congress, although lacking sufficient consensus for timely action, were generally in sympathy with the new policies, adding their eventual ratification to the legislative agenda.

One might object that this defense of administrative and judicial freewheeling ignores the difficulty of congressional action; an administrative or judicial decision easily can fail to be reversed even though opposed by a majority of congressmen. But this objection carries weight, it would seem, only insofar as there is a strong presumption in favor of existing policies. Without such a presumption the opposite danger is just as disturbing—that a decision supported by a majority of congressmen can fail to be taken. To grant some independent initiative to courts and administrative agencies, institutions less encumbered by internal complexity, can be defended partly as a means of reducing that danger.

We conclude, then, that these cases of procompetitive deregulation exemplify the "new American political system" working well, in a way that reveals some of its virtues. Though it uses different avenues of change from those contemplated in models of party or presidential government, in which presidents or other party leaders lead and Congress dutifully follows, it is still capable of innovation. The pluralism of political leadership and loose definition of administrative and judicial roles are alternative sources of dynamism. In this mode of innovation, the political system probably generates more numerous and varied proposals for change than the centralized models, but requires more collaboration and wider agreement to adopt them. There are obvious advantages to this mix of tendencies, since not all innovations advanced by any category of leaders are worth adopting.

The major virtue of the current American political system, at least by comparison with the past, probably lies in the resources and rewards it offers for overcoming particularism. Responsive to mass sentiment almost

---

12. For the view that administrative discretion undermines democratic procedures, with intrinsically conservative effects, see Theodore J. Lowi, *The End of Liberalism: The Second Republic of the United States,* 2d ed. (Norton, 1979).

since its founding, the political system seems to be more so than ever today, when mass education and communication and new technologies make it possible for such sentiment to be formed, expressed, and measured with unprecedented speed. At the same time, expert analysis, oriented toward broad conceptions of the public interest, is more thoroughly institutionalized in and addressed to the national government than ever before. This creates an unprecedented potential for linking the forces of expert analysis and mass sentiment as the basis for action—and political leaders who by luck or skill manage to achieve that union have a good chance of defeating narrow, particularistic interests.[13]

Deregulation exposed the political weakness of such vaunted industrial and union giants as AT&T, the truckers, and the Teamsters, and it also revealed a good deal of responsiveness and malleability on the part of administrative agencies, which have often been thought so closely tied to clientele groups and committees of Congress and so committed to organizational missions as to be largely immune to the influence of presidential leadership and indifferent to broad, diffuse interests. We suspect that, whatever may have been true in the past, interest group regimes today derive much of their apparent power merely from the absence of challenges—that is, from the inattentiveness of political leaders and allied forces that might launch an attack on broadly based grounds—and not from any reliable ability to defeat such challenges when they occur. If so, interest group power in any given policy area depends on there being so many issues, programs, and interest group regimes that political leadership, analytic expertise, and public attention must be selective in applying their power. The power of interest group regimes therefore is often less than meets the eye. Contests never joined by their potential adversaries are of course contests that they may be said to have "won." But behind their bloodless victories and seeming immunity to challenge lies far more vulnerability than has generally been supposed.

13. Of course nothing guarantees that politicians will make this particular linkage rather than exploit the power of mass sentiment alone, despite its lack of critical capacity. What sources of support politicians use depends partly on the opportunities that arise—the way perceived problems, proposals, and analyses happen to combine. In the long run, their choices will depend also on the degree to which further developments in political institutions, electoral politics, and public understanding offer rewards for behaving responsibly, and on the character of the leaders selected. The successful working of the political system depends, not just on leaders' luck and skill in combining expert analysis and mass sentiment, but above all on the good judgment with which they evaluate and seek to integrate the two forces.

Index

259